Contents

This book is the trace of work done during a two-year seminar (1968–1969) at the Ecole pratique des Hautes Etudes.

I hope that the students, auditors, and friends who took part in this seminar will accept this dedication of a text which was written according to their attention to it.

S/Z

Roland Barthes

TRANSLATED BY
Richard Miller

PREFACE BY
Richard Howard

BLACKWELL
Publishers

Translation © 1974 by Farrar, Straus and Giroux, Inc.

Originally published in French as S/Z
Copyright © 1973 by Éditions du Seuil, Paris

First published in the United Kingdom 1990
Reprinted 1992, 1993, 1995, 1996

Blackwell Publishers Ltd
108 Cowley Road
Oxford OX4 1JF, UK

Published by arrangement with
Hill and Wang, a division of Farrar, Straus & Giroux, Inc.,
19 Union Square West
New York, NY 10003, USA

British Library Cataloguing in Publication Data
A CIP catalogue record for this book is available from the British Library

ISBN   0–631–17607–1

Printed and bound in Great Britain by Athenæum Press Ltd,
Gateshead, Tyne & Wear

A Note on S/Z

"It will afford profit and pleasure to that numerous class of persons who have no instinctive enjoyment of literature," writes a British reviewer of the French text of S/Z. *Instinctive enjoyment of literature!* Surely all of Roland Barthes's ten books exist to unmask such an expression, to expose such a myth. It is precisely our "instinctive enjoyment" which is acculturated, determined, in bondage. Only when we know—and it is a knowledge gained by taking pains, by renouncing what Freud calls instinctual gratification—what we are doing when we read, are we free to enjoy what we read. As long as our enjoyment is—or is said to be—instinctive it is not enjoyment, it is terrorism. For literature is like love in La Rochefoucauld: no one would ever have experienced it if he had not first read about it in books. We require an education in literature as in the sentiments in order to discover that what we assumed—with the complicity of our teachers—was nature is in fact culture, that what was given is no more than a way of taking. And we must learn, when we take, the cost of our participation, or else we shall pay much more. We shall pay our capacity to read at all.

Barthes calls his study an essay, and in it a consideration of more than just the tale by Balzac is desirable if we hope to discern what it is that is being *tried* here. For the work on the text by Balzac, the dissection—into 561 numbered fragments, or lexias, varying in length from one word to several lines—of *Sarrasine*, is not performed for the sake of identifying the five notorious codes (hermeneutic, semantic, proairetic, cultural, and symbolic), or even for the sake of discriminating the classical text (with its *parsimonious* plurality of interpretation and its closure of significance) from the modern text which has no such restrictions, no such closure (for the final closure of the modern text is *suspension*). Rather, the work so joyously performed here is undertaken for the sake of the 93 divagations (I use Mallarmé's term advisedly, for it is with Mallarmé, Barthes has said, that our "modernity" begins) identified by Roman numerals and printed in large type, amounting in each case to a page or two. These divagations, taken together, as they interrupt and are generated by the lexias of the analyzed text, constitute the most sustained yet pulverized meditation on *reading* I know in all of Western critical literature. They afford—though Barthes can afford *them* only because of the scrupulous density of his attention, his presence of mind where one is used to little more than pasturage—a convinced, euphoric, even a militant critique of what it is we do when we read. For reading is still the principal thing we do by ourselves in culture, and it has too long been granted —as when Valery Larbaud calls it the one unpunished vice—the amnesty of our society. We have "forgiven" masturbation in our erotic jurisdiction, but have we even learned to "indict" reading?

"What do you read now?" the hungry interviewer asked the famous writer, a woman of commercial success in the theater whose autobiography has defined a character of considerable literary sophistication. And the famous writer answered:

> I don't read novels any more, I'm sorry to say. A writer should read novels. When I do, I go back to the ones I've read before. Dickens. Balzac . . . I find now when I go to get a book off the shelf, I pick something I've read before, as if I didn't dare try anything new.

Aside from the underlining fact that it is a writer speaking, this is a familiar experience, this preference for what Barthes calls the *readerly* over what he calls the *writerly* (I believe Richard Miller has been both plausible and adroit in his translation of *lisible* and

scriptible; the dilemma is characteristic of the problem any trans-
lator of Barthes confronts, and the solution is characteristic of Mr.
Miller, properly concerned with his reader's comprehension, not
his comfort). It is a familiar experience because only what is au-
thentically writerly can *become* readerly. If we were to set out to
write a readerly text, we should be no more than hacks in bad
faith; yet, as readers, how hard it is to face the open text, the plurality of signification, the suspension of meaning. It explains that
hesitation at the bookshelf, the hand falling on the Balzac story,
the known quantity. Known . . . How often we need to be assured of what we know in the old ways of knowing—how seldom
we can afford to venture beyond the pale into that chromatic fantasy where, as Rilke said (in 1908!), "begins the revision of categories, where something past comes again, as though out of the
future; something formerly accomplished as something to be completed." (A perfect description, by the way, of the book in hand.)
Why we read in this repressed and repressive way; what it is, in
the very nature of reading, which fences us in, which closes us off,
it is Barthes's genius to explore, not merely to deplore. His re-
searches into the structure of narrative have granted him a conviction (or a reprieve), a conviction that all telling modifies what is
being told, so that what the linguists call the message is a param-
eter of its performance. Indeed, his conviction of reading is that
what is told is always the telling. And this he does not arraign, he
celebrates.

So exact are Barthes's divagations, so exacting are their discover-
ies about the nature of reading, that we may now and again be
dismayed—if we are in the main readers of the *readerly*—by the
terms he has come to (he usually assumes Greek has a word for it)
in which they must be rendered. For Barthes's text is *writerly*—at
least his divagations are. This criticism is literature. It makes upon
us strenuous demands, exactions. And because of them, precisely,
we too are released, reprieved; we are free to read both the readerly
(and can we ever again read Balzac *in all innocence?* can we ever
want to?) and the writerly, *en connaissance de cause,* knowing the
reason why. Essentially an erotic meditation, then, because it concerns what is inexpressible (which is the essence of eros), Barthes's

ix

essay is the most useful, the most intimate, and the most suggestive book I have ever read about why I have ever read a book. It is, by the way, useful, intimate, and suggestive about Balzac's tale *Sarrasine*, which the reader of the readerly will find reassembled at the end of this writerly book, *en appendice,* as the French say.

RICHARD HOWARD

S/Z

I. EVALUATION

There are said to be certain Buddhists whose ascetic practices enable them to see a whole landscape in a bean. Precisely what the first analysts of narrative were attempting: to see all the world's stories (and there have been ever so many) within a single structure: we shall, they thought, extract from each tale its model, then out of these models we shall make a great narrative structure, which we shall reapply (for verification) to any one narrative: a task as exhausting (ninety-nine percent perspiration, as the saying goes) as it is ultimately undesirable, for the text thereby loses its difference. This difference is not, obviously, some complete, irreducible quality (according to a mythic view of literary creation), it is not what designates the individuality of each text, what names, signs, finishes off each work with a flourish; on the contrary, it is a difference which does not stop and which is articulated upon the infinity of texts, of languages, of systems: a difference of which each text is the return. A choice must then be made: either to place all texts in a demonstrative oscillation, equalizing them under the scrutiny of an in-different science, forcing them to rejoin, inductively, the Copy from which we will then make them derive; or else to restore each text, not to its individuality, but to its function, making it cohere, even before we talk about it, by the infinite paradigm of difference, subjecting it from the outset to a basic typology, to an evaluation. How then posit the value of a text? How establish a basic typology of texts? The primary evaluation of all texts can come neither from science,

3

for science does not evaluate, nor from ideology, for the ideological value of a text (moral, aesthetic, political, alethiological) is a value of representation, not of production (ideology "reflects," it does not do work). Our evaluation can be linked only to a practice, and this practice is that of writing. On the one hand, there is what it is possible to write, and on the other, what it is no longer possible to write: what is within the practice of the writer and what has left it: which texts would I consent to write (to re-write), to desire, to put forth as a force in this world of mine? What evaluation finds is precisely this value: what can be written (rewritten) today: the *writerly*. Why is the writerly our value? Because the goal of literary work (of literature as work) is to make the reader no longer a consumer, but a producer of the text. Our literature is characterized by the pitiless divorce which the literary institution maintains between the producer of the text and its user, between its owner and its customer, between its author and its reader. This reader is thereby plunged into a kind of idleness —he is intransitive; he is, in short, *serious:* instead of functioning himself, instead of gaining access to the magic of the signifier, to the pleasure of writing, he is left with no more than the poor freedom either to accept or reject the text: reading is nothing more than a *referendum*. Opposite the writerly text, then, is its countervalue, its negative, reactive value: what can be read, but not written: the *readerly*. We call any readerly text a classic text.

II. INTERPRETATION

There may be nothing to say about writerly texts. First of all, where can we find them? Certainly not in reading (or at least very rarely: by accident, fleetingly, obliquely in certain limit-

4

works): the writerly text is not a thing, we would have a hard time finding it in a bookstore. Further, its model being a productive (and no longer a representative) one, it demolishes any criticism which, once produced, would mix with it: to rewrite the writerly text would consist only in disseminating it, in dispersing it within the field of infinite difference. The writerly text is a perpetual present, upon which no *consequent* language (which would inevitably make it past) can be superimposed; the writerly text is *ourselves writing*, before the infinite play of the world (the world as function) is traversed, intersected, stopped, plasticized by some singular system (Ideology, Genus, Criticism) which reduces the plurality of entrances, the opening of networks, the infinity of languages. The writerly is the novelistic without the novel, poetry without the poem, the essay without the dissertation, writing without style, production without product, structuration without structure. But the readerly texts? They are products (and not productions), they make up the enormous mass of our literature. How differentiate this mass once again? Here, we require a second operation, consequent upon the evaluation which has separated the texts, more delicate than that evaluation, based upon the appreciation of a certain quantity—of the *more or less* each text can mobilize. This new operation is *interpretation* (in the Nietzschean sense of the word). To interpret a text is not to give it a (more or less justified, more or less free) meaning, but on the contrary to appreciate what *plural* constitutes it. Let us first posit the image of a triumphant plural, unimpoverished by any constraint of representation (of imitation). In this ideal text, the networks are many and interact, without any one of them being able to surpass the rest; this text is a galaxy of signifiers, not a structure of signifieds; it has no beginning; it is reversible; we gain access to it by several entrances, none of which can be authoritatively declared to be the main one; the codes it mobilizes extend *as*

5

far as the eye can reach, they are indeterminable (meaning here is never subject to a principle of determination, unless by throwing dice); the systems of meaning can take over this absolutely plural text, but their number is never closed, based as it is on the infinity of language. The interpretation demanded by a specific text, in its plurality, is in no way liberal: it is not a question of conceding some meanings, of magnanimously acknowledging that each one has its share of truth; it is a question, against all in-difference, of asserting the very existence of plurality, which is not that of the true, the probable, or even the possible. This necessary assertion is difficult, however, for as nothing exists outside the text, there is never a *whole* of the text (which would by reversion form an internal order, a reconciliation of complementary parts, under the paternal eye of the representative Model): the text must simultaneously be distinguished from its exterior and from its totality. All of which comes down to saying that for the plural text, there cannot be a narrative structure, a grammar, or a logic; thus, if one or another of these are sometimes permitted to come forward, it is *in proportion* (giving this expression its full quantitative value) as we are dealing with incompletely plural texts, texts whose plural is more or less parsimonious.

III. CONNOTATION: AGAINST

For these moderately plural (i.e., merely polysemous) texts, there exists an average appreciator which can grasp only a certain median portion of the plural, an instrument at once too delicate and too vague to be applied to univocal texts, and too poor to be applied to multivalent texts, which are reversible and frankly indeterminable (integrally plural texts). This *modest* instrument is connotation. For Hjelmslev, who has defined it, connotation is a secondary meaning, whose signifier is itself constituted by a sign or system of primary signification, which is denotation: if E is the expression, C the content, and R the relation of the two which establishes the sign, the formula for the connotation is: (ERC) R C. Doubtless because it has not been limited, subjected to a typology of texts, connotation has not had a good press. Some (the philologists, let us say), declaring every text to be univocal, possessing a true, canonical meaning, banish the simultaneous, secondary meanings to the void of critical lucubrations. On the other hand, others (the semiologists, let us say) contest the hierarchy of denotated and connotated; language, they say, the raw material of denotation, with its dictionary and its syntax, is a system like any other; there is no reason to make this system the privileged one, to make it the locus and the norm of a primary, original meaning, the scale for all associated meanings; if we base denotation on truth, on objectivity, on law, it is because we are still in awe of the prestige of linguistics, which, until today, has been reducing language to the sentence and its lexical and syntactical components; now the endeavor of this hierarchy is a serious one: it is to return to the closure of Western discourse (scientific, critical, or philosophical), to its centralized organization, to arrange all the meanings of a text in a circle around the hearth of denotation (the hearth: center, guardian, refuge, light of truth).

IV. CONNOTATION: FOR, EVEN SO

This criticism of connotation is only half fair; it does not take into account the typology of the texts (this typology is basic: no text exists without being classified according to its value); for if there are readerly texts, committed to the closure system

7

of the West, produced according to the goals of this system, devoted to the law of the Signified, they must have a particular system of meaning, and this meaning is based on connotation. Hence, to deny connotation altogether is to abolish the differential *value* of the texts, to refuse to define the specific apparatus (both poetic and critical) for the readerly texts—it is to make the limited text equal to the limit-text, to deprive oneself of a typological instrument. Connotation is the way into the polysemy of the classic text, to that limited plural on which the classic text is based (it is not certain that there are connotations in the modern text). Connotation must therefore be rescued from its double contestation and kept as the namable, computable trace of a *certain* plural of the text (that limited plural of the classic text). Then, what is a connotation? Definitionally, it is a determination, a relation, an anaphora, a feature which has the power to relate itself to anterior, ulterior, or exterior mentions, to other sites of the text (or of another text): we must in no way restrain this relating, which can be given various names (*function* or *index*, for example), except that we must not confuse connotation with association of ideas: the latter refers to the system of a subject; connotation is a correlation immanent in the text, in the texts; or again, one may say that it is an association made by the text-as-subject within its own system. Topically, connotations are meanings which are neither in the dictionary nor in the grammar of the language in which a text is written (this is, of course, a shaky definition: the dictionary can be expanded, the grammar can be modified). Analytically, connotation is determined by two spaces: a sequential space, a series of orders, a space subject to the successivity of sentences, in which meaning proliferates by layering; and an agglomerative space, certain areas of the text correlating other meanings outside the material text and, with them, forming "nebulae" of signifieds. Topologically, connotation makes possible a (limited) dissemination of meanings, spread like gold dust on the apparent surface of the text (meaning is golden). Semiologically, each connotation is the starting point of a code (which will never be reconstituted), the articulation of a voice which is woven into the text. Dynamically, it is a subjugation which the text must undergo, it is the possibility of this subjugation (meaning is a force). Historically, by inducing meanings that are apparently recoverable (even if they are not lexical), connotation establishes a (dated) Literature of the Signified. Functionally, connotation, releasing the double meaning on principle, corrupts the purity of communication: it is a deliberate "static," painstakingly elaborated, introduced into the fictive dialogue between author and reader, in short, a countercommunication (Literature is an intentional cacography). Structurally, the existence of two supposedly different systems— denotation and connotation—enables the text to operate like a game, each system referring to the other according to the requirements of a certain *illusion*. Ideologically, finally, this game has the advantage of affording the classic text a certain *innocence*: of the two systems, denotative and connotative, one turns back on itself and indicates its own existence: the system of denotation; denotation is not the first meaning, but pretends to be so; under this illusion, it is ultimately no more than the *last* of the connotations (the one which seems both to establish and to close the reading), the superior myth by which the text pretends to return to the nature of language, to language as nature: doesn't a sentence, whatever meaning it releases, subsequent to its utterance, it would seem, appear to be telling us something simple, literal, primitive: something *true*, in relation to which all the rest (which comes *afterwards*, *on top*) is literature? This is why, if we want to go along with the classic text, we must keep denotation, the old deity, watchful, cunning, theatrical, foreordained to *represent* the collective innocence of language.

9

I read the text. This statement, consonant with the "genius" of the language (subject, verb, complement), is not always true. The more plural the text, the less it is written before I read it; I do not make it undergo a predicative operation, consequent upon its being, an operation known as *reading,* and *I* is not an innocent subject, anterior to the text, one which will subsequently deal with the text as it would an object to dismantle or a site to occupy. This "I" which approaches the text is already itself a plurality of other texts, of codes which are infinite or, more precisely, lost (whose origin is lost). *Objectivity* and *subjectivity* are of course forces which can take over the text, but they are forces which have no affinity with it. Subjectivity is a plenary image, with which I may be thought to encumber the text, but whose deceptive plenitude is merely the wake of all the codes which constitute me, so that my subjectivity has ultimately the generality of stereotypes. Objectivity is the same type of replenishment: it is an imaginary system like the rest (except that here the castrating gesture is more fiercely characterized), an image which serves to name me advantageously, to make myself known, "misknown," even to myself. Reading involves risks of objectivity or subjectivity (both are imaginary) only insofar as we define the text as an expressive object (presented for our own expression), sublimated under a morality of truth, in one instance laxist; in the other, ascetic. Yet reading is not a parasitical act, the reactive complement of a writing which we endow with all the glamour of creation and anteriority. It is a form of work (which is why it would be better to speak of a lexeological act—even a lexeographical act, since I write my reading), and the method of this work is topological: I am not hidden within the text, I am simply irrecoverable from it: my task is to move, to shift systems whose perspective ends neither at the text nor at the "I":

in operational terms, the meanings I find are established not by "me" or by others, but by their *systematic* mark: there is no other *proof* of a reading than the quality and endurance of its systematics; in other words: than its functioning. To read, in fact, is a labor of language. To read is to find meanings, and to find meanings is to name them; but these named meanings are swept toward other names; names call to each other, reassemble, and their grouping calls for further naming: I name, I unname, I rename: so the text passes: it is a nomination in the course of becoming, a tireless approximation, a metonymic labor. —With regard to the plural text, forgetting a meaning cannot therefore be seen as a fault. Forgetting in relation to what? What is the *sum* of the text? Meanings can indeed be forgotten, but only if we have chosen to bring to bear upon the text a singular scrutiny. Yet reading does not consist in stopping the chain of systems, in establishing a truth, a legality of the text, and consequently in leading its reader into "errors"; it consists in coupling these systems, not according to their finite quantity, but according to their plurality (which is a being, not a discounting): I pass, I intersect, I articulate, I release, I do not count. Forgetting meanings is not a matter for excuses, an unfortunate defect in performance; it is an affirmative value, a way of asserting the irresponsibility of the text, the pluralism of systems (if I closed their list, I would inevitably reconstitute a singular, theological meaning): it is precisely because I forget that I read.

VI. STEP BY STEP

If we want to remain attentive to the plural of a text (however limited it may be), we must renounce structuring this text in large masses, as was done by classical rhetoric and by

11

secondary-school explication: no *construction* of the text: everything signifies ceaselessly and several times, but without being delegated to a great final ensemble, to an ultimate structure. Whence the idea, and so to speak the necessity, of a gradual analysis of a single text. Whence, it would seem, several implications and several advantages. The commentary on a single text is not a contingent activity, assigned the reassuring alibi of the "concrete": the single text is valid for all the texts of literature, not in that it represents them (abstracts and equalizes them), but in that literature itself is never anything but a single text: the one text is not an (inductive) access to a Model, but entrance into a network with a thousand entrances; to take this entrance is to aim, ultimately, not at a legal structure of norms and departures, a narrative or poetic Law, but at a perspective (of fragments, of voices from other texts, other codes), whose vanishing point is nonetheless ceaselessly pushed back, mysteriously opened: each (single) text is the very theory (and not the mere example) of this vanishing, of this difference which indefinitely returns, insubmissive. Further, to study this text down to the last detail is to take up the structural analysis of narrative where it has been left till now: at the major structures; it is to assume the power (the time, the elbow room) of working back along the threads of meanings, of abandoning no site of the signifier without endeavoring to ascertain the code or codes of which this site is perhaps the starting point (or the goal); it is (at least we may hope as much, and work to this end) to substitute for the simple representative model another model, whose very gradualness would guarantee what may be productive in the classic text; for the *step-by-step* method, through its very slowness and dispersion, avoids penetrating, reversing the tutor text, giving an internal image of it: it is never anything but the *decomposition* (in the cinematographic sense) of the work of reading: a *slow motion*, so to speak, neither wholly image nor

12

wholly analysis; it is, finally, in the very writing of the commentary, a systematic use of digression (a form ill-accommodated by the discourse of knowledge) and thereby a way of observing the reversibility of the structures from which the text is woven; of course, the classic text is incompletely reversible (it is modestly plural): the reading of this text occurs within a necessary order, which the gradual analysis will make precisely its order of writing; but the step-by-step commentary is of necessity a renewal of the entrances to the text, it avoids structuring the text *excessively*, avoids giving it that additional structure which would come from a dissertation and would close it: it stars the text, instead of assembling it.

VII. THE STARRED TEXT

We shall therefore star the text, separating, in the manner of a minor earthquake, the blocks of signification of which reading grasps only the smooth surface, imperceptibly soldered by the movement of sentences, the flowing discourse of narration, the "naturalness" of ordinary language. The tutor signifier will be cut up into a series of brief, contiguous fragments, which we shall call *lexias*, since they are units of reading. This cutting up, admittedly, will be arbitrary in the extreme; it will imply no methodological responsibility, since it will bear on the signifier, whereas the proposed analysis bears solely on the signified. The lexia will include sometimes a few words, sometimes several sentences; it will be a matter of convenience: it will suffice that the lexia be the best possible space in which we can observe meanings; its dimension, empirically determined, estimated, will depend on the density of connotations, variable according to the moments of the text: all we require is that each lexia should have at most three or four meanings to be

13

enumerated. The text, in its mass, is comparable to a sky, at once flat and smooth, deep, without edges and without landmarks; like the soothsayer drawing on it with the tip of his staff an imaginary rectangle wherein to consult, according to certain principles, the flight of birds, the commentator traces through the text certain zones of reading, in order to observe therein the migration of meanings, the outcropping of codes, the passage of citations. The lexia is only the wrapping of a semantic volume, the crest line of the plural text, arranged like a berm of possible (but controlled, attested to by a systematic reading) meanings under the flux of discourse: the lexia and its units will thereby form a kind of polyhedron faceted by the word, the group of words, the sentence or the paragraph, i.e., with the language which is its "natural" excipient.

VIII. THE BROKEN TEXT

What will be noted is, across these artificial articulations, the shifting and repetition of the signifieds. Discerning these signifieds systematically for each lexia does not aim at establishing the truth of the text (its profound, strategic structure), but its plurality (however parsimonious); the units of meaning (the connotations), strung out separately for each lexia, will not then be regrouped, provided with a metameaning which would be the ultimate construction to be given them (we shall merely reconnect, as an appendix, certain sequences which might have become lost in the unraveling of the tutor text). We shall not set forth the criticism of a text, or a criticism of *this* text; we shall propose the semantic substance (divided but not distributed) of several kinds of criticism (psychological, psychoanalytical, thematic, historical, structural); it will then be up to each kind of criticism (if it should so desire) to come

14

into play, to make its voice heard, which is the hearing of one of the voices of the text. What we seek is to sketch the stereographic space of writing (which will here be a classic, readerly writing). The commentary, based on the affirmation of the plural, cannot therefore work with "respect" to the text; the tutor text will ceaselessly be broken, interrupted without any regard for its natural divisions (syntactical, rhetorical, anecdotic); inventory, explanation, and digression may deter any observation of suspense, may even separate verb and complement, noun and attribute; the work of the commentary, once it is separated from any ideology of totality, consists precisely in *manhandling* the text, *interrupting* it. What is thereby denied is not the *quality* of the text (here incomparable) but its "naturalness."

IX. HOW MANY READINGS?

We must further accept one last freedom: that of reading the text as if it had already been read. Those who like a good story may certainly turn to the end of the book and read the tutor text first; it is given as an appendix in its purity and continuity, as it came from the printer, in short, as we habitually read it. But for those of us who are trying to establish a plural, we cannot stop this plural at the gates of reading: the reading must also be plural, that is, without order of entrance: the "first" version of a reading must be able to be its last, as though the text were reconstituted in order to achieve its artifice of continuity, the signifier then being provided with an additional feature: shifting. Rereading, an operation contrary to the commercial and ideological habits of our society, which would have us "throw away" the story once it has been consumed ("devoured"), so that we can then move on to another story, buy another book, and which is tolerated only in certain marginal categories of readers (children, old people, and professors), rereading is here suggested at the outset, for it alone saves the text from repetition (those who fail to reread are obliged to read the same story everywhere), multiplies it in its variety and its plurality: rereading draws the text out of its internal chronology ("this happens *before* or *after* that") and recaptures a mythic time (without *before* or *after*); it contests the claim which would have us believe that the first reading is a primary, naïve, phenomenal reading which we will only, afterwards, have to "explicate," to intellectualize (as if there were a beginning of reading, as if everything were not already read: there is no *first* reading, even if the text is concerned to give us that illusion by several operations of *suspense*, artifices more spectacular than persuasive); rereading is no longer consumption, but play (that play which is the return of the different). If then, a deliberate contradiction in terms, we *immediately* reread the text, it is in order to obtain, as though under the effect of a drug (that of recommencement, of difference), not the *real* text, but a plural text: the same and new.

X. SARRASINE

The text I have chosen (Why? All i know is that for some time I have wanted to make a complete analysis of a short text and that the Balzac story was brought to my attention by an article by Jean Reboul,[1] who in turn is supposed to have been inspired by Georges Bataille's reference; and thus I was caught up in this "series" whose scope I was to discover by means of the text itself) is Balzac's *Sarrasine*.[2]

[1] Jean Reboul: "Sarrasine ou la castration personnifiée," in *Cahiers pour l'Analyse*, March–April, 1967.
[2] *Scènes de la Vie Parisienne*.

(1) *SARRASINE* ★ The title raises a question: *What is Sarrasine?* A noun? A name? A thing? A man? A woman? This question will not be answered until much later, by the biography of the sculptor named Sarrasine. Let us designate as *hermeneutic code* (HER) all the units whose function it is to articulate in various ways a question, its response, and the variety of chance events which can either formulate the question or delay its answer; or even, constitute an enigma and lead to its solution. Thus, the title *Sarrasine* initiates the first step in a sequence which will not be completed until No. 153 (HER. Enigma 1—the story will contain others—: question). ★★ The word *Sarrasine* has an additional connotation, that of femininity, which will be obvious to any French-speaking person, since that language automatically takes the final "e" as a specifically feminine linguistic property, particularly in the case of a proper name whose masculine form (*Sarrazin*) exists in French onomastics. Femininity (connoted) is a signifier which will occur in several places in the text; it is a shifting element which can combine with other similar elements to create characters, ambiances, shapes, and symbols. Although every unit we mention here will be a signifier, this one is of a very special type: it is the signifier par excellence because of its connotation, in the usual meaning of the term. We shall call this element a signifier (without going into further detail), or a *seme* (semantically, the seme is the unit of the signifier), and we shall indicate these units by the abbreviation SEM, designating each time by an approximate word the connotative signifier referred to in the lexia (SEM. Femininity).

(2) *I was deep in one of those daydreams* ★ There will be nothing wayward about the daydream introduced here: it will be solidly constructed along the most familiar rhetorical lines, in a series of antitheses: garden and salon, life and death, cold and heat, outside and interior. The lexia thus lays the groundwork, in introductory form, for a vast symbolic structure, since it can lend itself to many substitutions, variations, which will lead us from the garden to the castrato, from the salon to the girl with whom the narrator is in love, by way of the mysterious old man, the full-bosomed Mme de Lanty, or Vien's moonlit Adonis. Thus, on the symbolic level, an immense province appears, the province of the antithesis, of which

17

this forms the first unit, linking at the start its two adversative terms (A/B) in the word *daydream*. (We shall mark all the units in this symbolic area with the letters SYM. Here—SYM. Antithesis: AB.) ★★ The state of absorption formulated here (*I was deep in* . . .) already implies (at least in "readerly" discourse) some event which will bring it to an end (. . . *when I was roused by a conversation* . . . No. 14). Such sequences imply a logic in human behavior. In Aristotelian terms, in which *praxis* is linked to *proairesis,* or the ability rationally to determine the result of an action, we shall name this code of actions and behavior *proairetic* (in narrative, however, the discourse, rather than the characters, determines the action). This code of actions will be abbreviated ACT; furthermore, since these actions produce effects, each effect will have a generic name giving a kind of title to the sequence, and we shall number each of the terms which constitute it, as they appear (ACT. "To be deep in": 1: to be absorbed).

(3) *which overtake even the shallowest of men, in the midst of the most tumultuous parties.* ★ The fact "there is a party" (given here obliquely), soon to be followed by further data (a private house in the Faubourg Saint-Honoré), forms a pertinent signifier: the wealth of the Lanty family (SEM. Wealth). ★★ The phrase is a conversion of what might easily be a real proverb: *"Tumultuous parties: deep daydreams."* The statement is made in a collective and anonymous voice originating in traditional human experience. Thus, the unit has been formed by a gnomic code, and this code is one of the numerous codes of knowledge or wisdom to which the text continually refers; we shall call them in a very general way *cultural codes* (even though, of course, all codes are cultural), or rather, since they afford the discourse a basis in scientific or moral authority, we shall call them reference codes (REF. Gnomic code).

XI. THE FIVE CODES

As chance would have it (but what is chance?), the first three lexias—the title and the first sentence of the story—have already provided us with the five major codes under which all the textual signifiers can be grouped: without straining a point, there will be no other codes throughout the story but these five, and each and every lexia will fall under one of these five codes. Let us sum them up in order of their appearance, without trying to put them in any order of importance. Under the hermeneutic code, we list the various (formal) terms by which an enigma can be distinguished, suggested, formulated, held in suspense, and finally disclosed (these terms will not always occur, they will often be repeated; they will not appear in any fixed order). As for the semes, we merely indicate them—without, in other words, trying either to link them to a character (or a place or an object) or to arrange them in some order so that they form a single thematic grouping; we allow them the instability, the dispersion, characteristic of motes of dust, flickers of meaning. Moreover, we shall refrain from structuring the symbolic grouping; this is the place for multivalence and for reversibility; the main task is always to demonstrate that this field can be entered from any number of points, thereby making depth and secrecy problematic. Actions (terms of the proairetic code) can fall into various sequences which should be indicated merely by listing them, since the proairetic sequence is never more than the result of an artifice of reading: whoever reads the text amasses certain data under some generic titles for actions (*stroll, murder, rendezvous*), and this title embodies the sequence; the sequence exists when and because it can be given a name, it unfolds as this process of naming takes place, as a title is sought or confirmed; its basis is therefore more empirical than rational, and it is useless to attempt to force it into a statutory order; its only logic is that of the "already-done" or "already-read"—whence the variety of sequences (some trivial, some melodramatic) and the variety of terms (numerous or few); here again, we shall not attempt to put them into any order. Indicating them (externally and

internally) will suffice to demonstrate the plural meaning en-
tangled in them. Lastly, the cultural codes are references to a
science or a body of knowledge; in drawing attention to them,
we merely indicate the type of knowledge (physical, physiological, medical, psychological, literary, historical, etc.) referred to, without going so far as to construct (or reconstruct)
the culture they express.

XII. THE WEAVING OF VOICES

The five codes create a kind of network, a *topos* through which
the entire text passes (or rather, in passing, becomes text).
Thus, if we make no effort to structure each code, or the five
codes among themselves, we do so deliberately, in order to
assume the multivalence of the text, its partial reversibility.
We are, in fact, concerned not to manifest a structure but to
produce a structuration. The blanks and looseness of the
analysis will be like footprints marking the escape of the text;
for if the text is subject to some form, this form is not unitary,
architectonic, finite: it is the fragment, the shards, the broken
or obliterated network—all the movements and inflections of
a vast "dissolve," which permits both overlapping and loss of
messages. Hence we use *Code* here not in the sense of a list, a
paradigm that must be reconstituted. The code is a perspective
of quotations, a mirage of structures; we know only its departures and returns; the units which have resulted from it (those
we inventory) are themselves, always, ventures out of the text,
the mark, the sign of a virtual digression toward the remainder
of a catalogue (*The Kidnapping* refers to every kidnapping
ever written); they are so many fragments of something that
has always been *already* read, seen, done, experienced; the code
is the wake of that *already*. Referring to what has been written,

i.e., to the Book (of culture, of life, of life as culture), it makes the text into a prospectus of this Book. Or again: each code is one of the forces that can take over the text (of which the text is the network), one of the voices out of which the text is woven. Alongside each utterance, one might say that off-stage voices can be heard: they are the codes: in their interweaving, these voices (whose origin is "lost" in the vast perspective of the *already-written*) de-originate the utterance: the convergence of the voices (of the codes) becomes *writing*, a stereographic space where the five codes, the five voices, intersect: the Voice of Empirics (the proairetisms), the Voice of the Person (the semes), the Voice of Science (the cultural codes), the Voice of Truth (the hermeneutisms), the Voice of Symbol.

(4) *Midnight had just sounded from the clock of the Elysée-Bourbon.* ★ A metonymy leads from the Elysée-Bourbon to the seme *Wealth*, since the Faubourg Saint-Honoré is a wealthy neighborhood. This wealth is itself connoted: a neighborhood of *nouveaux riches*, the Faubourg Saint-Honoré refers by synechdoche to the Paris of the Bourbon Restoration, a mythic place of sudden fortunes whose origins are suspect; where gold is produced without an origin, diabolically (the symbolic definition of speculation) (SEM. Wealth).

(5) *Seated in a window recess* ★ The development of an antithesis normally includes the exposition of each of its parts (A, B). A third term is possible: a joint presentation. This term can be purely rhetorical, if we are concerned to *introduce* or *summarize* the antithesis; but it can also be literal, if we are concerned to denote the physical conjunction of antithetical sites: a function which here devolves upon *recess*, an intermediate place between garden and salon, death and life (SYM. Antithesis: mediation).

(6) *and hidden behind the sinuous folds of a silk curtain,* ★ ACT. "Hiding place": 1: to be hidden.

21

(7) *I could contemplate at my leisure the garden of the mansion where I was spending the evening.* ★ *I could contemplate* means *I am going to describe.* The first term of the antithesis (garden) is introduced here from a rhetorical viewpoint (according to the code): there is a manipulation of the discourse, not of the story (SYM. Antithesis: A: introduction). We may note here, to return to it later, that *contemplation,* a visual posture, the arbitrary delimitation of a field of observation (the *templum* of the augurs), relates the whole description to the model of painting. ★★ SEM. Wealth (a party, the Faubourg Saint-Honoré, a mansion).

XIII. CITAR

The *Party,* the *Faubourg,* the *Mansion* are anodyne data, seemingly lost in the *natural* flow of the discourse; in fact, they are touches designed to bring out the image of Wealth in the tapestry of the daydream. Thus, on several occasions the seme is "cited"; we would like to give this word its tauromachian meaning: the *citar* is the stamp of the heel, the torero's arched stance which summons the bull to the banderilleros. Similarly, one cites the signified (wealth) to make it come forth, while avoiding it in the discourse. This fleeting citation, this surreptitious and discontinuous way of stating themes, this alternating of flux and outburst, create together the *allure* of the connotation; the semes appear to float freely, to form a galaxy of trifling data in which we read no order of importance: the narrative technique is impressionistic: it breaks up the signifier into particles of verbal matter which make sense only by coalescing: it plays with the distribution of a discontinuity (thus creating a character's "personality"); the greater the syntagmatic distance between two data, the more skillful the narrative; the performance consists in manipulating a certain degree of impressionism: the touch must be light, as though it weren't

22

worth remembering, and yet, appearing again later in another guise, it must already be a memory; the readerly is an effect based on the operations of solidarity (the readerly "sticks"); but the more this solidarity is renewed, the more the intelligible becomes intelligent. The (ideological) goal of this technique is to naturalize meaning and thus to give credence to the reality of the story: for (in the West) meaning (system), we are told, is antipathetic to nature and reality. This naturalization is possible only because the significant data released—or summoned—in a homeopathic rhythm are carried, borne along, by a purportedly "natural" medium: language: paradoxically, language, the integral system of meaning, is employed to de-systematize the secondary meanings, to naturalize their production and to authenticate the story: connotation is concealed beneath the regular sound of the "sentences," "wealth" beneath utterly natural syntax (subject and adverbial object) which says that a party is being given in a mansion which is located in a particular neighborhood.

(8) *The trees, partially covered with snow, stood out dimly against the grayish background of a cloudy sky, barely whitened by the moon. Seen amid these fantastic surroundings, they vaguely resembled ghosts half out of their shrouds, a gigantic representation of the famous Dance of the Dead.* ★ SYM. Antithesis: A: the outdoors. —★★ The snow here refers to cold, but this is not inevitable, it is even rare: the snow, a soft, downy cloak, rather connotes the warmth of homogeneous substances, the protection of a shelter. Here the cold is created by the partial nature of the snow covering: it is not the snow but the partialness that is cold; the sinister form is the partially covered form: the plucked, the skinned, the patchy, everything left of a wholeness preyed on by a nothingness (SEM. Cold). The moon, too, contributes to this deficiency: frankly sinister here, forming a defect in the landscape it lights; we will come upon it again endowed with an ambiguous softness when, in the

form of an alabaster lamp, it will illumine and feminize Vien's Adonis (No. 111), a portrait which is the (explicit) reflection of Girodet's Endymion (No. 547). The moon is the *nothingness* of light, warmth reduced to its deficiency: it illuminates by mere reflection without itself being an origin; thus, it becomes the luminous emblem of the castrato, a deficiency manifested by the empty glitter he borrows from femininity while young (an Adonis) and of which nothing remains but a leprous gray when he is old (the old man, the garden) (SEM. Selenity). Furthermore, the fantastic designates and will designate what is outside the limits of the human: supernatural, extra-terrestrial, this transgression is the castrato's, represented (later) as both sub-woman and sub-man (SEM. Fantastic). ★★★ REF. Art (The Dance of the Dead).

(9) *Then, turning in the other direction,* ★ Here the passage from one term of the Antithesis (outside, the garden) to the other (inside, the salon) is a bodily movement; thus it is not an artifice of discourse (part of the rhetorical code) but a physical act of conjunction (part of the symbolic level) (SYM. Antithesis: mediation).

(10) *I could admire the Dance of the Living!* ★ The Dance of the Dead (No. 8) was a stereotype, a fixed syntagm. Here, this syntagm is divided, a new syntagm is created (the *Dance of the Living*). Two codes are simultaneously understood: a code of connotation (in the *dance of death* the meaning is universal, arising from a coded knowledge, that of art history) and a code of denotation (in the *dance of the living,* each word, according to its dictionary meaning, is added to its predecessor); this divergence, this sort of double vision, defines the play on words. This play on words is constructed like a diagram for an Antithesis (a form whose symbolic importance we know): a common stem, *dance,* is diversified into two opposing syntagms (*death/life*), just as the narrator's body is the unique dividing line between the garden and the salon (REF. Play on words). ★★ *I could contemplate* set forth the first part (A) of the Antithesis (No. 7). "*I could admire*" symmetrically announces the second (B). The contemplation had reference to an actual painted picture; admiration, bringing forth shapes, colors, sounds, and scents, makes the description of the salon (still to come) like a theatrical scene (the stage). We will

return to this subjection of literature (particularly in its "realist" form) to other representational codes (SYM. Antithesis: B: statement).

(11) *a splendid salon decorated in silver and gold, with glittering chandeliers, sparkling with candles. There, milling about, whirling around, flitting here and there, were the most beautiful women of Paris, the richest, the noblest, dazzling, stately, resplendent with diamonds, flowers in their hair, on their bosoms, on their heads, strewn over dresses or in garlands at their feet. Light, rustling movements, voluptuous steps, made the laces, the silk brocades, the gauzes, float around their delicate forms. Here and there, some overly animated glances darted forth, eclipsing the lights, the fire of the diamonds, and stimulated anew some too-ardent hearts. One might also catch movements of the head meaningful to lovers, and negative gestures for husbands. The sudden outbursts of the gamblers' voices at each unexpected turn of the dice, the clink of gold, mingled with the music and the murmur of conversation, and to complete the giddiness of this mass of people intoxicated by everything seductive the world can hold, a haze of perfume and general inebriation played upon the fevered mind.* ★ SYM. Antithesis: B: indoors. ★★ The women are transformed into flowers (they are wearing them everywhere); this seme of *flora* will later be attached to the woman the narrator is in love with (whose outlines are "verdant"); further, *flora* connotes a certain conception of life in its pure state (because organic) which forms an antithesis with the dead "thing" the old man will represent (SEM. Flora). The rustling of laces, the gauzy floatings, the haze of perfumes, evoke the seme *vaporous*, antithetical to *angular* (No. 80), to the geometrical (No. 76), the wrinkled (No. 82), all of which are forms which will be semes for the old man. In the old man, by way of contrast, what is intended is the *machine*; can we conceive (at least in readerly discourse) of a *vaporous machine?* (SEM. Vaporous.) ★★★ SEM. Wealth. ★★★★ Allusively, an adulterous ambiance is designated; it connotes Paris as an immoral city (Parisian fortunes, the Lantys' included, are immoral) (REF. Ethnic psychology: Paris).

(12) *Thus, on my right, the dark and silent image of death; on my left, the seemly bacchanalias of life: here, cold nature, dull, in*

25

mourning; there, human beings enjoying themselves. ★ SYM. Antithesis: AB: résumé.

(13) *On the borderline between these two so different scenes,
which, a thousand times repeated in various guises, make Paris the
world's most amusing and most philosophical city, I was making
for myself a moral macédoine, half pleasant, half funereal. With
my left foot I beat time, and I felt as though the other were in the
grave. My leg was in fact chilled by one of those insidious drafts
which freeze half our bodies while the other half feels the humid
heat of rooms, an occurrence rather frequent at balls.* ★ *Macédoine* connotes a composite, the mixture *without combination* of
disparate elements. This seme will move from the narrator to Sarrasine (No. 195), thus weakening the notion that the narrator is
merely a secondary, introductory character: symbolically, the two
are equals. The *composite* is set against a condition which will
have vast importance in Sarrasine's story, since it will be linked
with the discovery of his first pleasure: the *lubricated* (No. 213).
The failure of the narrator and of Sarrasine is the failure of a substance which does not "take" (SEM. Composite). ★★ Two cultural codes make their voices heard here: ethnic psychology (REF.
"Paris") and popular medicine ("an easy way to catch cold is to
stand in a window recess") (REF. Medicine). ★★★ The narrator's
participation in the profound symbolism of the Antithesis is here
made ironic, trivialized, minimized by reference to a physical causation which is vulgar, contemptible: the narrator pretends to reject
the symbolic, which in his eyes is a "draft"; however, he will be
punished for his disbelief (SEM. Asymbolism).

XIV. ANTITHESIS I: THE SUPPLEMENT

The several hundred figures propounded by the art of rhetoric
down through the centuries constitute a labor of classification
intended to name, to lay the foundations for, the world.
Among all these figures, one of the most stable is the Antithesis; its apparent function is to consecrate (and domesticate)
by a name, by a metalinguistic object, the division between

opposi ~ and the very irreducibility of this division. The antithesis separates for eternity; it thus refers to a nature of opposites, and this nature is untamed. Far from differing merely by the presence or lack of a simple relationship (as is ordinarily the case with paradigmatic opposites), the two terms of an antithesis are each *marked*: their difference does not arise out of a complementary, dialectical movement (empty as opposed to full): the antithesis is the battle between two plenitudes set ritually face to face like two fully armed warriors; the Antithesis is the figure of the *given* opposition, eternal, eternally recurrent: the figure of the inexpiable. Every joining of two antithetical terms, every mixture, every conciliation—in short, every passage through the wall of the Antithesis—thus constitutes a transgression; to be sure, rhetoric can reinvent a figure designed to name the transgressive; this figure exists: it is the *paradoxism* (or alliance of words): an unusual figure, it is the code's ultimate attempt to affect the inexpiable. Hidden in the *recess*, between outside and inside, installed at the interior limit of adversation, spanning the wall of the Antithesis, the narrator brings this figure into play: he induces or supports a transgression. This transgression is in no way catastrophic, for the moment; ironized, trivialized, tamed, it is the object of an innocuous word, without relationship to the horror of the symbol (to the symbol as horror); and yet its outrageousness is immediately clear. How? Rhetorically, the antithesis of garden and salon has been saturated: the whole (AB) has been stated, each term has been individually introduced and described, and then once again, to sum up, the whole antithesis has been recapitulated in a harmoniously closed loop:

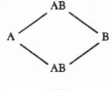

Now an element has thrust itself into this group which has been (rhetorically) completed. This element is the narrator's position (encoded as "mediation").

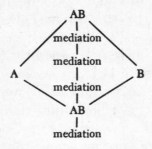

Mediation upsets the rhetorical—or paradigmatic—harmony of the Antithesis (AB/A/B/AB) and this difficulty arises not out of a lack but out of an excess: there is one element *in excess*, and this untoward supplement is the body (of the narrator). As supplement, the body is the site of the transgression effected by the narrative: it is at the level of the body that the two *inconciliabilia* of the Antithesis (outside and inside, cold and heat, death and life) are brought together, are made to touch, to mingle in the most amazing of figures in a composite substance (without *holding together*), here whimsical (the macédoine) and later chimerical (the arabesque created by the old man and the girl when seated side by side). It is by way of this *excess* which enters the discourse after rhetoric has properly saturated it that something can be told and the narrative begin.

XV. THE FULL SCORE

The area of the (readerly) text is comparable at every point to a (classical)musical score. The divisions of the syntagm (in its gradual movement) correspond to the divisions of the sonic flow into measures (one is hardly more arbitrary than the other). What stands out, what flashes forth, what emphasizes and impresses are the semes, the cultural citations and the symbols, analogous in their heavy timbre, in the value of their discontinuity, to the brass and percussion. What sings, what flows smoothly, what moves by accidentals, arabesques, and controlled ritardandos through an intelligible progression (like the melody often given the woodwinds) is the series of enigmas, their suspended disclosure, their delayed resolution: the development of an enigma is really like that of a fugue; both contain a *subject*, subject to an *exposition*, a *development* (embodied in the retards, ambiguities, and diversions by which the discourse prolongs the mystery), a *stretto* (a tightened section where scraps of answers rapidly come and go), and a *conclusion*. Finally, what sustains, flows in a regular way, brings everything together, like the strings, are the proairetic sequences, the series of actions, the cadence of familiar gestures:

LEXIAS	1	2	3	4	5	6	7	8	9	10	11	12	13
Semes	♪		♪	♪			♪	♫			♫		♫
Cultural codes			♪					♪		♪	♪		♫
Antithesis		♩			♩		♩	♩	♩	♩	♩	♩	♩
Enigma 1	𝅝												
"Deep in"		𝅗𝅥											
"Hidden"						𝅗𝅥							

The analogy can be carried even further. We can attribute to two lines of the polyphonic table (the hermeneutic and the

29

proairetic) the same tonal determination that melody and harmony have in classical music: the readerly text is a *tonal* text (for which habit creates a reading process just as conditioned as our hearing: one might say there is a *reading eye* as there is a tonal ear, so that to unlearn the readerly would be the same as to unlearn the tonal), and its tonal unity is basically dependent on two sequential codes: the revelation of truth and the coordination of the actions represented: there is the same constraint in the gradual order of melody and in the equally gradual order of the narrative sequence. *Now, it is precisely this constraint which reduces the plural of the classic text.* The five codes mentioned, frequently heard simultaneously, in fact endow the text with a kind of plural quality (the text is actually polyphonic), but of the five codes, only three establish permutable, reversible connections, outside the constraint of time (the semic, cultural, and symbolic codes); the other two impose their terms according to an irreversible order (the hermeneutic and proairetic codes). The classic text, therefore, is actually tabular (and not linear), but its tabularity is vectorized, it follows a logico-temporal order. It is a multivalent but incompletely reversible system. What blocks its reversibility is just what limits the plural nature of the classic text. These blocks have names: on the one hand, truth; on the other, empiricism: against—or between—them, the modern text comes into being.

(14) *"Monsieur de Lanty hasn't owned this house for very long, has he?"*

"Oh yes. Maréchal Carigliano sold it to him nearly ten years ago."

"Ah!"

"These people must have a huge fortune."

"They must have."

"*What a party! It's shockingly elegant.*"

"*Do you think they're as rich as M. de Nucingen or M. de Gondreville?*" ★ ACT. "To be deep in": 2: to come back again. ★★ REF. Chronological code (ten years . . .). ★★★ Here the Lantys' wealth (already indicated by linking the party, the mansion, and the neighborhood) is openly stated; and since this wealth will be the subject of an enigma (where does it come from?), the lexia must be regarded as a term of the hermeneutic code; we shall designate as *theme* the object (or subject) of the enigma; the enigma is not yet formulated, but its theme has already been introduced, or, if we prefer, speaking casually, brought out (HER. Enigma 2: theme).

(15) "*You mean you don't know?*" . . .

I stuck my head out and recognized the two speakers as members of that strange race which, in Paris, deals exclusively with "whys" and "hows," with "Where did they come from?" "What's happening?" "What has she done?" They lowered their voices and walked off to talk in greater comfort on some isolated sofa. Never had a richer vein been offered to seekers after mystery. ★ ACT. "Hiding place: 2: to come out of hiding. ★★ REF. Ethnic psychology (Paris, worldly, slanderous, taletelling). ★★★ Here we have two further terms of the hermeneutic code: the proposal of the enigma each time the discourse tells us, in one way or another, "There is an enigma," and the *avoided* (or *suspended*) *answer*: for had the discourse not moved the two speakers off to a secluded sofa, we would have quickly learned the answer to the enigma, the source of the Lanty fortune (however, then there would have been no story to tell) (HER. Enigma 2: proposal and suspended answer).

(16) *Nobody knew what country the Lanty family came from,* ★ A new enigma, thematized (the Lantys are a family), proposed (there is an enigma), and formulated (What is their origin?): these three morphemes are here combined in a single phrase (HER. Enigma 3: theme, proposal, and formulation).

(17) *or from what business, what plunder, what piratical activity, or what inheritance derived a fortune estimated at several millions.* ★ HER. Enigma 2: (the Lanty fortune): formulation.

31

(18) *All the members of the family spoke Italian, French, Spanish, English, and German perfectly enough to create the belief that they must have spent a long time among these various peoples. Were they gypsies? Were they freebooters?* ★ A seme is hinted at here: the international character of the Lantys, who speak the five cultivated languages of the day. This seme points to the truth (the great-uncle is a former international star and the languages mentioned are those of musical Europe), but it is far too soon for it to serve in unveiling it: the important thing, for the morale of the discourse, is that the seme not contradict the truth prospectively (SEM. Internationalism). ★★ Narratively, an enigma leads from a question to an answer, *through a certain number of delays.* Of these delays, the main one is unquestionably the feint, the misleading answer, the lie, what we will call the *snare.* The discourse has already lied by preterition, by omitting from among the possible sources of the Lantys' fortune (*commerce, plunder, piracy, inheritance*) the real one, which is the stardom of an uncle, a famous and kept castrato; here the discourse lies positively by means of an enthymeme with a false premise: 1. Only gypsies and freebooters speak several languages. 2. The Lantys are polygot. 3. The Lantys are gypsies or freebooters (HER. Enigma 3: snare, set by the discourse for the reader).

(19) *"Even if it's the devil," some young politicians said, "they give a marvelous party."*
   "Even if the Count de Lanty had robbed a bank, I'd marry his daughter any time!" cried a philosopher. ★ REF. Ethnic psychology: cynical Paris.

(20) *Who wouldn't have married Marianina, a girl of sixteen whose beauty embodied the fabled imaginings of the Eastern poets! Like the sultan's daughter, in the story of the Magic Lamp, she should have been kept veiled. Her singing put into the shade the partial talents of Malibran, Sontag, and Fodor, in whom one dominant quality has always excluded over-all perfection; whereas Marianina was able to bring to the same level purity of sound, sensibility, rightness of movement and pitch, soul and science, correctness and feeling. This girl was the embodiment of that secret poetry, the common bond among all the arts, which always eludes*

*those who search for it. Sweet and modest, educated and witty, no
one could eclipse Marianina, save her mother.* ★ REF. Chronology (Marianina was six years old when her father purchased the
Carigliano mansion, etc.). ★★ REF. Gnomic code (*"There is in
every art,"* etc.) and literary code (Oriental poets, *The Thousand
and One Nights,* Aladdin). ★★★ Why is Marianina's musicianship
so perfect? because she unites talents which are usually scattered.
Similarly, why does Sarrasine find La Zambinella so seductive? because her body unites perfections the sculptor has only seen divided
among many models (No. 220). In both cases, we have the theme
of the dismembered body—or the body as a whole (SYM. The reassembled body). ★★★★ The young girl's beauty is referred to a
cultural code, in this instance literary (it can elsewhere be pictorial or sculptural). This is a vast commonplace of literature: the
Woman copies the Book. In other words, every body is a citation:
of the "already-written." The origin of desire is the statue, the
painting, the book (Sarrasine will be identified with Pygmalion,
No. 229) (SYM. Replication of bodies).

XVI. BEAUTY

Beauty (unlike ugliness) cannot really be explained: in each
part of the body it stands out, repeats itself, but it does not
describe itself. Like a god (and as empty), it can only say: *I
am what I am.* The discourse, then, can do no more than assert
the perfection of each detail and refer "the remainder" to the
code underlying all beauty: Art. In other words, beauty cannot
assert itself save in the form of a citation: that Marianina resembles the sultan's daughter is the only way something can
be said about her beauty; it derives from its Model not only
beauty but also language; left on its own, deprived of any anterior code, beauty would be mute. Every direct predicate is
denied it; the only feasible predicates are either tautology (*a
perfectly oval face*) or simile (*lovely as a Raphael Madonna,*

33

like a dream in stone, etc.); thus, beauty is referred to an infinity of codes: *lovely as Venus?* But Venus lovely as what? As herself? As Marianina? There is only one way to stop the replication of beauty: hide it, return it to silence, to the ineffable, to aphasia, refer the referent back to the invisible, veil the sultan's daughter, affirm the code without realizing (without compromising) its original. There is one rhetorical figure which fills this blank in the object of comparison whose existence is altogether transferred to the language of the object to which it is compared: catachresis (there is no other possible word to denote the "wings" of a house, or the "arms" of a chair, and yet "wings" and "arms" are *instantly*, *already* metaphorical): a basic figure, more basic perhaps than metonymy, since it speaks around an empty object of comparison: the figure of beauty.

(21) *Have you ever encountered one of those women whose striking beauty defies the inroads of age and who seem at thirty-six more desirable than they could have been fifteen years earlier? Their visage is a vibrant soul, it glows; each feature sparkles with intelligence; each pore has a special brilliance, especially in artificial light. Their seductive eyes refuse, attract, speak or remain silent; their walk is innocently knowledgeable; their voices employ the melodious wealth of the most coquettishly soft and tender notes. Based on comparisons, their praises flatter the self-love of the most sentient. A movement of their eyebrows, the least glance, their pursed lips, fill with a kind of terror those whose life and happiness depend upon them. Inexperienced in love and influenced by words, a young girl can be seduced; for this kind of woman, however, a man must know, like M. de Jaucourt, not to cry out when he is hiding in a closet and the maid breaks two of his fingers as she shuts the door on them. In loving these powerful sirens, one gambles with one's life. And this, perhaps, is why we love them so passionately. Such was the Countess de Lanty.* ★ REF. Chronology

(Mme de Lanty is thirty-six when . . . : the information is either functional or signifying, as it is here). ★★ REF. The legends of love (M. de Jaucourt) and the amorous typology of women (the mature woman as superior to the inexperienced virgin). ★★★ Marianina copied *The Thousand and One Nights*. Mme. de Lanty's body is drawn from another Book, the Book of Life (*"Have you ever encountered one of those women . . ."*). This book was written by men (like M. de Jaucourt) who are themselves a part of the *legend*, a part of what must be read in order for love to be spoken (SYM. Replication of bodies). ★★★★ In contrast to her daughter, Mme de Lanty is described so that her symbolic role is clear: the biological axis of the sexes (which would force us, quite pointlessly, to put all the women in the story in the same class) is replaced by the symbolic axis of castration (SYM. Axis of castration).

XVII. THE CASTRATION CAMP

At first glance, *Sarrasine* sets forth a complete structure of the sexes (two opposing terms, a mixed and a neuter). This structure might then be defined in phallic terms: (1) to be the phallus (the men: the narrator, M. de Lanty, Sarrasine, Bouchardon); (2) to have it (the women: Marianina, Mme de Lanty, the girl the narrator is in love with, Clotilde); (3) to have it and not to be it (the androgynous: Filippo, Sappho); not to have it or to be it (the castrato). Now this distribution is unsatisfactory. The women, though they belong to the same biological class, do not have the same symbolic role: the mother and the daughter are opposites (as the text tells us often enough), Mme de Rochefide is divided, alternately child and queen, Clotilde is a nothing; Filippo, who has both feminine and masculine features, has no relationship to the Sappho who terrifies Sarrasine (No. 443); finally, and most notably, the men in the story do badly where full virility is concerned: one is shrunken (M. de Lanty), another is maternal (Bouchardon),

the third is in thrall to the Queen-Woman (the narrator), and
the last (Sarrasine) "run down" to the point of castration.
Thus, sexual classification is not the right one. Another pertinence must be found. It is Mme de Lanty who reveals the
proper structure: in opposition to her (passive) daughter,
Mme de Lanty is totally active: she dominates time (defying
the inroads of age); she radiates (radiation is action at a distance, the highest form of power); bestowing praises, making
comparisons, instituting the language in relation to which
man can recognize himself, she is the primal Authority, the
Tyrant, whose silent *numen* decrees life, death, storm, peace;
finally and above all, she mutilates man (M. de Jaucourt loses
his "finger" because of her). In short, the precursor of Sappho
who so terrifies Sarrasine, Mme de Lanty is the castrating
woman, endowed with all the hallucinatory attributes of the
Father: power, fascination, instituting authority, terror, power
to castrate. Thus, the symbolic field is not that of the biological sexes; it is that of castration: of *castrating/castrated, ac-
tive/passive*. It is in this field, and not in that of the biological
sexes, that the characters in the story are pertinently distributed. On the side of active castration, we must include Mme
de Lanty, Bouchardon (who keeps Sarrasine away from sexuality), and Sappho (a mythic figure threatening the sculptor).
On the passive side, whom do we find? the "men" in the story:
Sarrasine and the narrator, both led into castration, which the
former desires and the latter recounts. As for the castrato himself, we would be wrong to place him of necessity among the
castrated: he is the blind and mobile flaw in this system; he
moves back and forth between active and passive: castrated, he
castrates; the same is true of Mme de Rochefide: contami-
nated by the castration she has just been told about, she impels
the narrator into it. As for Marianina, her symbolic existence
could not be defined apart from that of her brother Filippo.

(22) *Filippo, Marianina's brother, shared with his sister in the Countess's marvelous beauty. To be brief, this young man was a living image of Antinous, even more slender. Yet how well these thin, delicate proportions are suited to young people when an olive complexion, strongly defined eyebrows, and the fire of velvet eyes give promise of future male passion, of brave thoughts! If Filippo resided in every girl's heart as an ideal, he also resided in the memory of every mother as the best catch in France.* ★ REF. Antique art. ★★ SEM. Wealth (the best catch in France), and Mediterranean type (olive complexion, velvet eyes). ★★★ Young Filippo exists only as a copy of two models: his mother and Antinous: the biological, chromosomatic Book, and the Book of statuary (without which it would be impossible to speak of beauty: Antinous, *"to be brief"*: but what else is to be said? and what then to be said about Antinous?) (SYM. Replication of bodies). ★★★★ SYM. Axis of castration. Filippo's feminine features, although quickly amended by euphemism (*strongly defined eyebrows, male passions*), since saying a boy is handsome is already sufficient to feminize him, place him in the women's camp, on the side of active castration: however, Filippo plays no part in the story: then what purpose, symbolically, can Marianina and Filippo serve?

XVIII. THE CASTRATO'S POSTERITY

In the story, neither Marianina nor Filippo serve much purpose: Marianina only provides the minor episode of the ring (an episode intended to deepen the Lanty mystery) and Filippo has no semantic existence other than to form a link (by his ambiguous physique, his tender and concerned treatment of the old man) with the women's camp. As we have seen, this camp is not one of biological sex, but of castration. Now, neither Marianina nor Filippo have the characteristics of castrators. Then what symbolic purpose do they serve? This one: both feminine, brother and sister create a feminine progeny for Mme de Lanty (their maternal atavism is emphasized); *in other words, for La Zambinella* (whose niece Mme de Lanty is): they exist to embody a kind of explosion of Zambinellan femininity. The meaning is as follows: if La Zambinella had had children (a paradox indicative of the deficiency which makes her what she is), they would have been these hereditarily and delicately feminine creatures, Marianina and Filippo: as though in La Zambinella there had been a dream of normality, a teleological essence from which the castrato had been excluded, and this essence was femininity itself, a realm and posterity reconstituted in Marianina and Filippo above the blank of castration.

(23) *The beauty, the fortune, the wit, the charms of these two children, came solely from their mother.* ★ What is the source of the Lanty fortune? To this enigma 2, there is now an answer: the countess, the woman. Thus, according to the hermeneutic code, there is a solution (partial, at least), a scrap of an answer. Yet the truth is submerged in a list whose parataxis sweeps it along, hides it, holds it back, and finally does not reveal it at all: thus there is a decoy, a snare, an obstacle (or a delay) in the solving. We will call this mixture of truth and snare, this ineffective solving, an *equivocation* (HER. Enigma 2: equivocation). ★★ (SYM. Replication of bodies) (the bodies of the children copy their mother's).

(24) *The Count de Lanty was small, ugly, and pock-marked; dark as a Spaniard, dull as a banker. However, he was taken to be a deep politician, perhaps because he rarely laughed, and was always quoting Metternich or Wellington.* ★ REF. Psychology of peoples and professions (Spaniard, banker). ★★ Monsieur de Lanty's role is small; as a banker, host of the party, he links the story to the myth of Parisian High Finance. His function is symbolic: his deprecatory portrait excludes him from the heritage of La Zambinella (from femininity); he is a negligible, lost father, and joins the discarded men of the story, all castrated, cut off from pleasure; he helps fill out the paradigm *castrating/castrated* (SYM. Axis of castration).

(25) *This mysterious family had all the appeal of one of Lord Byron's poems, whose difficulties each person in the fashionable world interpreted in a different way: an obscure and sublime song in every strophe.* ★ REF. Literature (Byron). ★★ HER. Enigma 3: theme and proposal ("this mysterious family"). ★★★ The family, out of the Byronic Book, is itself a book, set forth strophe by strophe: the realistic author spends his time referring back to books: reality is what has been written (SYM. Replication of bodies).

(26) *The reserve maintained by M. and Mme de Lanty about their origin, their past life, and their relationship with the four corners of the globe had not lasted long as a subject of astonishment in Paris. Nowhere perhaps is Vespasian's axiom better understood. There, even bloodstained or filthy money betrays nothing and stands for everything. So long as high society knows the amount of your fortune, you are classed among those having an equal amount, and no one asks to see your family tree, because everyone knows how much it cost. In a city where social problems are solved like algebraic equations, adventurers have every opportunity in their favor. Even supposing this family were of gypsy origin, it was so wealthy, so attractive, that society had no trouble in forgiving its little secrets.* ★ REF. Gnomic code (*Non olet*, the Latin supplement of a dictionary) and the mythology of Parisian Gold. ★★ SEM. Internationality. ★★★ HER. Enigma 3 (origin of the Lantys): proposal (there is a mystery) and snare (the Lantys are perhaps of gypsy origin). ★★★★ HER. Enigma 2 (source of the fortune): proposal (no one knows where this fortune comes from).

XIX. INDEX, SIGN, MONEY

In the past (says the text), money "revealed"; it was an index, it furnished a fact, a cause, it had a nature; today it "represents" (everything): it is an equivalent, an exchange, a representation: a sign. Between index and sign, a common mode, that of inscription. Shifting from a monarchy based on land to an industrial monarchy, society changed the Book, it passed from the Letter (of nobility) to the Figure (of fortune), from title deeds to ledgers, but it is always subject to a writing. The difference between feudal society and bourgeois society, index and sign, is this: the index has an origin, the sign does not: to shift from index to sign is to abolish the last (or first) limit, the origin, the basis, the prop, to enter into the limitless process of equivalences, representations that nothing will ever stop, orient, fix, sanction. Parisian indifference to the origin of money equates symbolically with the non-origin of money; a money that has no smell is money withdrawn from the basic order of the index, from the consecration of origin: this money is as empty as being-castrated: for Parisian Gold, what corresponds to the physiological impossibility of procreating is the impossibility of having an origin, a moral heredity: the signs (monetary, sexual) are wild because, contrary to the indices (the meaningful regime of the old society), they are not based on an original, irreducible, incorruptible, immovable otherness of their component parts: in the index, what is indicated (nobility) is of a different nature from what indicates (wealth): there is no possible mingling; in the sign, which establishes an order of representation (and no longer of determination, of creation, as does the index), the two elements *interchange*, signified and signifier revolving in an endless process: what is bought can be sold, the signified can become signifier, and so on. Replacing the feudal index, the bourgeois sign is a metonymic confusion.

(27) *Unfortunately, however, the mystery of the Lantys presented a continuing source of curiosity, rather like that contained in the novels of Ann Radcliffe.* ★ REF. Literature (Ann Radcliffe). ★★ HER. Enigma 3 (where do the Lantys come from?) : proposal.

(28) *Observers, people who make it a point to know in what shop you buy your candlesticks, or who ask the amount of your rent when they find your apartment attractive, had noticed, now and then, in the midst of the Countess's parties, concerts, balls, and routs, the appearance of a strange personage.* ★ REF. Code of Novelists, Moralists, Psychologists: observation of those who observe. ★★ Here a new enigma is proposed (a strange feeling) and thematized (a personage) (HER. Enigma 4: theme and proposal).

(29) *It was a man.* ★ The old man, in fact, is not a man: here, the discourse is misleading the reader (HER. Enigma 4: snare).

XX. THE DISSOLVE OF VOICES

Who is speaking? Is it a scientific voice which from the type "personage" infers, in passing, a species, "man," in order later to give it another species, "castrato"? Is it a phenomenalist voice naming what it sees, the wholly masculine garb of the old man? Here it is impossible to attribute an origin, a point of view, to the statement. Now, this impossibility is one of the ways in which the plural nature of a text can be appreciated. The more indeterminate the origin of the statement, the more plural the text. In modern texts, the voices are so treated that any reference is impossible: the discourse, or better, the language, speaks: nothing more. By contrast, in the classic text the majority of the utterances are assigned an origin, we can identify their parentage, who is speaking: either a consciousness (of a character, of the author) or a culture (the anonymous is still an origin, a voice: the voice we find, for example, in the gnomic code); however, it may happen that in the classic text, always haunted by the appropriation of speech, the voice gets lost, as though it had leaked out through a hole in the discourse. The best way to conceive the classical plural is then to listen to the text as an iridescent exchange carried on by

41

multiple voices, on different wavelengths and subject from time to time to a sudden *dissolve*, leaving a gap which enables the utterance to shift from one point of view to another, without warning: the writing is set up across this tonal instability (which in the modern text becomes atonality), which makes it a glistening texture of ephemeral origins.

(30) *The first time he had appeared in the mansion was during a concert, when he seemed to have been drawn to the salon by Marianina's enchanting voice.* ★ SEM. Musicianship (the seme is a truthful indicator, since the old man is a former soprano, but it lacks as yet the strength to reveal the whole truth).

(31) *"All of a sudden, I'm cold," a lady had said who was standing with a friend by the door.*
The stranger, who was standing next to the women, went away.
"That's odd! I'm warm now," she said, after the stranger had gone. "And you'll say I'm mad, but I can't help thinking that my neighbor, the man dressed in black who just left, was the cause of my chill." ★ SEM. Cold (first proposed in the garden, the migrating signifier has attached itself to the old man). ★★ SYM. Antithesis: cold/hot (the antithesis of garden and salon, animate and inanimate, repeated a second time).

(32) *Before long, the exaggeration native to those in high society gave birth to and accumulated the most amusing ideas, the most outrageous expressions, the most ridiculous anecdotes about this mysterious personage.* ★ REF. Worldliness. ★★ HER. Enigma 4 (who is the old man?): false replies: statement. As a term in the hermeneutic code, the *false reply* differs from the snare in that error is distinguished as such by the discourse.

(33) *Although not a vampire, a ghoul, or an artificial man, a kind of Faust or Robin Goodfellow, people fond of fantasy said he had something of all these anthropomorphic natures about him.* ★ HER. Enigma 4: false reply No. 1. ★★ SEM. Extra-

terrestrial and extra-temporal (the old man is death itself, who alone does not die: in the dead man who does not die there is an extra, supplemental death).

(34) *Here and there, one came across some Germans who accepted as fact these clever witticisms of Parisian scandal-mongering.* ★ REF. Ethnic psychology: a paradigm of the period: the naïve German, the witty Parisian.

(35) *The stranger was merely an old man.* ★ HER. Enigma 4: snare (the stranger is not "merely" an old man). ★★ The narrator (or the discourse?) reduces the mysterious to the simple; he stands as the defender of fact, dismisses any recourse to fable, myth, symbol, renders language useless by means of a tautology (*the old man was an old man*): the narrator (or discourse) here resorts to an *imaginary* figure: asymbolism (SEM. Asymbolism).

(36) *Many of the young men who were in the habit of settling the future of Europe every morning in a few elegant phrases would have liked to see in this stranger some great criminal, the possessor of vast wealth. Some storytellers recounted the life of this old man and provided really curious details about the atrocities he had committed while in the service of the Maharaja of Mysore. Some bankers, more positive by nature, invented a fable about money. "Bah," they said, shrugging their shoulders in pity, "this poor old man is a tête génoise!"* ★ HER. Enigma 4: false replies Nos. 2, 3, and 4 (the false replies derive from cultural codes: cynical youths, storytellers, bankers). ★★ SYM. Wealth.

(37) *"Sir, without being indiscreet, could you please tell me what you mean by a tête génoise?"*
"A man, sir, with an enormous lifetime capital and whose family's income doubtless depends on his good health." ★ True, there is a link between the fortune of the former star and the Lantys' fortune; it is doubtful that the family's affection for the old man is an interested one, however: the whole creates an ambiguity (HER. Enigma 4: equivocation).

(38) *I remember having heard at Mme d'Espard's a hypnotist proving on highly suspect historical data that this old man,*

43

*preserved under glass, was the famous Balsamo, known as Caglios-
tro. According to this contemporary alchemist, the Sicilian adventurer had escaped death and passed his time fabricating gold
for his grandchildren. Last, the bailiff of Ferette maintained that
he had recognized this odd personage as the Count of Saint-
Germain.* ★ HER. Enigma 4: false reply No. 5. ★★ SEM. Beyond
time. Two (weakened) accessory connotations are heard here:
under glass recalls the revulsion some people feel at the sight of a
mummy, an embalmed, preserved body; and alchemist's gold is
empty gold, without origin (the same gold as the gold of specu-
lators).

(39) *These stupidities, spoken in witty accents, with the mocking
air characteristic of atheistic society in our day, kept alive vague
suspicions about the Lanty family.* ★ REF. Psychology of peoples:
cynical Paris. ★★ HER. Enigma 3: proposal and thematization
(there is an enigma, and it concerns the Lanty family). ★★★ HER.
Enigma 4: false response No. 6. In the hermeneutic sequence, the
false replies create a *byte* (a basic or subroutine configuration in
cybernetic language); this *byte* is itself subject to a rhetorical code
(the code of exposition): a statement (No. 32), six false replies, a
résumé (No. 39).

XXI. IRONY, PARODY

Stated by the discourse itself, the ironic code is, in principle, an
explicit quotation of what someone has said; however, irony
acts as a signpost, and thereby it destroys the multivalence we
might expect from quoted discourse. A multivalent text can
carry out its basic duplicity only if it subverts the opposition
between true and false, if it fails to attribute quotations (even
when seeking to discredit them) to explicit authorities, if it
flouts all respect for origin, paternity, propriety, if it destroys
the voice which could give the text its ("organic") unity, in
short, if it coldly and fraudulently abolishes quotation marks

which must, as we say, in all *honesty*, enclose a quotation and juridically distribute the ownership of the sentences to their respective proprietors, like subdivisions of a field. For multivalence (contradicted by irony) is a transgression of ownership. The wall of voices must be passed through to reach the writing: this latter eschews any designation of ownership and thus can never be *ironic*; or, at least, its irony is never certain (an uncertainty which marks several great texts: Sade, Fourier, Flaubert). Employed in behalf of a subject that puts its imaginary elements at the distance it pretends to take with regard to the language of others, thereby making itself even more securely a subject of the discourse, parody, or irony at work, is always *classic* language. What could a parody be that did not advertise itself as such? This is the problem facing modern writing: how breach the wall of utterance, the wall of origin, the wall of ownership? *But why want to?*

(40) *Finally, through a strange combination of circumstances, the members of this family justified everyone's conjectures by behaving somewhat mysteriously toward this old man, whose life was somehow hidden from all investigation.* ★ HER. Enigma 4: proposal. The "mystery" surrounding the old man's identity will be embodied in a certain number of actions, in themselves mysterious.

(41) *Whenever this person crossed the threshold of the room he was supposed to inhabit in the Lanty mansion, his appearance always created a great sensation among the family. One might have called it an event of great importance. Filippo, Marianina, Mme de Lanty, and an old servant were the only persons privileged to assist the old man in walking, rising, sitting down. Each of them watched over his slightest movement.* ★ SYM. The feminine camp. ★★ HER. Enigma 4: proposal (enigmatic behavior).

(42) *It seemed that he was an enchanted being upon whom depended the happiness, the life, or the fortune of them all.* ★ SEM.

45

Fascination. This signifier could lead to the truth, it being the castrato's nature to *enchant*, like a supernatural medium: thus Farinelli, who cured, or at least assuaged, the morbid melancholia of Philip V of Spain by singing to him daily (always the same melody for years on end).

(43) *Was it affection or fear? Those in society were unable to discover any clue to help them solve this problem.* ★ HER. Enigma 4: proposal and jamming of the answer.

(44) *Hidden for whole months in the depths of a secret sanctuary, this family genie would suddenly come forth, unexpectedly, and would appear in the midst of the salons like those fairies of bygone days who descended from flying dragons to interrupt the rites to which they had not been invited.* ★ SEM. Fascination. ★★ REF. Fairy tales.

(45) *Only the most avid onlookers were then able to perceive the uneasiness of the heads of the house, who could conceal their feelings with unusual skill.* ★ HER. Enigma 4: proposal (enigmatic behavior).

(46) *Sometimes, however, while dancing a quadrille, Marianina, naïve as she was, would cast a terrified glance at the old man when she spied him among the crowd. Or else Filippo would slip quickly through the throng to his side and would stay near him, tender and attentive, as though contact with others or the slightest breath would destroy this strange creature. The Countess would make a point of drawing near, without seeming to have any intention of joining them; then, assuming a manner and expression of servitude mixed with tenderness, submission, and power, she would say a few words, to which the old man nearly always deferred, and he would disappear, led off, or, more precisely, carried off, by her.* ★ SEM. Fragility and childishness. ★★ HER. Enigma 4: proposal (enigmatic behavior). ★★★ Since the old man is a castrato and the castrato is outside the sexes, he should be referred to in the neuter; however, since there is no neuter in French, the discourse, when it is trying not to "lie," denotes the castrato in ambiguous terms: nouns morphologically feminine, semantically applicable to

46

both sexes (both masculine and feminine simultaneously): thus the word *creature* (and further, *this feminine organization*) (SYM. The neuter of castration).

(47) *If Mme de Lanty were not present, the Count used a thousand stratagems to reach his side; however, he seemed to have difficulty making himself heard, and treated him like a spoiled child whose mother gives in to his whims in order to avoid a scene.* ★ HER. Enigma 4: proposal (enigmatic behavior). ★★ The Count is excluded from the women's camp: their elegant and successful actions are contrasted to his, which are laborious and ineffectual. M. de Lanty (the man of the family) is not a descendant of La Zambinella. Yet once again the symbolic distribution is set forth: the woman (Mme de Lanty) has the effective control, that of the father; it is the man (M. de Lanty) who exercises a haphazard and disregarded authority, that of the mother (SYM. Axis of castration).

(48) *Some bolder persons having thoughtlessly ventured to question the Count de Lanty, this cold, reserved man had appeared never to understand them. And so, after many tries, all futile because of the circumspection of the entire family, everyone stopped trying to fathom such a well-kept secret. Weary of trying, the companionable spies, the idly curious, and the politic all gave up bothering about this mystery.* ★ The discourse declares the enigma it has proposed to be unresolved: in the hermeneutic code, this is jamming (frequent in detective fiction) (HER. Enigma 4: jamming).

(49) *However, even now perhaps in these glittering salons there were some philosophers who, while eating an ice or a sherbet, or placing their empty punch glass on a side table, were saying to each other: "It wouldn't surprise me to learn that those people are crooks. The old man who hides and only makes his appearance on the first day of spring or winter, or at the solstices, looks to me like a killer . . ."*
"Or a confidence man . . ."
"It's almost the same thing. Killing a man's fortune is sometimes worse than killing the man." ★ REF. Psychology of peoples

(Paris) and gnomic code (*Killing a man's fortune . . .*). ★★ SEM. Fascination (the old man is said, albeit ironically, to appear at the magical times of the year, like a sorcerer).

(50) *"Sir, I have bet twenty louis, I should get back forty."*
  "But, sir, there are only thirty on the table."
  "Ah well, you see how mixed the crowd is, here. It's impossible to play."
  "True . . . But it's now nearly six months since we've seen the Spirit. Do you think he's really alive?"
  "Hah! at best . . ."
  These last words were spoken near me by people I did not know, as they were moving off, ★ SEM. Supernatural (out of the world and ultra-temporal). ★★ That which disappears in the gaming as though blown away is symbolically equivalent to the gold which appears without anyone's knowing or trying to find out its origin: without source and without destination, (Parisian) Gold is a substitute for the emptiness of castration (SYM. Gold, emptiness).

(51) *and as I was resuming, in an afterthought, my mixed thoughts of white and black, life and death. My vivid imagination as well as my eyes looked back and forth from the party, which had reached the height of its splendor, and the somber scene in the gardens.* ★ SYM. Antithesis: AB: résumé.

(52) *I do not know how long I meditated on these two faces of the human coin;* ★ ACT. "To meditate": 1: to be in the process of meditation. ★★ The coin is symbolic of the incommunicability of the two sides: like the paradigmatic slash mark of an antithesis, metal cannot be traversed: yet it will be, the Antithesis will be transgressed (SYM. Antithesis: AB: double participation).

(53) *but all at once I was awakened by the stifled laugh of a young woman.* ★ ACT. "To meditate": 2: to stop meditating. ★★ ACT. "To laugh": 1: to burst out laughing.

(54) *I was stunned by the appearance of the image which arose before me.* ★ The image: a generic term which announces (rhetorically) a third version of the antithesis: after the contrast of garden and party, heat and cold, we have here the groundwork for

48

the contrast of the girl and the old man. Like the other forms of Antithesis, this one is also corporeal: the image will be that of two mingled antithetical bodies. Now, this carnal antithesis is revealed, called forth, by a carnal act: laughter. A substitute for the cry, an hallucinatory agent, laughter breaches the wall of the Antithesis, removes from the coin the duality of reverse and obverse; erases the paradigmatic slash mark "reasonably" separating cold and heat, life and death, animate and inanimate. In addition, in the story itself, laughter is linked to castration: La Zambinella, "for a laugh," participates in the farce prepared by her friends at Sarrasine's expense; in the face of laughter, Sarrasine protests his virility (SYM. Antithesis: AB: statement).

(55) *By one of those tricks of nature, the half-mournful thought turning in my mind had emerged, and it appeared living before me, it had sprung like Minerva from the head of Jove, tall and strong, it was at once a hundred years old and twenty-two years old; it was alive and dead.* ★ SYM. Antithesis: AB: mingling (the wall of Antithesis is breached). ★★ REF. Mythology. What is amazing in the myth of Minerva is not that the goddess sprang from her father's head but that she emerged "tall and strong," already fully armed and fully developed. The (hallucinatory) image for which Minerva serves as model is not elaborated upon: we encounter it abruptly, as a reality, in the salon; when born, it is *already* written: there is only a shift of writings, trans-scription, without maturation, without organic origin. ★★★ REF. Chronology. The girl is twenty-two, the old man is one hundred. *Twenty-two*: this precise figure produces the effect of reality; metonymically, this precision leads us to believe that the old man is exactly one hundred years old (rather than being somewhere around one hundred).

(56) *Escaped from his room like a lunatic from his cell, the little old man had obviously slipped behind a hedge of people who were listening to Marianina's voice, finishing the cavatina from* Tan-credi. ★ SEM. Supernature (madness is outside "nature"). ★★ SEM. Musicianship. ★★★ REF. Music history (Rossini).

(57) *He seemed to have come out from underground, impelled by some piece of stage machinery.* ★ SEM. Machine, mechanical-

ness (likened to a machine, the old man is a part of the extra-human, of the inanimate).

(58) *Motionless and somber, he stood for a moment gazing at the party, the noises of which had perhaps reached his ears. His almost somnambulatory preoccupation was so concentrated on things that he was in the world without seeing it.* ★ SEM. Supernature, out-of-the-world. ★★ SYM. Antithesis: A: the old man.

(59) *He had unceremoniously sprung up next to one of the most ravishing women in Paris,* ★ SYM. Antithesis: AB: mixture of elements. The mixing of bodies (transgression of the Antithesis) is signified not by proximity (*next to*) but by sudden appearance. This implies that the space in which one appears was not expecting one, that it was completely occupied by something other: the young woman and the old man both find themselves occupying the same area, which was intended for only one of them.

(60) *a young and elegant dancer, delicately formed, with one of those faces as fresh as that of a child, pink and white, so frail and transparent that a man's glance seems to penetrate it like a ray of sunlight going through ice.* ★ SYM. Antithesis: B: the young woman. ★★ The body is a duplicate of the Book: the young woman originates in the Book of Life ("*one of those faces . . .*": the plural refers to a total of stored-up and recorded experiences) (SYM. Replication of bodies). ★★★ It is premature to place the young girl in the symbolic field: her (semic) portrait has just begun. Moreover, it will vary: the child-woman, transparent, fragile, fresh, will become, in No. 90, a fully drawn woman, outgoing rather than receptive, in short, *active* (whereupon, as we have seen, she will join the castrators); for the moment, probably due to the needs of the Antithesis, the discourse can only contrast the old man-machine with the child-woman (SYM. child-woman).

(61) *They were both there before me, together, united, and so close that the stranger brushed against her, her gauzy dress, her garlands of flowers, her softly curled hair, her floating sash.* ★ The mingling of the two bodies is signified by two connotators: on the one hand, the staccato rhythm of the short syntagms (*both/together/united/and so close*), which are built up diagrammatically,

describes the breathless pressure of bodies; and on the other hand, the image of a supple material (*gauze, garland, curled hair, floating sash*) has something of the vegetal in its development (SYM. Antithesis: AB: mingling). ★★ Symbolically, we here witness the castrato's marriage: opposites come together, the castrato has taken the woman (who, with equivocal fascination which will be emphasized later, bends toward him): an active metonymy through which castration will contaminate the young woman, the narrator, and Sarrasine (SYM. Marriage of the castrato).

(62) *I had brought this young woman to Mme de Lanty's ball. Since this was her first visit to the house, I forgave her her stifled laugh, but I quickly gave her a signal which completely silenced her and filled her with awe for her neighbor.* ★ SYM. The child-woman (the young woman is treated like a child who has been naughty). ★★ ACT. "To laugh": 2: to stop.

XXII. VERY NATURAL ACTIONS

There is a belief that great structures, serious symbols, grand meanings are built upon an unimpressive foundation of ordinary acts that the discourse notes as a matter of form, "to speak truly": all criticism therefore rests on the notion that *the text contains insignificant elements* or, in effect, nature: the meaning is supposed to take its preeminence from an "over meaning," which is noted, whose subordinate role is supposed to be purely by way of contrast. Now, the notion of structure does not support the separation of foundation and design, insignificant and significant; structure is not a design, a schema, a diagram: everything signifies something. For proof, we have only to examine the basic (and thus seemingly unimportant) proairetisms, the usual paradigm of which is something like *begin/end, continue/stop.* In these common examples (in the present text: *to laugh, to be deep in, to hide, to meditate, to join, to threaten, to undertake,* etc.), the nature of the phenomenon established by the notation is capped by a *conclusion* and consequently seems to be subject to some logic (as long as temporality appears: the classic narrative is basically subject to the logico-temporal order). Writing "the end" (a phrase which is precisely both temporal and logical) thus posits everything that has been written as having been a tension which "naturally" requires resolution, a consequence, an end, i.e., something like a *crisis*. The crisis is a cultural model: the same model that has marked Western thinking about the organic (with Hippocrates), the poetic and the logical (Aristotelian *catharsis* and syllogism), and more recently the socioeconomic. By participating in the need to set forth the *end* of every action (conclusion, interruption, closure, dénouement), the readerly declares itself to be historical. In other words, it can be subverted, but not without scandal, since it is the *nature* of the discourse which then appears to have been betrayed: the girl *can* not stop laughing, the narrator *can* never be aroused from his daydream, or at least the discourse could suddenly *think of something else*, abandon its obsession with telling the whole story, change direction in order to produce a more effective network; curiously, we call the *knot* (of the story) what needs to be unknotted (*dénouement*), we situate the knot at the peak of the crisis, not at its outcome; yet the knot is what closes, terminates, concludes the action in progress, like a flourish below a signature; to deny this final word (to deny the end as a word) would in fact scandalously dismiss the *signature* we seek to give each of our "messages."

(63) *She sat down next to me.* ★ ACT. "To join": 1: to sit down.

(64) *The old man did not want to leave this lovely creature, to whom he had attached himself with that silent and seemingly baseless stubbornness to which the extremely old are prone, and which makes them appear childish.* ★ REF. Psychology of the old.

★★ SEM. Childishness. ★★★ The castrato is attracted to the young woman, opposite to opposite, the reverse of the coin by its obverse (SYM. Marriage of the castrato).

(65) *In order to sit near her, he had to take a folding chair. His slightest movements were full of that cold heaviness, the stupid indecision, characteristic of the gestures of a paralytic. He sat slowly down on his seat, with circumspection,* ★ ACT. "To join": 2: to sit next to. ★★ REF. Psychology of the old.

(66) *muttering some unintelligible words. His worn-out voice was like the sound made by a stone falling down a well.* ★ The noise of a stone falling down a well is not a "worn-out sound"; however, the chain of connotation of the sentence is more important than the exactitude of the simile; this chain links the following elements: the inanimate inertia of the stone, the sepulchral depth of the well, the discontinuity of the aged voice, antinomic to the perfect, unified, "lubricated" voice: the signified is the "thing," artificial and creaky as a machine (SEM. Mechanicalness).

(67) *The young woman held my hand tightly, as if seeking protection on some precipice, and she shivered when this man at whom she was looking* ★ SEM. Fascination.

(68) *turned upon her two eyes without warmth, glaucous eyes which could only be compared to dull mother-of-pearl.* ★ Worse than cold: chilled (dulled). The lexia connotes the corpse, death in human form, by bringing out what is most disquieting about him: his *open eyes* (to close the eyes of the dead is to exorcise whatever life remains, to make the dead die for good, to make the dead totally dead). As for *glaucous*, it has no denotative importance here (the exact color of *glaucous* is not important); connotatively (culturally), it is the color of a blind eye, a dead eye: a death of color which is yet not colorless (SEM. Cold).

(69) *"I'm afraid," she said, leaning toward my ear.* ★ SEM. Fascination.

(70) *"You can talk," I answered. "He is very hard of hearing."*
"Do you know him?"

"Yes." ★ The old man's deafness (justified by his great age) serves the following purpose: it informs us (obliquely) that the narrator holds the key to the suspended enigmas: hitherto presented to us merely as the "poet" of the Antithesis, the narrator is here presented as being in a position to narrate. A proairetism is opened: *"to know the story/to tell it,"* etc. Taken as a whole, this proairetism will, as we shall see, be heavily laden with symbolism (ACT. "To narrate": 1: to know the story).

(71) *Thereupon, she gathered up enough courage to look for a moment at this creature for which the human language had no name, a form without substance, a being without life, or a life without action.* ★ The neuter, the gender proper to the castrato, is signified by lack of a soul (or animation: the inanimate, in the Indo-European languages, is the determinant of the neuter): the privative repetition (*without* . . .) is the diagrammatical form of castration, the appearance of life in one lacking life (SYM. The neuter). ★★ The old man's portrait, which will follow and which is here rhetorically indicated, takes form within a *framework* established by the young woman (*gathered up enough courage to look* . . .), but by means of a dissolve of the original voice, the description will be carried out by the discourse: the body of the old man copies a painted model (SYM. Replication of bodies).

XXIII. PAINTING AS A MODEL

Every literary description is a *view.* It could be said that the speaker, before describing, stands at the window, not so much to see, but to establish what he sees by its very frame: the window frame creates the scene. To describe is thus to place the empty frame which the realistic author always carries with him (more important than his easel) before a collection or continuum of objects which cannot be put into words without this obsessive operation (which could be as laughable as a "gag"); in order to speak about it, the writer, through this initial rite, first transforms the "real" into a depicted (framed) object; having done this, he can take down this object, *remove* it from his picture: in short: de-depict it (to depict is to unroll the carpet of the codes, to refer not from a language to a referent but from one code to another). Thus, realism (badly named, at any rate often badly interpreted) consists not in copying the real but in copying a (depicted) copy of the real: this famous *reality*, as though suffering from a fearfulness which keeps it from being touched directly, is *set farther away*, postponed, or at least captured through the pictorial matrix in which it has been steeped before being put into words: code upon code, known as realism. This is why realism cannot be designated a "copier" but rather a "pasticheur" (through secondary mimesis, it copies what is already a copy); naïve or shameless, Joseph Brideau has no scruple about painting a Raphael (since the painter too must copy another code, an anterior code), any more than Balzac has in declaring this pastiche to be a masterpiece. Once the infinite circularity of codes is posited, the body itself cannot escape it: the real body (fictionally given as such) is the replication of a model set forth by that code of the arts, so that the most "natural" of bodies, that of Balzac's crayfish-gatherer (*La Rabouilleuse*), is always only the *promise* of the artistic code from which it has previously issued (*"The doctor, who was enough of an anatomist to recognize a delectable figure, understood all that the arts would lose, if this charming model were destroyed by working in the fields"*). Thus, even within realism, the codes never stop: bodily replication cannot be interrupted save by leaving nature: either toward Superlative Woman (the "masterpiece") or toward the sub-human (the castrato). All of which raises a twofold problem: first, where and when did this preeminence of the pictorial code in literary mimesis begin? Why has it disappeared? Why has the writer's dream of painting died out? What has replaced it? Nowadays, the representational codes are shattered to make room for a multiple space no longer based on painting (the "picture") but rather on the theater (the stage), as Mallarmé predicted, or at least wished. And then: if literature and painting are no longer held in a hierarchical reflection, one being the *rear-view mirror* for the other, why maintain them any longer as objects at once united and separate, in short, *classed together?* Why not wipe out the difference between them (purely one of substance)? Why not forgo the plurality of the "arts" in order to affirm more powerfully the plurality of "texts"?

(72) *She was under the spell of that timorous curiosity which leads women to seek out dangerous emotions, to go see chained tigers, to look at boa constrictors, frightening themselves because they are separated from them only by weak fences.* ★ SEM. Fascination. ★★ The Woman and the Snake.

(73) *Although the little old man's back was stooped like a laborer's, one could easily tell that he must have had at one time a normal shape. His excessive thinness, the delicacy of his limbs, proved that he had always been slender.* ★ REF. Rhetorical code: prosopography (the "portrait" was a rhetorical genre particularly in favor in the neo-rhetoric of the second century A.D., a brilliant and *detachable* fragment which the discourse will here imbue with semic intentions). ★★ SEM. Beauty (past).

(74) *He was dressed in black silk trousers which fell about his bony thighs in folds, like an empty sail.* ★ SEM. Emptiness. The image of the empty sail adds a connotation of default; in other words, of temporality: the wind, the life have departed.

(75) *An anatomist would have promptly recognized the symptoms of galloping consumption by looking at the skinny legs supporting this strange body.* ★ SEM. Monster (Extra-nature). ★★ HER. Enigma 4: theme and proposal (because of his body, the old man is the subject of an enigma).

(76) *You would have said they were two bones crossed on a tomb-stone.* ★ SEM. Death (the signifier connotes the angular, the geo-metrical, the broken line, a form antithetical to *gauzy* or *vegetal*, i.e., to life).

(77) *A feeling of profound horror for mankind gripped the heart when one saw the marks that decrepitude had left on this fragile machine.* ★ SEM. Mechanicalness.

(78) *The stranger was wearing an old-fashioned gold-embroidered white waistcoat, and his linen was dazzlingly white. A frill of some-what yellowed lace, rich enough for a queen's envy, fell into ruffles on his breast. On him, however, this lace seemed more like a rag than like an ornament. Centered on it was a fabulous diamond which glittered like the sun.* ★ SEM. Superannuation, Femininity (coquetry), Wealth.

(79) *This outmoded luxury, this particular and tasteless jewel, made the strange creature's face even more striking.* ★ HER. Enigma 4 (Who is the old man?): theme and purpose. The lack of taste refers to his dress, in which the feminine essence and wealth are displayed, with no concern for whether it is asethetically pleasing or socially fitting (the "particular jewel"): similarly, vulgarity suits a transvestite's dress more strikingly than distinction, because it makes femininity into an essence, not a value; vulgarity is on the side of the code (which enables it to be fascinating), distinction on the side of performance.

(80) *The setting was worthy of the portrait. This dark face was angular and all sunk in. The chin was sunken, the temples were sunken; the eyes were lost in yellowish sockets. The jawbones stood out because of his indescribable thinness, creating cavities in the center of each cheek.* ★ REF. Rhetorical code: the portrait. ★★ The old man's extreme thinness is an index of age, but also of emptiness, of reduction through deficiency. This latter seme is ob-viously in contrast to the stereotype of the fat, bloated eunuch, puffed up with empty pride; this is because in this instance the connotation can lead in two directions: syntagmatically, emptiness ought not contradict the lines of old age; paradigmatically, thin-

ness seen as emptiness is in contrast to the strong, vegetal, full bloom of the young woman (SEM. Emptiness).

(81) *These deformations, more or less illuminated by the candles, produced shadows and strange reflections which succeeded in erasing any human characteristics from his face.* ★ SEM. Out of the World.

(82) *And the years had glued the thin, yellow skin of his face so closely to his skull that it was covered all over with a multitude of circular wrinkles, like the ripples on a pond into which a child has thrown a pebble, or star-shaped, like a cracked windowpane, but everywhere deep and close-set as the edges of pages in a closed book.* ★ SEM. Superannuation (the excessively wrinkled, the mummy).

XXIV. TRANSFORMATION AS GAME

The excess of metaphor (water, windowpane, book) is a game played by the discourse. The game, which is a regulated activity and always subject to return, consists then not in piling up words for mere verbal pleasure (logorrhea) but in multiplying one form of language (in this case, comparison), as though in an attempt to exhaust the nonetheless infinite variety and inventiveness of synonyms, while repeating and varying the signifier, so as to affirm the plural existence of the text, its return. Thus, in the elevator at Balbec, where Proust's narrator wants to initiate a conversation with the young operator, the latter does not reply, *"either because of astonishment at my words, attention to his work, a regard for etiquette, hardness of hearing, respect for the surroundings, fear of danger, slow-wittedness, or orders from the manager."* The game here is grammatical in essence (and therefore much more exemplary): it consists in presenting, acrobatically, for as long as possible, the plural diversity of possibilities within a singular syntagm, to "transform" the verbal proposition behind each cause (*"because he was hard of hearing"*) into a double substantive (*"hardness of hearing"*); in short, to produce a constant model carried out to infinity, which is to constrain language as one wishes: whence the very pleasure of power.

(83) *Some old people have presented more hideous portraits; what contributed the most, however, in lending the appearance of an artificial creature to the specter which had risen up before us was the red and white with which he glistened. The eyebrows of his mask took from the light a luster which revealed that they were painted on. Fortunately for the eye depressed by the sight of such ruin, his cadaverous skull was covered by a blond wig whose innumerable curls were evidence of an extraordinary pretension.* ★ REF. The physique of the aged. ★★ SEM. Outside nature. Femininity. Thing. Beauty, as we have seen, cannot be induced through catachresis other than from some great cultural model (written or pictorial): it is stated, not described. Contrariwise, ugliness can be abundantly described: it alone is "realistic," confronting the referent without an intermediate code (whence the notion that realism, in art, is concerned solely with ugliness). Yet here we have a turning back, a reversion to the code: the old man is himself "very well painted"; thus he is reintegrated with the replication of bodies; he is his own double: like a mask, he copies from himself *what is underneath*; only, since he is his own copy, his duplication is tautological, sterile as the duplication of painted things.

(84) *For the rest, the feminine coquetry of this phantasmagorical personage was rather strongly emphasized by the gold ornaments hanging from his ears, by the rings whose fine stones glittered on his bony fingers, and by a watch chain which shimmered like the brilliants of a choker around a woman's neck.* ★ SEM. Femininity. Out of the world. Wealth.

(85) *Finally, this sort of Japanese idol* ★ The Japanese idol (perhaps, strangely enough, Buddha) connotes an inhuman mixture of

impassivity and make-up: it designates the mysterious insensibility of the thing, the thing copying life and making life into a thing (SEM. Thing).

(86) *had on his bluish lips a fixed and frozen smile, implacable and mocking, like a skull.* ★ The fixed, frozen smile leads to the image of stretched skin (as in plastic surgery), of life lacking that minimum skin which is the very stuff of life. In the old man, life is endlessly copied, but the copy always offers the *less* of castration (as in his lips, which lack the fresh red of life) (SEM. Fantastic. Out of the world).

(87) *Silent and motionless as a statue, it exuded the musty odor of old clothes which the heirs of some duchess take out for inventory.* ★ SEM. Thing, Superannuation.

(88) *Although the old man turned his eyes toward the crowd, it seemed that the movements of those orbs, incapable of sight, were accomplished only by means of some imperceptible artifice; and when the eyes came to rest on something, anyone looking at them would have concluded that they had not moved at all.* ★ SEM. Cold, artifice, death (the eyes of a doll).

XXV. THE PORTRAIT

Meanings abound in the portrait, proliferating through a form which nonetheless disciplines them: this form is both a rhetorical order (declaration and detail) and an anatomical cataloguing (body and face); these two protocols are also codes; these codes are superimposed on the anarchy of signifiers, they appear as the operators of nature—or of "rationality." The ultimate image afforded by the discourse (by the "portrait") is that of a natural form, pregnant with meaning, as though meaning were merely the ulterior predicate of a primal body. Indeed, the naturalness of the portrait arises from the fact that in their superimposition the multiple codes undergo a shift: their units are no longer in the same place, do not have the same size, and this disparity, built up unevenly, produces what we shall call the "shifting" of the discourse—its *naturalness*: when two codes function simultaneously but according to un-equal wavelengths, they produce an image of movement, an image of life—at this juncture, a portrait. The portrait (in the present text) is not a realistic representation, a related copy, an idea such as we might get from figurative painting; it is a scene made up by blocks of meaning, at once varied, repeated, and discontinuous (outlined); out of the arrangement of these blocks comes a diagram of the body, not its copy (in which the portrait remains totally subject to a linguistic structure, lan-guage recognizing only diagrammatical analogies: analogies in the etymological sense: proportions): the old man's body is not "detached" like a real referent from the background of the words or of the salon; it is itself the semantic space—becoming meaning, it becomes space. In other words, the reading of the "realistic" portrait is not a realistic reading: it is a cubist read-ing: the meanings are cubes, piled up, altered, juxtaposed, and yet feeding on each other, whose shift produces the entire space of a painting and makes this very space into a *supple-mentary* meaning (accessory and atopical): that of the human body: the figure is not the sum, the frame, or the support of the meanings; it is an additional meaning, a kind of diacritical paradigm.

XXVI. SIGNIFIED AND TRUTH

All the signifieds which compose the portrait are "true," for they are all part of the definition of the old man: the Empty, the Inanimate, the Feminine, the Superannuated, the Monstrous, the Wealthy, each of these semes stands in a congruent relationship to the demonstrative truth of the old man, who is an extremely old castrato, a fabulously wealthy ex-international star; all these semes distinguish the truth, but even when taken together, they do not suffice to name it (and this failure is fortunate, since from the point of view of the story, the truth must not be revealed prematurely). Thus, clearly, the signified has a hermeneutic value: every action of the meaning is an action of truth: in the classic text (dependent upon an historical ideology), meaning is mingled with truth, signification is the path of truth: if we succeed in *denoting* the old man, his truth (castration) is immediately revealed. Yet, in the hermeneutic system, the connotative signified occupies a special place: it brings into being an insufficient half truth, powerless to name itself: it is the incompleteness, the insufficiency, the powerlessness of truth, and this partial deficiency has a qualifying value; this birth defect is a coded factor, a hermeneutic morpheme, whose function is to thicken the enigma by outlining it: a powerful enigma is a dense one, so that, provided certain precautions are taken, the more signs there are, the more the truth will be obscured, the harder one will try to figure it out. The connotative signified is literally an *index*: it points but does not tell; what it points to is the name, the truth as name; it is both the temptation to name and the impotence to name (induction would be more effective than designation in producing the name): it is the *tip of the tongue* from which the name, the truth, will later fall. Thus, with its designating, silent movement, a pointing finger always accompanies the classic text: the truth is thereby long desired and avoided, kept in a kind of pregnancy for its full term, a pregnancy whose end, both liberating and catastrophic, will bring about the utter end of the discourse; and the character, the very arena of these signifieds, is only the enigma's passage, the passage for this nominative form of the enigma with which

62

Oedipus (in his debate with the Sphynx) mythically impregnated all Western discourse.

(89) *To see, next to this human wreckage, a young woman* ★
SYM. Antithesis: B: (young woman): introduction.

(90) *whose neck, bosom, and arms were bare and white, whose figure was in the full bloom of its beauty, whose hair rose from her alabaster forehead and inspired love, whose eyes did not receive but gave off light, who was soft, fresh, and whose floating curls and sweet breath seemed too heavy, too hard, too powerful for this shadow, for this man of dust:* ★ SEM. Antithesis: B: (the young woman). ★★ SEM. Vegetality (organic life). ★★★ The young woman was at the outset a child-woman, passively penetrated by the man's gaze (No. 60). Here, her symbolic situation is reversed; we find her in the field of action: *"her eyes did not receive but gave off light"*; she joins the Castrating Woman, of whom Mme de Lanty was the first example. This mutation can be explained by the purely paradigmatic needs of the Antithesis: in No. 60, as opposed to the petrified old man, it required a fresh young woman, frail, floreal; here, as opposed to "human wreckage," it requires a powerful vegetality that reassembles, that unites. This new paradigm, which turns the young woman into a castrating figure, will gradually establish itself and draw the narrator himself into its orbit; he will no longer have control over the young woman (as in No. 62), but, reversing his own symbolic role, he will shortly appear in the passive position of a dominated subject (SYM. The queen-woman).

(91) *ah! here were death and life indeed, I thought, in a fantastic arabesque, half hideous chimera, divinely feminine from the waist up.*
"Yet there are marriages like that often enough in the world," I *said to myself.* ★ From a realistic viewpoint, the old man and the young woman, pressed close together into a single fantastic creature, ought to be vertically bipartite, like Siamese twins. Yet the force of symbolism reverses—or redresses—this meaning: their bi-

partite nature is seen as horizontal: the chimera (half lion, half goat) has opposing top and bottom—leaving the castrated zone, of course, in its proper anatomical position ("female from the waist up") (SYM. Marriage of the castrato). ★★ REF. Code of marriages.

(92) *"He smells like a graveyard," cried the terrified young woman,* ★ SEM. Death.

(93) *pressing against me for protection, and whose uneasy movements told me she was frightened.* ★ SYM. The child-woman (the symbolic mutation has not yet been stabilized: the discourse returns from the queen-woman to the child-woman).

(94) *"What a horrible sight," she went on. "I can't stay here any longer. If I look at him again, I shall believe that death itself has come looking for me. Is he alive?"* ★ SEM. Death. ★★ *"Is he alive?"* The question could be purely rhetorical, merely varying the funereal signified in the old man. Now, by an unexpected turn, the question (which the young woman is asking herself) becomes a literal one and calls for an answer (or verification) (ACT. "Question": 1: to ask oneself a question).

(95) *She reached out to the phenomenon* ★ ACT. "Question": 2: to verify (ACT. "To touch": 1: touching).

(96) *with that boldness women can summon up out of the strength of their desires;* ★ REF. Female psychology.

(97) *but she broke into a cold sweat, for no sooner had she touched the old man than she heard a cry like a rattle. This sharp voice, if voice it was, issued from a nearly dried up throat.* ★ ACT. "To touch": 2: reaction. ★★ The rattle connotes a granular, discontinuous sound; the shaking voice, a problematical humanity; the dried-up throat, a deficiency of a kind specific to organic life: the lubricated (SEM. Extra-natural). ★★★ SYM. Marriage of the castrato (here: its catastrophic conclusion).

(98) *Then the sound was quickly followed by a little, convulsive, childish cough of a peculiar sonorousness.* ★ SEM. Childishness

(the convulsive once again connotes an evil, funereal discontinuity, contrasted to the unified life *uno tenore*).

XXVII. ANTITHESIS II: THE MARRIAGE

The antithesis is a wall without a doorway. Leaping this wall is a transgression. Subject to the antithesis of inside and outside, heat and cold, life and death, the old man and the young woman are in fact separated by the most inflexible of barriers: that of meaning. Thus, anything that draws these two antipathetic sides together is rightly scandalous (the most blatant scandal: that of form). It was already shocking (*"one of those rare tricks of nature"*) to see the two terms of the antithesis so closely linked, pressed together, the young woman's body and the old man's; however, when the young woman *touches* the old man, there is a paroxysm of transgression; it is no longer restricted spatially, it becomes substantial, organic, chemical. The young woman's gesture is an *acting out*: whether taken as conversion hysteria (a substitute for orgasm) or as a breaching of the Wall (of Antithesis and of hallucination), the physical contact between these two completely separate substances, the woman and the castrato, the animate and the inanimate, produces a catastrophe: there is an explosive shock, a paradigmatic conflagration, a headlong flight of the two bodies brought together in so unseemly a manner: each of the partners forms the locus of an overt physiological revolution: sweat and exclamation: each, by the other, is *reversed*; touched by an extraordinarily powerful chemical agent (for the castrato, the woman; for the woman, castration), the depths are emptied, as in vomiting. This is what happens when the arcana of meaning are subverted, when the sacred separation of the paradigmatic poles is abolished, when one removes the separating barrier, the basis of all "pertinence." The marriage of the young

65

woman and the castrato is doubly catastrophic (or, if we prefer, it creates a double-entry system): symbolically, it affirms the non-viability of the dual body, the chimeric body, doomed to the dispersion of its parts: when a supplementary body is introduced, added to the distribution of opposites already effected, this supplement (ironically posited in No. 13, which is there intended to exorcise it) is dammed: the *excess* explodes: gathering becomes scattering; and structurally, as we know, the major figure of rhetorical wisdom, Antithesis, cannot be transgressed with impunity: *meaning* (and its classifying basis) is a question of life or death: similarly, in copying woman, in assuming her position on the other side of the sexual barrier, the castrato will transgress morphology, grammar, discourse, and because of this abolition of meaning Sarrasine will die.

(99) *At this sound, Marianina, Filippo, and Mme de Lanty looked in our direction, and their glances were like bolts of lightning. The young woman wished she were at the bottom of the Seine.* ★ ACT. "To touch": 3: generalized reaction. ★★ The feminine camp, its exclusive relationship to the old man, is here reaffirmed: Mme de Lanty, Marianina, Filippo, all of La Zambinella's feminine lineage (SYM. Axis of castration).

(100) *She took my arm and led me into a side room. Men, women, everyone made way for us. At the end of the public rooms, we came into a small, semicircular chamber.* ★ ACT. "To touch": 4: to flee. ★★ Worldly intelligence: others make way for the blunderers; symbolic meaning: castration is contagious: the young woman who has made contact with it is marked (SYM. Contagion of castration). The semicircular shape of the chamber connotes a theatrical site, where the Adonis can fittingly be "contemplated."

(101) *My companion threw herself onto a divan, trembling with fright, oblivious to her surroundings.* ★ ACT. "To touch": 5: to hide.

(102) *"Madame, you are mad," I said to her.* ★ SYM. The child-woman. The narrator scolds the young woman as if she were an irresponsible child; in another sense, however, the young woman's madness is literal: her gesture, touching, is indeed the eruption of the signifier into reality through the wall of symbolism: it is a psychotic act.

(103) *"But," she replied, after a moment's silence, during which I gazed at her in admiration,* ★ The narrator's symbolic role is beginning to change: first presented as some sort of patron to the young woman, here he admires her, is silent, and desires her: he now has something to ask (SYM. The man-subject).

(104) *"is it my fault? Why does Mme de Lanty allow ghosts to wander about in her house?"* ★ SEM. Supernature.

(105) *"Come," I replied, "you are being ridiculous, taking a little old man for a ghost."* ★ The narrator's imaginary world, i.e., the symbolic system in which he does not know his own position, has exactly this *asymbolic* character: he is, he says, the one who does not believe in stories (symbols) (SEM. Asymbolism). ★★ SYM. The child-woman.

XXVIII. CHARACTER AND FIGURE

When identical semes traverse the same proper name several times and appear to settle upon it, a character is created. Thus, the character is a product of combinations: the combination is relatively stable (denoted by the recurrence of the semes) and more or less complex (involving more or less congruent, more or less contradictory figures); this complexity determines the character's "personality," which is just as much a combination as the odor of a dish or the bouquet of a wine. The proper name acts as a magnetic field for the semes; referring in fact to a body, it draws the semic configuration into an evolving (biographical) tense. In principle, the character who says "I" has no name (Proust's narrator is an outstanding example); in fact, however, *I* immediately becomes a name, his name. In the story (and in many conversations), *I* is no longer a pronoun, but a name, the best of names: to say *I* is inevitably to attribute signifieds to oneself; further, it gives one a biographical duration, it enables one to undergo, in one's imagination, an intelligible "evolution," to signify oneself as an object with a destiny, to give a meaning to time. On this level, *I* (and notably the narrator of *Sarrasine*) is therefore a character. The figure is altogether different: it is not a combination of semes concentrated in a legal Name, nor can biography, psychology, or time encompass it: it is an illegal, impersonal, anachronistic configuration of symbolic relationships. As figure, the character can oscillate between two roles, without this oscillation having any meaning, for it occurs outside biographical time (outside chronology): the symbolic structure is completely reversible: it can be read in any direction. Thus, the child-woman and the narrator-father, momentarily effaced, can return, can overtake the queen-woman and the narrator-slave. As a symbolic ideality, the character has no chronological or biographical standing; he has no Name; he is nothing but a site for the passage (and return) of the figure.

(106) *"Be still,"* she said, *with that forceful and mocking air all women so easily assume when they want to be in the right.* ★ The queen-woman *orders* silence (all domination begins by prohibiting language), she *forces* (placing her partner in a subject position), she *mocks* (denies the narrator as father) (SYM. The queen-woman). ★★ REF. Feminine psychology.

(107) *"What a pretty room!"* she cried, *looking around. "Blue satin always makes such wonderful wall hangings. How refreshing it is!* ★ ACT. "Tableau": 1: to look around. Blue satin, freshness,

can either create a mere effect of reality (to create "truth," one must be at once precise and insignificant), or they can connote the flightiness of the young woman's words, speaking of furnishings a moment after having indulged in an outlandish act, or they pave the way for the euphoric state in which the portrait of Adonis will be read.

(108) *Oh! what a beautiful painting!" she went on, getting up and going to stand before a painting in a magnificent frame.*
   We stood for a moment in contemplation of this marvel, ★ ACT. "Tableau": 2: to perceive.

(109) *which seemed to have been painted by some supernatural brush.* ★ Metonymically, the trans-natural element in the referent (La Zambinella is outside nature) enters into both the picture's subject (Adonis is *"too beautiful for a man"*) and its fabrication (the *"supernatural brush"* suggests that the painter's hand was guided by some god: so Christ, when the picture was completed, descended from heaven to superimpose himself on the icon which the Byzantine artist had just completed) (SYM. Supernature).

(110) *The picture was of Adonis lying on a lion's skin.* ★ The portrait of Adonis is the theme (subject) of a new enigma (the fifth) which will shortly be formulated: of whom is this Adonis the portrait? (HER. Enigma 5: thematization). ★★ The "lion's skin" of this Adonis harks back to countless academic representations of Greek shepherds (REF. Mythology and painting).

(111) *The lamp hanging from the ceiling of the room in an alabaster globe illuminated this canvas with a soft glow which enabled us to make out all the beauties of the painting.*

XXIX. THE ALABASTER LAMP

The light diffused by the lamp is outside the picture; however, metonymically, it becomes the interior light of the painted scene: alabaster (soft, white)—a conducting rather than an

emitting substance, a luminous and cold reflection—this boudoir alabaster is in fact the moon which illuminates the young
shepherd. Thus Adonis, which No. 547 will tell us inspired
Girodet in painting his Endymion, becomes a lunar lover.
Here there is a threefold inversion of the codes: Endymion
transmits his meaning, story, and reality to Adonis: Endymion
is read with the same words which describe Adonis; Adonis is
read according to the situation of Endymion. In Endymion-
Adonis, everything connotes femininity (cf. description in No.
113): the "exquisite grace," the "contours" (a word used only
for the flaccid academic paintings of romantic women or mythological ephebes), the elongated pose, slightly turned, open to
possession, the pale and diffuse color—white (beautiful women
of the period were always very white), the abundant, curling
hair, *"everything, in short"*; this final attribute, like any *et
cetera*, censors what is not named, that is, what must be both
concealed and pointed out: the Adonis is placed on the back
wall of a theater (the semicircular chamber) and the Endymion is discovered, uncovered by a Cupid who pulls back the
curtain of greenery, like the curtain of a stage, thus focusing on
the very center of what must be seen, inspected: the sexual
member, shadowed in the Girodet, as it is in La Zambinella,
mutilated by castration. In love with Endymion, Selena visits
him; her active light caresses the sleeping and unprotected
shepherd and steals into him; although feminine, the Moon is
active; although masculine, the boy is passive: a double inversion, that of the two biological sexes and of the two terms of
castration throughout the story, in which the women are castrators and the men castrated: thus music will insinuate itself
into Sarrasine, *lubricating* him, giving him the most intense
pleasure, just as the moonlight possesses Endymion, in a kind
of insinuating bath. This is the exchange which controls the
symbolic interplay: a terrifying essence of passivity, castration
is paradoxically superactive: its nothingness contaminates

everything it encounters: deficiency makes everything radiant. Now, by a final—and curious—cultural reversal, we can *see* all this (and not merely read it); the Endymion in our text is the same Endymion which is in a museum (our museum, the Louvre), so that, retracing the duplicative chain of bodies and copies, we possess the most literal image of La Zambinella: a photograph. Since reading is a traversal of codes, nothing can stop its journey; the photograph of the fictitious castrato is part of the text; retracing the line of the codes, we are entitled to go to the Bulloz establishment in the rue Bonaparte and ask to be shown the box (most likely filed under "mythological subjects") in which we will discover the castrato's photograph.

(112) *"Does such a perfect creature exist?" she asked me,* ★ HER. Enigma 5: formulation (does the model for the painting exist in "nature"?). ★★ SEM. Supernature (Outside of nature).

XXX. BEYOND AND SHORT

Perfection is one end of the Code (origin or terminus, whichever); it exalts (or euphorizes) insofar as it puts a stop to the leak of replications, wipes out the distance between code and performance, between origin and result, between model and copy; and since this distance is part of the human condition, perfection, which annuls it, lies outside of anthropological limits, in supernature, where it joins the other, inferior, transgression: *more* and *less* can be generically placed in the same class, that of excess, what is *beyond* no longer differs from what is *short* of a limit; the essence of the code (perfection) has in the end the same status as what is outside the code (the monster, the castrato), for life, the norm, mankind, are but intermediary migrations in the field of replications. Thus, La Zambinella is Super-Woman, essential, perfect woman (in any theology, perfection is the essence, and Zambinella is a "masterpiece"), but at the same time, by the same impulse, she is sub-man, castrated, deficient, definitively *less*; in her, absolutely desirable, in him, absolutely execrable, the two transgressions are united. This confusion is warranted because transgression is actually a *mark* (La Zambinella is marked both by perfection and by deficiency); it enables the discourse to engage in a game of equivocations: to speak of the "supernatural" perfection of the Adonis is also to speak of the "sub-natural" deficiency of the castrato.

(113) *after having, with a soft smile of contentment, examined the exquisite grace of the contours, the pose, the color, the hair; in short, the entire picture.* ★ SEM. Femininity. ★★ Described in this way, the picture connotes a whole atmosphere of fulfillment, of sexual gratification: a harmony, a kind of erotic fulfillment occurs, between the painted Adonis and the young woman, who expresses it by a *"soft smile of contentment."* Now, through the devices of the story, the young woman's pleasure is drawn from three different sources, superimposed in the Adonis: (1) *a man:* Adonis himself, the mythological subject of the painting; the narrator's jealousy will be aroused by this interpretation of the young woman's desire; (2) *a woman:* the young woman perceives the feminine nature of the Adonis and feels herself in harmony, complicity, even Sapphism, in any event once again frustrating the narrator, who is denied access to the glamorous field of femininity; (3) *a castrato:* who obviously continues to fascinate the young woman (SYM. Marriage of the castrato).

(114) *"He is too beautiful for a man,"* she added, *after an examination such as she might have made of some rival.* ★ The bodies in *Sarrasine*, oriented—or disoriented—by castration, cannot with any certainty be situated on either side of the sexual paradigm;

implicit in it are a Female *beyond* (perfection) and a Male *short of it* (being-castrated). To say that the Adonis is not a man is to refer both to the truth (he is a castrato) and to a false clue, a snare (he is a woman) (HER. Enigma 5: truth and snare: equivocation).

(115) *Oh! how jealous I then felt; something* ★ SYM. Narrator's desire.

(116) *in which a poet had vainly tried to make me believe, the jealousy of engravings, of pictures, wherein artists exaggerate human beauty according to the doctrine which leads them to idealize everything.* ★ REF. Literary code of passion (or code of literary passion). ★★ SYM. Replication of bodies (to be in love with a copy: this is the theme of Pygmalion, developed in just this way in No. 229).

(117) *"It's a portrait,"* I replied, *"the product of the talent of Vien.* ★ SYM. Replication of bodies.

(118) *But that great painter never saw the original and maybe you'd admire it less if you knew that this daub was copied from the statue of a woman."* ★ SYM. Replication of bodies (the duplication of bodies is linked to the instability of the sexual paradigm, which makes the castrato waver between boy and woman). ★★ The picture was copied from a statue: true, but this statue was copied from a false woman; in other words, the statement is true with regard only to the statue and false with regard to the woman; the lie is carried along by the sentence, made a part of the truth with which it begins, as the genitive is a part of the statue: how can a simple genitive lie? (HER. Enigma 5: equivocation).

XXXI. THE DISTURBED REPLICATION

Without the—always anterior—Book and Code, no desire, no jealousy: Pygmalion is in love with a link in the code of statuary; Paolo and Francesca love each other *according to* the passion of Lancelot and Guinevere (Dante, *Inferno,* V): itself a lost origin, writing becomes the origin of emotion. Into this organized drift, castration brings disturbance: emptiness perturbs the chain of signs, the engendering of replications, the regularity of the code. Deceived, Sarrasine sculpts La Zambinella as a woman. Vien transforms this woman into a boy and thereby returns to the original sex of his model (a Neapolitan *ragazzo*): in a final reversal, the narrator arbitrarily stops the chain at the statue and makes the original a woman. Thus three trajectories intersect: an operative trajectory, a "real" producer of copies (retracing from the male Adonis to the female statue, then to the transvestite boy); a mystifying trajectory, deviously drawn by the jealous narrator (retracing from the male Adonis to the female statue and then, implicitly, to the female model); a symbolic trajectory, which passes only through femininities: that of Adonis, that of the statue, that of the castrator: this is the only homogeneous area, within which no one tells a lie. This confusion has a hermeneutic role: the narrator knowingly distorts the true origin of the Adonis; he produces a snare designed for the young woman— and for the reader; symbolically, however, this same narrator, through his bad faith, *indicates* (by referring it to a woman) the model's lack of virility; his lie is thus an inductor of truth.

(119) *"But who is it?"*
   I hesitated.
   "I want to know," she added, *impetuously.* ★ SYM. The queen-woman (the narrator desires the young woman, the young woman desires to know who the Adonis is; the terms of a contract are suggested). ★★ HER. Enigma 5: formulation (who is the model for the Adonis?).

(120) *"I believe,"* I replied, *"that this Adonis is a . . . a relative of Mme de Lanty."* ★ ACT. "To narrate": 2: to know the story

74

(we know that the narrator knows the old man's identity from No. 70; here we learn that he also knows the origin of the Adonis: thus, he has the power to solve the enigmas, to tell the story). ** HER. Enigma 5: suspended answer. *** SYM. Taboo on the noun castrato.

XXXII. DELAY

Truth is brushed past, avoided, lost. This accident is a structural one. In fact, the hermeneutic code has a function, the one we (with Jakobson) attribute to the poetic code: just as rhyme (notably) structures the poem according to the expectation and desire for recurrence, so the hermeneutic terms structure the enigma according to the expectation and desire for its solution. The dynamics of the text (since it implies a truth to be deciphered) is thus paradoxical: it is a static dynamics: the problem is to *maintain* the enigma in the initial void of its answer; whereas the sentences quicken the story's "unfolding" and cannot help but move the story along, the hermeneutic code performs an opposite action: it must set up *delays* (obstacles, stoppages, deviations) in the flow of the discourse; its structure is essentially reactive, since it opposes the ineluctable advance of language with an organized set of stoppages: between question and answer there is a whole dilatory area whose emblem might be named "reticence," the rhetorical figure which interrupts the sentence, suspends it, turns it aside (Virgil's *Quos ego . . .*). Whence, in the hermeneutic code, in comparison to these extreme terms (question and answer), the abundance of dilatory morphemes: the *snare* (a kind of deliberate evasion of the truth), the *equivocation* (a mixture of truth and snare which frequently, while focusing on the enigma, helps to thicken it), the *partial answer* (which only exacerbates the expectation of the truth), the *suspended answer* (an aphasic stoppage of the disclosure), and *jamming*

75

(acknowledgment of insolubility). The variety of these terms (their inventive range) attests to the considerable labor the discourse must accomplish if it hopes to *arrest* the enigma, to keep it open. Expectation thus becomes the basic condition for truth: truth, these narratives tell us, is what is *at the end* of expectation. This design brings narrative very close to the rite of initiation (a long path marked with pitfalls, obscurities, stops, suddenly comes out into the light); it implies a return to order, for expectation is a disorder: disorder is supplementary, it is what is forever added on without solving anything, without finishing anything; order is complementary, it completes, fills up, saturates, and dismisses everything that risks adding on: truth is what completes, what closes. In short, based on the articulation of question and answer, the hermeneutic narrative is constructed according to our image of the sentence: an organism probably infinite in its expansions, but reducible to a diadic unity of subject and predicate. To narrate (in the classic fashion) is to raise the question as if it were a subject which one delays predicating; and when the predicate (truth) arrives, the sentence, the narrative, are over, the world is adjectivized (after we had feared it would not be). Yet, just as any grammar, however new, once it is based on the diad of subject and predicate, noun and verb, can only be a historical grammar, linked to classical metaphysics, so the hermeneutic narrative, in which truth predicates an incomplete subject, based on expectation and desire for its imminent closure, is dated, linked to the kerygmatic civilization of meaning and truth, appeal and fulfillment.

XXXIII. AND/OR

When the narrator hesitates to tell us who the Adonis is (and dislocates or drowns the truth), the discourse mixes two codes:

the symbolic code—from which is derived the ban on the noun *castrato*, the aphasia this word provokes whenever anyone risks saying it—and the hermeneutic code, according to which this aphasia is merely a suspension of the answer, required by the dilatory structure of the narrative. Of these two codes, simultaneously referred to in the same words (the same signifier), is one more important than the other? Or, more precisely: if we want to "explicate" the sentence (and consequently the narrative), must we *decide* on one code or the other? Ought we to say that the narrator's hesitation is determined by the constraint of the symbol (according to which the castrato must be censored), or by the finality of the disclosure (according to which this disclosure must be at once suggested and delayed)? Nobody in the world (no knowing subject, no god of narrative) can decide this: In narrative (and this is perhaps its "definition"), the symbolic and the operative are non-decidable, subject to the rule of an *and/or*. Thus, to choose, to decide on a hierarchy of codes, on a predetermination of messages, as in secondary-school explications, is *impertinent*, since it overwhelms the articulation of the writing by a single voice, here psychoanalytic, there poetic (in the Aristotelian sense). Furthermore, to miss the plurality of the codes is to censor the work of the discourse: non-decidability defines a *praxis*, the performance of the narrator: just as a successful metaphor affords, between its terms, no hierarchy and removes all hindrances from the polysemic chain (in contrast to the comparison, an originated figure), so a "good" narrative fulfills both the plurality and the circularity of the codes: ceaselessly correcting the causalities of the anecdote by the metonymy of the symbols and, inversely, the simultaneity of the meanings by the operations which lead on and use up expectation to its end.

(121) *I had the pain of seeing her rapt in the contemplation of this figure. She sat in silence; I sat down next to her and took her hand without her being aware of it! Forgotten for a painting!* ★ SYM. Marriage of the castrato (here, the union of the young woman and the castrato is euphorized: we know that the symbolic configuration is not subject to a diegetic development: what has exploded catastrophically can return peacefully united). ★★ SYM. Replication of bodies (to be in love with a portrait, like Pygmalion with a statue).

(122) *At this moment, the light footsteps of a woman in a rustling dress broke the silence.* ★ The short episode which begins here (and which will end at No. 137) is a *byte* (in computer terminology), a section of program fed into the machine, a sequence equivalent, as a whole, to only one signified: the gift of the ring reopens Enigma 4: *who is the old man?* This episode includes several pro-airetisms (ACT. "To enter": 1: to announce oneself by a sound).

(123) *Young Marianina came in, and her innocent expression made her even more alluring than did her grace and her lovely dress; she was walking slowly and escorting with maternal care, with filial solicitude, the costumed specter who had made us flee from the music room,* ★ ACT. "To enter": 2: the entrance itself. ★★ HER. Enigma 3: proposal and formulation (enigmatic as they are, the relations between Marianina and the Old Man strengthen the enigma of the Lanty family: where do they come from? who are they?). ★★★ SEM. Childishness.

(124) *and whom she was leading, watching with what seemed to be concern as he slowly advanced on his feeble feet.* ★ HER. Enigma 3: formulation (What can be the motive for Marianina's anxious solicitude, what relationship between them? Who are the Lantys?)

XXXIV. THE PRATTLE OF MEANING

For any fictional action (given in the discourse of the classic novel) there exist three possible realms of *expression*. Either

78

the meaning is stated, the action named but not detailed (*to accompany with anxious solicitude*). Or, while the meaning is being set forth, the action is more than named, it is described (*to watch with concern the ground where the person one is guiding is setting his feet*). Or else the action is described, but its meaning is kept tacit: the action is merely connoted (in the strict sense of the word) from an implicit signified (*to watch the old man slowly advance on his feeble feet*). The first two realms, in terms of which signification is *excessively* named, impose a dense plenitude of meaning or, if one prefers, a certain redundancy, a kind of semantic prattle typical of the archaic—or infantile—era of modern discourse, marked by the excessive fear of failing to communicate meaning (its basis); whence, in reaction, in our latest—or "new"—novels, the practice of the third system: to state the event without accompanying it with its signification.

(125) *They went together with some difficulty to a door hidden behind a tapestry.* ★ ACT. "Door I" (there will be other "Doors"): 1: to reach a door (moreover, the *hidden* door connotes a mysterious atmosphere, which restates Enigma 3).

(126) *There, Marianina knocked softly.* ★ ACT. "Door I": 2: to knock.

(127) *At once, as if by magic, a tall, stern man, a kind of family genie, appeared.* ★ ACT. "Door I": 3: to appear at a door (that is, to open it). ★★ REF. The novelistic (the appearance of a "genie"). The tall, stern man is the servant mentioned in No. 41, associated with the female clan protecting the old man.

(128) *Before entrusting the old man to the care of his mysterious guardian,* ★ ACT. "Farewell": 1: to entrust to another (before leaving).

(129) *the child respectfully kissed the walking corpse, and her chaste caress was not devoid of that graceful cajolery of which some privileged women possess the secret.* ★ ACT. "Farewell": 2: to embrace. ★★ HER. Enigma 3: proposal and formulation (what kind of relationship can a "chaste caress," a "graceful cajolery" imply? family? conjugal?). ★★★ REF. Code of proverbs: Superior Women.

(130) *"Addio, addio," she said, with the prettiest inflection in her youthful voice.* ★ ACT. "Farewell": 3: to say farewell. ★★ SEM. Italianness.

(131) *She added to the final syllable a marvelously well-executed trill, but in a soft voice, as if to give poetic expression to the emotions in her heart.* ★ SEM. Musicality.

XXXV. THE REAL, THE OPERABLE

What would happen if one actually performed Marianina's *"addio"* as it is described in the discourse? Something incongruous, no doubt, extravagant, and not musical. More: is it really possible to perform the act described? This leads to two propositions. The first is that the discourse has no responsibility vis-à-vis the real: in the most realistic novel, the referent has no "reality": suffice it to imagine the disorder the most orderly narrative would create were its descriptions taken at face value, converted into operative programs and simply *executed*. In short (this is the second proposition), what we call "real" (in the theory of the realistic text) is never more than a code of representation (of signification): it is never a code of execution: *the novelistic real is not operable.* To identify—as it would, after all, be "realistic" enough to do—the real with the operable would be to subvert the novel at the limit of its genre (whence the inevitable destruction of novels when they are transferred from writing to film, from a system of meaning to an order of the operable).

(132) *Suddenly struck by some memory, the old man stood on the threshold of this secret hideaway. Then, through the silence, we heard the heavy sigh that came from his chest:* ★ SEM. Musicality (the old man remembers having been a soprano). ★★ ACT. "Gift": 1: to incite (or be incited) to the gift.

(133) *he took the most beautiful of the rings which adorned his skeletal fingers, and placed it in Marianina's bosom.* ★ ACT. "Gift": 2: to give the gift.

(134) *The young girl broke into laughter, took the ring, and slipped it onto her finger over her glove;* ★ ACT. "Gift": 3: to accept the gift (the laugh, the glove, are effects for the sake of reality, notations whose very insignificance authenticates, signs, signifies "reality").

(135) *then she walked quickly toward the salon, from which there could be heard the opening measures of a quadrille.* ★ ACT. "To leave": 1: to want to leave.

(136) *She saw us:*
   "Ah, you were here," she said, blushing.
   After having seemed as if about to question us, ★ ACT. "To leave": 2: to delay. *As if* is the basic operator of meaning, the key that introduces the substitutions, the equivalences, that takes us from action (*to look at questioningly*) to its manner (*as if about to question*), from the operable to the signifier.

(137) *she ran to her partner with the careless petulance of youth.* ★ ACT. "To leave": 3: to leave again.

What is a series of actions? the unfolding of a name. To *enter?* I can unfold it into "to appear" and "to penetrate." *To leave?* I can unfold it into "to want to," "to stop," "to leave again." *To give?*: "to incite," "to return," "to accept." Inversely, to establish the sequence is to find the name: the sequence is the currency, the *exchange value* of the name. By what divisions is this exchange established? What is there in "Farewell," "Door," "Gift"? What subsequent, constitutive actions? Along what folds can we close the fan of the sequence? Two systems of folding (two "logics") seem to be required alternately. The first breaks down the title (noun or verb) according to its constituent moments (the articulation can be orderly: *begin/ continue* or confused: *begin/stop/leave*). The second system attaches contingent actions to a guide word (*to say farewell/to confide/to embrace*). These systems, one analytical, the other catalytical, one definitional, the other metonymical, have in fact no logic other than that of the *already-seen, already-read, already-done*: that of empirics and culture. The unfolding of the sequence, or, inversely, its folding, occurs by and through the authority of the great models, cultural (*to give thanks for a gift*), organic (*to disturb the course of an action*), or phenomenal (*the sound precedes the phenomenon*), etc. The proairetic sequence is indeed a series, i.e., "a multiplicity possessing a rule of order" (Leibnitz), but the rule of order here is cultural (*habit*,in short), and linguistic (the possibility of the word, the word pregnant with its possibilities). Similarly, sequences can be arranged among themselves (converged, articulated) in such a way as to form a kind of network, a table (as in the sequences "To enter," "Door," "Farewell," "To leave"), but the "luck" of this table (narratively, *this* episode) is linked to the possibility of a metaname (the metasequence of the Ring, for example). Thus, to read (to perceive the *readerly*

82

aspect of the text) is to proceed from name to name, from fold to fold; it is to fold the text according to one name and then to unfold it along the new folds of this name. This is proairetism: an artifice (or art) of reading that seeks out names, that tends toward them: an act of lexical transcendence, a labor of classification carried out on the basis of the classification of language—a *maya* activity, as the Buddhists would say, an account of appearances, but as discontinuous forms, as names.

(138) *"What did that mean?" my young companion asked me. "Is he her husband?* ★ HER. Enigma 3: formulation (What is the family relationship of the Lantys and the old man?). ★★ Even if false, the hypothesis provides a name, that is, a way out, for the symbol: it once again *marries* the castrato to youth, to beauty, to life: a marriage achieved either with the young woman or with Marianina: the symbol has no regard for persons (SYM. Marriage of the castrato).

(139) *I must be dreaming. Where am I?"*
"You," I replied, *"you, madame, superior as you are, you who understand so well the most hidden feelings, who know how to inspire in a man's heart the most delicate of feelings without blighting it, without breaking it at the outset, you who pity heartache and who combine the wit of a Parisienne with a passionate soul worthy of Italy or Spain—"*
She perceived the bitter irony in my speech; then, without seeming to have heard, she interrupted me: "Oh, you fashion me to your own taste. What tyranny! You don't want me for myself!"
"Ah, I want nothing," I cried, taken aback by her severity. ★ Here there are two cultural codes, one controlling the other: 1) "Flirtatious and witty conversation," all the more coded for being labored, due either to voluntary parody on the narrator's part or to a Balzacian conception of the "lightness" of worldly conversation. 2) Irony, equally labored, probably for the same reasons (REF. "Flirtatiousness, irony"). ★★ REF. Marivaudage, Southern passion ★★★ The narrator, at first fatherly, is here entirely the suitor; the Woman has him in her power; at the slightest word

from his mistress (spoken "without seeming to have heard"), the subject-male beats a retreat, emphasizing a subjection necessary for the (immediate) continuation of the story (SYM. The Queen-Woman and the narrator-subject).

(140) *"Is it true, at least, that you enjoy hearing stories of those vivid passions that ravishing Southern women inspire in our hearts?"* ★ The narrator knows the story of the enigmatic old man and the mysterious Adonis (Nos. 70 and 120); for her part, the young woman is interested in hearing it (No. 119): the conditions are met for a narrative contract. We now come to an explicit proposition of narrative. This proposition will first of all (here) be tantamount to a propitiatory gift meant to compensate for the narrator's offense against the Queen-Woman, who must be mollified. The imminent narrative is henceforth constituted as an offering, before becoming merchandise (in a transaction to be explained later on) (ACT. "To narrate": 3: to offer to tell). ★★ REF. Passion (the delights of analogy: a *hotter* sun creates *burning* passions, love being a *flame*). Meridionality, already connoted in Filippo's olive complexion, is the genus containing the species "Italy" in advance. ★★★ The utterance proposes a false enthymeme: (1) the story to be told is the story of a woman; (2) it will be the story of La Zambinella; (3) thus, La Zambinella will be a woman. The narrator sets a snare for his listener (and the reader): even before the narrative begins, a false clue is given for Enigma 6 (*Who is La Zambinella?*) (HER. Enigma 6: thematization and snare).

XXXVII. THE HERMENEUTIC SENTENCE

The proposition of truth is a "well-made" sentence; it contains a subject (theme of the enigma), a statement of the question (formulation of the enigma), its question mark (proposal of the enigma), various subordinate and interpolated clauses and catalyses (delays in the answer), all of which precede the ultimate predicate (disclosure). Canonically, Enigma 6 (*Who is La Zambinella?*) would be set forth as follows:

Question: *"This is La Zambinella.* *Who is she*   ?
               (subject, theme)   (formulation)   (proposal)

             "I will tell you: *a woman,*   *a creature*
             (promise of answer)   (snare)   *outside nature*
Delays: ⎰ *a . . .*   *relative of*   (ambiguity)
             (suspended answer)   *the Lantys,*
             no one knows.   (partial answer)
             (jammed answer)

Answer: A *castrato dressed as a woman.*
         (disclosure)

This canon can be modified (just as there are several kinds of sentence), provided that the principal hermeneutemes (the "knots" or "kernels") are present at some point in the discourse: the discourse can condense several hermeneutemes into a single statement (into a single signifier) by making some of them implicit (thematization, proposal, and formulation); it can also invert the terms of the hermeneutic order: an answer can be given before the question has been asked (it is suggested that La Zambinella is a woman even before she appears in the story); or a snare can remain set after the truth has been revealed (Sarrasine continues to ignore La Zambinella's true sex even though it has been revealed to him). This freedom of the hermeneutic sentence (which is something like the freedom of the flexional sentence) exists because the classic narrative combines two points of view (two pertinences): a rule of communication, which keeps the networks of destination separate, so that each one can continue to operate even if its neighbor is already "burned out" (Sarrasine can continue to receive a false message although the reader's circuit is already saturated: the sculptor's blindness becomes a new message, object of a new system henceforth destined solely for the reader); and a pseudo-logical rule, which tolerates a certain freedom in the order in which predicates are presented, once the subject has been proposed: this freedom actually reinforces the preeminence of the subject (of the star), whose perturbation (literally, whose jeopardy) seems accidental and provisional; or rather: from the question's provisional nature, we infer its accidents: once the subject is provided with its *"true"* predicate, everything falls into place, the sentence can end.

(141) *"Yes, so?"*

"So, I'll call tomorrow around nine and reveal this mystery to you." ★ In the sequence "To narrate" we could set up a sub-sequence or byte, "Rendezvous" (*suggested/refused/accepted*), inasmuch as the Rendezvous is a common weapon in the novelistic arsenal (there is another later on in the story, given Sarrasine by the duenna [No. 288]). Nevertheless, since this rendezvous, in its specific structure (*refused/accepted*), diagrammatically represents the bargain struck between the narrator and the young woman concerning the subject "Story," we shall integrate it directly into the "To narrate" sequence, where it will become an intermediate term: ACT. "To narrate": 4: to suggest a rendezvous for the undisturbed telling of a story (a fairly frequent act in the code of everyday life: *"I'll tell it to you . . ."*).

(142) *"No," she replied, "I want to know now."*

"You haven't yet given me the right to obey you when you say: I want to." ★ ACT. "To narrate": 5: to discuss the time of the rendezvous. ★★ The Queen-Woman appears to be demanding an immediate narration out of pure caprice—a way of connoting her domination—but the narrator reminds her of the precise—and serious—nature of the bargain: you haven't yet given me anything, and thus I am not obligated to you. Which means: if you give yourself to me, I will tell you the story: tit for tat: a moment of love in exchange for a good story (SYM. The Queen-Woman and the subject-narrator).

(143) *"At this moment," she replied with maddening coquetry, "I have the most burning desire to know the secret. Tomorrow, I*

might not even listen to you . . ." ★ SYM. The (capricious) Queen-woman. To demand delivery of the goods on the spot (narration of the story) is to scant the other half of the bargain, since the narrator's desire cannot be fulfilled in the Lantys' salon: the young woman has some desire to "cheat."

(144) *She smiled and we parted; she just as proud, just as forbidding, and I just as ridiculous as ever. She had the audacity to waltz with a young aide-de-camp; and I was left in turn angry, pouting, admiring, loving, jealous.* ★ SEM. The Queen-Woman and subject-narrator. Here, the symbolic situation of the partners is transcribed by one of the interested parties in a psychological metalanguage.

(145) *"Till tomorrow,"* she said, around two in the morning, as *she left the ball.* ★ ACT. "To narrate": 6: to agree to the rendezvous.

(146) *"I won't go,"* I thought to myself. *"I'll give you up. You are more capricious, perhaps a thousand times more fanciful . . . than my imagination."* ★ ACT. "To narrate": 7: to reject the rendezvous. The complicated maneuver of the rendezvous (refused by one, agreed to by the other, and vice versa) diagrammatically embodies the very essence of the bargain, which is a seesaw of proposals and refusals: through the rendezvous episode, a very precise economy of exchange is established. —The story of La Zambinella, the narrator informs us in passing, is perhaps fictitious, in the fiction itself: counterfeit money surreptiously put in circulation.

(147) *The next evening, we were both seated before a good fire* ★ ACT. "To narrate": 8: to have accepted the rendezvous.

(148) *in a small, elegant salon, she on a low sofa, I on cushions almost at her feet, and my eyes below hers. The street was quiet. The lamp shed a soft light. It was one of those evenings pleasing to the soul, one of those never-to-be-forgotten moments, one of those hours spent in peace and desire whose charm, later on, is a matter for constant regret, even when we may be happier. Who can erase the vivid imprint of the first feelings of love?* ★ SYM. The Queen-

Woman and the subject-narrator (*"almost at her feet, and my eyes below hers"*). The décor (a good fire, comfortable furnishings, soft light) is ambivalent: it is as propitious for the telling of a good story as it is for a night of love. ★★ REF. Code of Passion, Regret, etc.

(149) *"Well,"* she said, *"I'm listening."* ★ ACT. "To narrate": 9: to command to tell.

(150) *"I don't dare begin. The story has some dangerous passages for its teller. If I become too moved, you must stop me."* ★ ACT. "To narrate": 10: to hesitate to tell. Perhaps a special morpheme should be constituted for this final hesitation of the discourse in beginning a story, a suspense which is purely discursive, analogous to the final moments of a striptease. ★★ SYM. The narrator and castration. Running the risk, as he says, of becoming too moved, the narrator identifies himself in advance with Sarrasine's "passion" for La Zambinella—and, consequently, with the castration which is at stake.

(151) *"Tell."* ★ ACT. "To narrate: 11: to repeat the command to tell.

(152) *"I will obey."* ★ ACT. "To narrate": 12: command accepted. By this final word, the narrative which now begins comes under the sign of the Queen-Woman, the Castrating Figure.

XXXVIII. CONTRACT-NARRATIVES

At the origin of Narrative, desire. To produce narrative, however, desire must *vary*, must enter into a system of equivalents and metonymies; or: in order to be produced, narrative must be susceptible of *change*, must subject itself to an *economic system*. In *Sarrasine*, for example: the secret of the Adonis has to do with his body; a knowledge of this secret is access to that body: the young woman desires the Adonis (No. 113) and its story (No. 119): a first desire is posited that determines a second, through metonymy: the narrator, jealous of the Adonis by cultural constraint (Nos. 115–16), is forced to desire the young woman; and since he knows the story of the Adonis, the conditions for a contract are met: A desires B, who desires something A has; and A and B will exchange this desire and this thing, this body and this narrative: a night of love for a good story. Narrative: legal tender, subject to contract, economic stakes, in short, *merchandise*, barter which, as here, can turn into haggling, no longer restricted to the publisher's office but represented, *en abyme*, in the narrative. This is the theory *Sarrasine* offers as a fable. This is the question raised, perhaps, by every narrative. *What should the narrative be exchanged for? What is the narrative "worth"?* Here, the narrative is exchanged for a body (a contract of prostitution); elsewhere it can purchase life itself (in *The Thousand and One Nights*, one story of Scheherazade equals one day of continued life); and elsewhere, in Sade, the narrator systematically alternates, as in a gesture of purchase, an orgy for a dissertation, in other words, for meaning (philosophy *is equivalent to* sex, the boudoir): by a dizzying device, narrative becomes the representation of the contract upon which it is based: in these exemplary fictions, narrating is the (economic) theory of narration: one does not narrate to "amuse," to "instruct," or to satisfy a certain anthropological function of meaning; one narrates in order to obtain by exchanging; and it is this exchange that is represented in the narrative itself: narrative is both product and production, merchandise and commerce, a stake and the bearer of that stake: a dialectic even more explicit in *Sarrasine* since the very "contents" of the Narrative-as-Merchandise (a story of castration) will prevent the bargain from being completed: the young woman, upset by the *narrated* castration, will withdraw from the transaction without honoring her pledge.

89

Since narrative is both merchandise and the relation of the contract of which it is the object, there can no longer be any question of setting up a rhetorical hierarchy between the two parts of the tale, as is common practice: the evening at the Lanty mansion is not a mere prologue, and Sarrasine's adventure is not the main story: the sculptor is not the hero and the narrator is not a mere protactic character: *Sarrasine* is not the story of a castrato, but of a contract; it is the story of a force (the narrative) and the action of this force on the very contract controlling it. Thus, the two parts of the text are not detached from one another according to the so-called principle of "nested narratives" (a narrative within the narrative). The nesting of the blocks of narrative is not (merely) ludic but (also) economic. Narrative does not engender itself by metonymic extension (subject to its passage through the stages of desire), by paradigmatic alternation: narrative is determined not by a desire to narrate but by a desire to exchange: it is a *medium of exchange*, an agent, a currency, a gold standard. What accounts for this central equivalence is not the "plan" of *Sarrasine*, but its structure. The structure is not the plot or plan. Therefore, this is not an "explication de texte."

(153) *Ernest-Jean Sarrasine was the only son of a lawyer in the Franche-Comté, I went on, after a pause. His father had amassed six or eight thousand livres of income honestly enough, a professional's fortune which at that time, in the provinces, was considered to be colossal. The elder Sarrasine, having but one child and anxious to overlook nothing where his education was concerned, hoped to make a magistrate of him, and to live long enough to see, in his old age, the grandson of Matthieu Sarrasine, farmer of Saint-Dié, seated beneath the lilies and napping through some trial for the greater glory of the law; however, heaven did not hold this*

pleasure in store for the lawyer. ★ A question was posed by the story's very title (No. 1): *What is Sarrasine?* Now that question has been answered (HER. Enigma 1: answer). ★★ SYM. Father and son: Antithesis: A: the favored son (he will be accursed in No. 168). The antithesis corresponds to a cultural code: Magistrate-Father, Artist-Son: by this inversion, societies are dissolved. ★★★ In this family chronicle, one place is empty: that of the mother (SYM. Father and son: the absent mother).

(154) *The younger Sarrasine, entrusted to the Jesuits at an early age,* ★ ACT. "Boarding school": 1: to go away to boarding school.

(155) *evidenced an unusual turbulence.* ★ SEM. Insubordination. Denotatively, turbulence is a character trait; here, however, this trait refers to a larger, vaguer, and more formal signified: the state of a substance that doesn't "take" or cannot be filtered, and remains unresolved, murky; Sarrasine is subject to this deep-seated vice: he has no unification, no organic lubrication; and finally, it is the etymological meaning of the word *turbulence* which is its connoted meaning.

(156) *He had the childhood of a man of talent.* ★ SEM. Vocation (indefinite for the moment).

(157) *He would study only what pleased him, frequently rebelled, and sometimes spent hours on end plunged in confused thought, occupied at times in watching his comrades at play, at times dreaming of Homeric heroes.* ★ SEM. Unsociability. ★★ SEM. Vocation (artistic: perhaps literary?).

(158) *Then, if he made up his mind to amuse himself, he threw himself into games with an extraordinary ardor. When a fight broke out between him and a friend, the battle rarely ended without bloodshed. If he was the weaker of the two, he would bite.* ★ SEM. Excess (what exceeds nature). ★★ SEM. Femininity (*to bite,* rather than to use the phallic fist, is a connotator of femininity). The appearance of blood in the sculptor's childhood already dramatizes his fate, however remotely.

(159) *Both active and passive by turns, without aptitude and not overly intelligent, his bizarre character* ★ SEM. The composite.

This maleficent seme has already appeared in other forms through the first part of the text: the *composite* (in romantic terminology, the *bizarre*), connoted by the alternation of opposites, designates an inability to attain the homogeneity or unity whose model is organic cohesion, in a word the *lubricated* (No. 213); not that Sarrasine lacks virility (energy, independence, etc.), but such virility is unstable, and instability leads the sculptor outside a plenary, reconciled unity toward defeat, toward deficiency (or signifies it).

XL. THE BIRTH OF THEMATICS

To state that Sarrasine is *"active or passive by turns"* is to attempt to locate something in his character "which doesn't take," to attempt to name that something. Thus begins a process of nomination which is the essence of the reader's activity: to read is to struggle to name, to subject the sentences of the text to a semantic transformation. This transformation is erratic; it consists in hesitating among several names: if we are told that Sarrasine had *"one of those strong wills that know no obstacle,"* what are we to read? *will, energy, obstinacy, stubbornness,* etc.? The connotator refers not so much to a name as to a synonymic complex whose common nucleus we sense even while the discourse is leading us toward other possibilities, toward other related signifieds: thus, reading is absorbed in a kind of metonymic skid, each synonym adding to its neighbor some new trait, some new departure: the old man who was first connoted as *fragile* is soon said to be *"of glass"*: an image containing signifieds of rigidity, immobility, and dry, cutting frangibility. This expansion is the very movement of meaning: the meaning skids, recovers itself, and advances simultaneously; far from analyzing it, we should rather describe it through its expansions, lexical transcendence, the generic word it continually attempts to join: the object of semantics

92

should be the synthesis of meanings, not the analysis of words. In a way, this semantics of expansions already exists: it is called Thematics. To thematize is, on the one hand, to leave the dictionary behind, to follow certain synonymic chains (*turbulent, murky, unstable, unresolved*), to yield to an expanding nomination (which can proceed from a certain sensualism), and, on the other, to return to these various substantive stations in order to create some constant form (*"which doesn't take"*), for the exchange value of a seme, its ability to participate in a thematic economy, depends on its repetition: in Sarrasine's aggressivity, it is worth noting a tendency (a repeated clue) toward petty destructiveness, since this element will crop up in other signifiers; similarly, the old man's *fantastic* quality has no semantic value unless the exceeding of human limits, which is one of the primitive "components" of the word (one of its other "names"), can recur elsewhere. To read, to understand, to thematize (at least a classic text), is therefore to *retreat* from name to name, starting from the signifying thrust (thus we retreat from Sarrasine's *violence* at least to the point of *excess*, a clumsy name for *what exceeds the limits and transcends nature*). This retreat is of course coded: when the unnesting of names ceases, a critical level is established, the work is closed, the language by which the semantic transformation is ended becomes nature, truth, the work's secret. Only an infinite thematics, open to endless nomination, can respect the enduring character of language, the production of reading, and no longer the list of its products. However, the metonymic production of language is not postulated in the classic text: whence the inevitability of a dice throw which can arrest and fix the skid of names: this is thematics.

(160) *made his teachers as wary of him as were his classmates.*
★ SEM. Danger.

(161) *Instead of learning the elements of Greek, he drew the Reverend Father as he explained a passage in Thucydides to them, sketched the mathematics teacher, the tutors, the Father in charge of discipline, and he scribbled shapeless designs on the walls.* ★ SEM. Unsociability (Sarrasine acts inappropriately, outside the norms, outside the limits of "nature"). ★★ SEM. Vocation (drawing). The signified is deduced from a cultural code: the inspired dunce succeeds outside regulated class activities.

(162) *Instead of singing the Lord's praises in church, he distracted himself during services by whittling on a pew;* ★ SEM. Impiety. Impiety here is provocation, not indifference: Sarrasine is (and thus will be) a transgressor. Transgression consists not in ignoring the service but in replacing it (in parodying it) with an inverted activity, erotic and hallucinatory: whittling. ★★ SEM. Whittling. The destruction of the whole object, the (deliberate) regression toward the partial object, the hallucination of fragmentation, the quest for a fetish, will reappear when Sarrasine endeavors to *undress* La Zambinella mentally in order to draw her body.

XLI. THE PROPER NAME

We occasionally speak of Sarrasine as though he existed, as though he had a future, an unconscious, a soul; however, what we are talking about is his *figure* (an impersonal network of symbols combined under the proper name "Sarrasine"), not his *person* (a moral freedom endowed with motives and an overdetermination of meanings): we are developing connotations, not pursuing investigations; we are not searching for the truth of Sarrasine, but for the systematics of a (transitory) site of the text: we mark this site (under the name Sarrasine) so it will take its place among the alibis of the narrative operation, in the indeterminable network of meanings, in the plurality of the codes. By restoring to the discourse its hero's proper name, we are merely acting in accordance with the economic nature of the Name: in the novelistic regime (and elsewhere?), it is an instrument of exchange: it allows the substitution of a nominal unit for a collection of characteristics by establishing an equivalent relationship between sign and sum: it is a bookkeeping method in which, the price being equal, condensed merchandise is preferable to voluminous merchandise. Except that the economic function (substitutive, semantic) of the Name is stated with varying degrees of frankness. Whence the variety of patronymic codes. To call characters, as Furetière does, *Javotte, Nicodème, Belastre* is (without keeping completely aloof from a certain half-bourgeois, half-classic code) to emphasize the structural function of the Name, to state its arbitrary nature, to depersonalize it, to accept the currency of the Name as pure convention. To say *Sarrasine, Rochefide, Lanty, Zambinella* (not to mention *Bouchardon*, who really existed) is to maintain that the patronymic substitute is *filled* with a person (civic, national, social), it is to insist that appellative currency be in gold (and not left to be decided arbitrarily). All subversion, or all novelistic submission, thus begins with the Proper Name: specific—as well specified—as is the Proustian narrator's social position, his perilously maintained lack of a name creates a serious deflation of the realistic illusion: the Proustian *I* is not of itself a name (in contrast to the substantive character of the novelistic pronoun, XXVIII); because it is undermined, troubled by the disturbances of age, it loses its biographical tense by a certain blurring. What is obsolescent in today's novel is not the novelistic, it is the character; what can no longer be written is the Proper Name.

(163) *or when he had stolen a piece of wood, he carved some holy figure. If he had no wood, paper, or pencil, he reproduced his ideas with bread crumbs.* ★ SEM. Vocation (sculptor). The kneading of bread crumbs, prefiguring the moment when Sarrasine kneads

95

the clay in which he copies La Zambinella's body, has a dual value: informative (the definition of Sarrasine is created by restriction from the genus "Artist" to the species "Sculptor"); symbolic (referring to the onanism of the solitary viewer, returned to in the scene on the sofa in No. 267).

(164) *Whether copying the characters in the pictures that decorated the choir, or improvising, he always left behind him some gross sketches whose licentiousness shocked the youngest Fathers; evil tongues maintained that the older Jesuits were amused by them.* ★ SEM. Licentiousness (kneading is an erotic activity). ★★ REF. Psychology of ages (the young are strict; the old, permissive).

(165) *Finally, if we are to believe school gossip, he was expelled* ★ ACT. "Boarding school": 2: to be expelled.

(166) *for having, while awaiting his turn at the confessional on Good Friday, shaped a big stick of wood into the form of Christ. The impiety with which this statue was endowed was too blatant not to have merited punishment of the artist. Had he not had the audacity to place this somewhat cynical figure on top of the tabernacle!* ★ SEM. Vocation (sculptor). ★★ SEM. Impiety (the transgression links religion and the erotic, cf. No. 162).

(167) *Sarrasine sought in Paris a refuge from the effects* ★ ACT. "Career": 1: to go to Paris.

(168) *of a father's curse.* ★ SYM. Father and son: Antithesis: B: the accursed son.

(169) *Having one of those strong wills that brook no obstacle, he obeyed the commands of his genius and entered Bouchardon's studio.* ★ SEM. Obstinacy (Sarrasine will also insist on loving La Zambinella, then on deceiving himself as to her nature; his "obstinacy" is only the protection of his illusions). ★★ ACT. "Career": 2: to study with a great master.

(170) *He worked all day, and in the evening went out to beg for his living.* ★ REF. Stereotype: the poor, courageous artist (earning his living by day, creating at night or, as here, vice versa).

96

(171) *Astonished at the young artist's progress and intelligence, Bouchardon* ★ SEM. Genius (genius crowns the artist's vocation, cf. No. 173).

(172) *soon became aware of his pupil's poverty; he helped him, grew fond of him, and treated him like his own son.* ★ Bouchardon replaces not the father but the mother, whose absence (No. 153) has led the child into licentiousness, excess, anomie; like a mother, Bouchardon understands, cares for, helps (SYM. Mother and son).

(173) *Then, when Sarrasine's genius was revealed* ★ SEM. Genius. Sarrasine's genius is, three times over, necessary ("credible"): according to the cultural (romantic) code, it makes Sarrasine a singular being, outside the norms; according to the dramatic code, it exposes the wicked fate which "exchanges" a great artist's death for a castrato's life, that is, *everything* for *nothing*; according to the narrative code, it justifies the perfection La Zambinella's statue will have, the source of the desire transmitted to the Adonis.

(174) *in one of those works in which future talent struggles with the effervescence of youth,* ★ REF. Code of ages and code of Art (talent as discipline, youth as effervescence).

XLII. CODES OF CLASS

What is the use of trying to reconstruct a cultural code, since the regulations governing it are never more than a *prospect* (to quote Poussin)? And yet the locus of an epoch's codes forms a kind of scientific vulgate which it will eventually be valuable to describe: what do we know "naturally" about art?—"it is a constraint"; about youth?—"it is turbulent," etc. If we collect all such knowledge, all such vulgarisms, we create a monster, and this monster is ideology. As a fragment of ideology, the cultural code *inverts* its class origin (scholastic and social) into

97

a natural reference, into a proverbial statement. Like didactic language and political language, which also never question the repetition of their utterances (their stereotypic essence), the cultural proverb vexes, provokes an intolerant reading; the Balzacian text is clotted with it: because of its cultural codes, it stales, rots, excludes itself from writing (which is always a *contemporary* task): it is the quintessence, the residual condensate of what cannot be rewritten. This extrusion of the stereotype is scarcely averted by irony, for, as we have seen (XXI), irony can only add a new code (a new stereotype) to the codes, to the stereotypes it claims to exorcise. The writer's only control over stereotypic vertigo (this vertigo is also that of "stupidity," "vulgarity") is to participate in it without quotation marks, producing a text, not a parody. This is what Flaubert did in *Bouvard et Pécuchet*: the two copyists are copiers of codes (they are, one may say, *stupid*), but since they too confront the class stupidity which surrounds them, the text presenting them sets up a circularity in which no one (not even the author) has an advantage over anyone else; and this is in fact the function of writing: to make ridiculous, to annul the power (the intimidation) of one language over another, to dissolve any metalanguage as soon as it is constituted.

(175) *the warmhearted Bouchardon endeavored to restore him to the old lawyer's good graces. Before the authority of the famous sculptor, the parental anger subsided. All Besançon rejoiced at having given birth to a great man of the future. In the first throes of the ecstasy produced by his flattered vanity, the miserly lawyer gave his son the means to cut a good figure in society.* ★ We have noted the paradigm: *favored/accursed.* We might conceive here a third term: reconciled. However, this dialectic is unacceptable, for it is valid only on the anecdotal, not the symbolic, level, where the curse (the casting out) exists outside time. This reconciliation is significant because of its agent, thereby confirmed in his maternal

98

nature: as the stake of the struggle, the mother can resolve the conflict between father and son (later we will see Bouchardon, like a mother, protecting Sarrasine from sexuality) (SYM. Mother and son).

(176) *For a long time, the lengthy and laborious studies demanded by sculpture* ★ REF. Code of Art (the difficult apprenticeship of sculpture). Sculpture is said to struggle with matter, not with representation, as in the case of painting; it is a demiurgic art, an art which extracts rather than covers, an art of the hand that takes hold.

(177) *tamed Sarrasine's impetuous nature and wild genius. Bouchardon, foreseeing the violence with which the passions would erupt in this young soul,* ★ SEM. Excess (the excessive, out of bounds).

(178) *which was perhaps as predisposed to them as Michelangelo's had been,* ★ REF. Art history, the psychological typology of a great artist (if Sarrasine had been a musician and Balzac had been born fifty years later, it would have been Beethoven; in literature, Balzac himself, etc.).

(179) *channeled his energy into constant labor. He succeeded in keeping Sarrasine's extraordinary impetuosity within limits by forbidding him to work; by suggesting distractions when he saw him being carried away by the fury of some idea, or by entrusting him with important work when he seemed on the point of abandoning himself to dissipation.* ★ SEM. Excess. ★★ Like a bourgeois mother who wants her son to become an engineer, Bouchardon keeps an eye on Sarrasine's work (but also, like the same bourgeois mother, on his sexual activities) (SYM. Mother and son).

(180) *However, gentleness was always the most powerful of weapons where this passionate soul was concerned, and the master had no greater control over his student than when he inspired his gratitude through paternal kindness.* ★ Gentleness is a maternal weapon: symbolically, a gentle father is the mother (SYM. Mother and son). ★★ REF. Gnomic code ("A *soft answer turneth away wrath*").

99

The utterances of the cultural code are implicit proverbs: they are written in that obligative mode by which the discourse states a general will, the law of a society, making the proposition concerned ineluctable or indelible. Further still: it is because an utterance can be transformed into a proverb, a maxim, a postulate, that the supporting cultural code is discoverable: stylistic transformation "proves" the code, bares its structure, reveals its ideological perspective. What is easy for proverbs (which have a very special syntactical, archaistic form) is much less so for the other codes of discourse, since the sentence-model, the example, the paradigm expressing each of them has not (yet) been isolated. Nevertheless, we can conceive that stylistics, which has hitherto been concerned only with departures and expressive phrases—in other words, with verbal *individuations*, with an author's ideolects—will radically change its object and concern itself essentially with isolating and classifying models (patterns) of sentences, clauses, armatures, deep structures; in short, we can conceive that stylistics, too, will become transformational; thereby it would cease to be a minor subdivision of literary analysis (limited to a few individual syntactical and lexical constants) and, transcending the opposition of form and content, would become an instrument of ideological classification; for, once these models are found, we could then, in the course of the text, expose each code as it occurs.

(181) *At twenty-two, Sarrasine was necessarily removed from the salutary influence Bouchardon had exercised over his morals and his habits.* ★ REF. Chronology (Sarrasine is twenty-two when he leaves for Italy). ★★ ACT. "Career": 3: to leave the master. ★★★ Since Sarrasine is "licentious," Bouchardon's "salutary influence,"

even though finally for art's sake, must be a moral one: the son's sexuality is protected, preserved, annulled by the mother. Sequestration from sex designates, in Sarrasine, *aphanisis*, castration, to which he was subject well before knowing La Zambinella: the castrato appears to rescue him from it for a time (thus Sarrasine's "first" pleasure in the theater), only to subject him to it definitively (*"You have dragged me down to your level,"* No. 525); thus, in the end, La Zambinella will be for Sarrasine only the *consciousness* of what he has been all along (SYM. Aphanisis).

(182) *He reaped the fruits of his genius by winning the sculpture prize* ★ ACT. "Career": 4: to win a prize.

(183) *established by the Marquis de Marigny, the brother of Mme de Pompadour, who did so much for the arts.* ★ REF. History (Mme de Pompadour).

(184) *Diderot hailed the statue by Bouchardon's pupil as a masterpiece.* ★ ACT. "Career": 5: to be praised by a great critic. ★★ REF. History of literature (Diderot as art critic).

XLIV. THE HISTORICAL CHARACTER

In *The Guermantes Way*, Proust writes: "We see . . . in a gazetteer of the works of Balzac, where the most illustrious personages figure only according to their connexion with the *Comédie humaine*, Napoleon occupy a space considerably less than that allotted to Rastignac, and occupy that space solely because he once spoke to the young ladies of Cinq-Cygne." It is precisely this minor importance which gives the historical character its *exact* weight of reality: this *minor* is the measure of authenticity: Diderot, Mme de Pompadour, later Sophie Arnould, Rousseau, d'Holbach, are introduced into the fiction laterally, obliquely, *in passing*, painted on the scenery, not represented on the stage; for if the historical character were to assume its *real* importance, the discourse would be forced to yield it a role which would, paradoxically, make it less real (thus the characters in Balzac's *Catherine de Médicis*, Alexandre Dumas's novels, or Sacha Guitry's plays: absurdly improbable): they would give themselves away. Yet if they are merely mixed in with their fictional neighbors, mentioned as having simply been present at some social gathering, their modesty, like a lock between two levels of water, equalizes novel and history: they reinstate the novel as a family, and like ancestors who are contradictorily famous and absurd, they give the novel the glow of reality, not of glory: they are superlative effects of the real.

(185) *The King's sculptor, not without great sorrow, saw off to Italy a young man* ★ ACT. "Career": 6: to leave for Italy. ★★ Bouchardon's sorrow, his fear, is that of a mother who has kept her son a virgin and who suddenly finds him sent off to do his military service in some hot-blooded country (SYM. Protection against sexuality).

(186) *whom he had kept, as a matter of principle, in total ignorance of the facts of life.* ★ The generous but abusive mother (abusive by her very generosity) has denied her son knowledge of the "facts of life" by overwhelming him with work (though allowing him a few social outings); Bouchardon has condemned Sarrasine to virginity and has played the role of his castrator (SYM. Protection against sexuality).

(187) *For six years, Sarrasine had boarded with Bouchardon.* ★ REF. Chronology (Sarrasine came to Bouchardon at the age of sixteen).

(188) *As fanatic in his art as Canova was later to be, he arose at dawn, went to the studio, did not emerge until nightfall,* ★ SEM. Excess. ★★ REF. History of art (Canova).

(189) *and lived only with his Muse.* ★ SYM. Protection against sexuality. ★★ SYM. Pygmalion. There is a dual (contradictory) connotation: Sarrasine never makes love, he is in a state of aphanisis (or loss of sexuality); like a Pygmalion, Sarrasine sleeps with his statues, he puts his eroticism into his art.

(190) *If he went to the Comédie-Française, he was taken by his master. He felt so out of place at Mme Geoffrin's and in high society, into which Bouchardon tried to introduce him, that he preferred to be alone, and shunned the pleasures of that licentious era.* ★ REF. Historical code: the century of Louis XV. ★★ SYM. Protection against sexuality.

(191) *He had no other mistress but sculpture* ★ Redundance of No. 189. ★★ SYM. Protection against sexuality. ★★★ SYM. Pygmalion.

(192) *and Clotilde, one of the luminaries of the Opéra.* ★ ACT: "Liaison": 1: to have a liaison.

(193) *And even this affair did not last.* ★ ACT: "Liaison": 2: indication of the end of the liaison. The indication is interior to the discourse, not to the story (to the liaison itself), in which case one would have been given the facts which led to the break: it is therefore a rhetorical indication. The brevity of the liaison (signified by the *"And even"*) connotes its insignificance: Sarrasine's sexual exile has not ended.

(194) *Sarrasine was rather ugly, always badly dressed, and so free in his nature, so irregular in his private life,* ★ Romantically (that is, by virtue of the romantic code), ugliness connotes genius, by the intermediary stage of a sign, a sign of exclusion (SEM. Genius). Unlike beauty, ugliness replicates no model, has no metonymic origin; its only reference (its only Authority) is the word *ugliness,* which denotes it.

(195) *that the celebrated nymph, fearing some catastrophe, soon relinquished the sculptor to his love of the Arts.* ★ ACT. "Liaison": 3: end of the liaison.

To begin a liaison/to indicate its end/to end it: the asyndeton signifies the adventure's absurd brevity (whereas ordinarily "liaison" is open to a thousand novelistic expansions and incidents). Basically, by its very structure (clearly revealed in the utter simplicity of the sequence), proairetism comparatively depreciates language ("action," it is said, speaks louder than "words"): once restored to its proairetic essence, the operative mocks the symbolic, *dismisses* it. By the asyndeton of behavioral statements, human action is trivialized, reduced to a horizon of stimulus and responses, the sexual is mechanized, voided. Thus, by the mere form of its sequence, the liaison of Sarrasine and Clotilde keeps the sculptor away from sex: proairetism, when reduced to its essential terms, like so many knives (the knives of asyndeton), itself becomes an instrument ᵒf castration, applied by the discourse to Sarrasine.

(196) *Sophie Arnould made one of her witticisms on this subject. She confessed her surprise, I believe, that her friend had managed to triumph over statuary.* ★ REF. Historical code: the century of Louis XV (licentious and witty). ★★ SYM. Sequestration from sex. ★★★ Pygmalion.

(197) *Sarrasine left for Italy in 1758.* ★ ACT. "Journey": 1: to depart (for Italy). ★★ REF. Chronology (Sarrasine is twenty-two in 1758, cf. No. 181).

(198) *During the journey, his vivid imagination caught fire beneath a brilliant sky and at the sight of the wonderful monuments which are to be found in the birthplace of the Arts. He admired the statues, the frescoes, the paintings, and thus inspired,* ★ ACT. "Journey": 2: to travel (this term in a famous sequence is infinitely catalyzable). ★★ REF. Art and Tourism (Italy Mother of the Arts, etc.).

(199) *he came to Rome,* ★ ACT. "Journey": 3: to arrive.

(200) *filled with desire to carve his name between Michelangelo's and M. Bouchardon's. Accordingly, at the beginning, he divided his time between studio tasks and examining the works of art in which Rome abounds.* ★ ACT. "Journey": 4: to stay. ★★ REF. History of Art.

XLVI. COMPLETENESS

To depart/to travel/to arrive/to stay: the journey is saturated. To end, to fill, to join, to unify—one might say that this is the basic requirement of the *readerly*, as though it were prey to some obsessive fear: that of omitting a connection. Fear of forgetting engenders the appearance of a logic of actions; terms and the links between them are posited (invented) in such a way that they unite, duplicate each other, create an illusion of continuity. The plenum generates the drawing intended to "express" it, and the drawing evokes the complement, coloring: as if the *readerly* abhors a vacuum. What would be the narrative of a journey in which it was said that one stays somewhere without having arrived, that one travels without having departed—in which it was never said that, having departed, one arrives or fails to arrive? Such a narrative would be a scandal, the extenuation, by hemorrhage, of readerliness.

(201) *He had already spent two weeks in the ecstatic state which overwhelms young minds at the sight of the queen of ruins,* ★ REF. Ancient Rome. ★★ REF. Chronology. (This notation—*two weeks*—will retroactively match the sculptor's ignorance of Italian and Roman customs: an ignorance of capital importance to the entire story, since it is the basis for all the snares by which Sarra-

sine is surrounded—and by which he surrounds himself—concerning the sex of La Zambinella.)

(202) *when he went one evening to the Teatro Argentina,* ★ ACT. "Theater": 1: to enter (the building).

(203) *before which a huge crowd was assembled.* ★ ACT. "Question" (which will follow): 1: a fact to be explained.

(204) *He inquired as to the causes of this gathering* ★ ACT. "Question": 2: to inquire.

(205) *and everyone answered with two names: Zambinella! Jomelli!* ★ ACT. "Question": 3: to receive an answer. ★★ The preceding proairetism ("Question") has an over-all connotative value; it serves to designate La Zambinella as a star; this signified has already been attached to the old man; it is linked to the international character of the Lanty family and is the source of their wealth (SEM. International star). ★★★ Who is, or rather: what (sex) is La Zambinella? This is the text's sixth enigma: here it is thematized, since its subject is emphatically introduced. (HER. Enigma 6: thematization).

XLVII. S/Z

SarraSine: customary French onomastics would lead us to expect *SarraZine*: on its way to the subject's patronymic, the Z has encountered some pitfall. Z is the letter of mutilation: phonetically, Z stings like a chastising lash, an avenging insect; graphically, cast slantwise by the hand across the blank regularity of the page, amid the curves of the alphabet, like an oblique and illicit blade, it cuts, slashes, or, as we say in French, *zebras*; from a Balzacian viewpoint, this Z (which appears in Balzac's name) is the letter of deviation (see the story Z. *Marcas*); finally, here, Z is the first letter of La Zambinella, the initial of castration, so that by this orthographical error committed in the middle of his name, in the center of his body, Sarrasine receives the Zambinellan Z in its true sense— the wound of deficiency. Further, S and Z are in a relation of graphological inversion: the same letter seen from the other side of the mirror: Sarrasine contemplates in La Zambinella his own castration. Hence the slash (/) confronting the S of SarraSine and the Z of Zambinella has a panic function: it is the slash of censure, the surface of the mirror, the wall of hallucination, the verge of antithesis, the abstraction of limit, the obliquity of the signifier, the index of the paradigm, hence of meaning.

XLVIII. THE UNFORMULATED ENIGMA

Zambinella can be *Bambinella*, little baby, or *Gambinella*, little leg, little phallus, each marked by the letter of deviation (Z). The name without its article (contrary to what occurs throughout the text, where discourse writes: *La Zambinella*), raised to its pure substantive state by the public's outcry, still avoids sexual snares; a decision will soon have to be made whether or not to lie, to say *Zambinella* or *La Zambinella*; for the moment there is neither snare nor question but merely the emphasis of a subject, affirmed before the enigma has been proposed or formulated; in fact, the enigma never will be proposed; for to ask what someone's sex might be, or even simply to hint at its mystery, would in itself be to answer too soon: to characterize sex is immediately to make it deviant; until its disclosure, the enigma will therefore be subject only to snares, equivocations. Yet this enigma is already operative; for to propose a subject, to thematize, to emphasize, to punctuate La Zambinella's name with an exclamation point, is to introduce the question of its predicate, the uncertainty of its complement; the hermeneutic structure is already wholly contained in the predicative cell of the sentence and of the anecdote; to speak of a subject (*Zambinella!*) is to postulate a truth. Like La Zambinella, every subject is a *star*: there is a confusion of the theatrical subject, the hermeneutic subject, and the logical subject.

(206) *He entered* ★ ACT. "Theater": 2: to enter the hall.

(207) *and took a seat in the orchestra,* ★ ACT. "Theater": 3: to be seated.

(208) *squeezed between two notably fat abbati;* ★ ACT. "Discomfort": 1: to be squeezed, made uncomfortable. (The proairetism *to be uncomfortable/to ignore it* will be an over-all connotation of Sarrasine's unawareness, captivated as he is by La Zambinella.) ★★ REF. Italianness (*abbati*, not clerics: local color).

(209) *however, he was lucky enough to be fairly close to the stage.* ★ Proximity to the stage, and thus to the desired object, serves as a (fortuitous) point of departure for a series of hallucinatory feelings which will lead Sarrasine to solitary pleasure (ACT. "Pleasure": 1: proximity to the desired object).

(210) *The curtain rose.* ★ ACT. "Theater": 4: curtain up.

(211) *For the first time in his life, he heard that music* ★ ACT. "Theater": 5: to hear the overture. ★★ We are soon to learn (213, 214, 215) that music has a frankly erotic effect on Sarrasine: it sends him into ecstasy, lubricates him, loosens the sexual constraints under which he has hitherto lived. Sarrasine's sexual exile is here broken *for the first time*. The first (sensual) pleasure is initiatory: it serves as a basis for memory, repetition, ritual: afterwards, everything is organized to recapture this *first time* (SYM. Aphanisis: first pleasure).

(212) *whose delights M. Jean-Jacques Rousseau had so eloquently praised to him at one of Baron d'Holbach's evenings.* ★ REF. Historical code: the century of Louis XV (Rousseau, the Encyclopedists, the Salons).

(213) *The young sculptor's senses were, so to speak, lubricated by the accents of Jomelli's sublime harmony. The languorous novelties of these skillfully mingled Italian voices plunged him into a delicious ecstasy.* ★ Although La Zambinella has not yet appeared, structurally Sarrasine's passion has begun, his *seduction* inaugurated by a preliminary ecstasy; a long series of bodily states will lead Sarrasine from capture to conflagration (ACT. "Seduction": 1: ecstasy). ★★ REF. Italian music. ★★★ Hitherto, Sarrasine has been sequestered from sex; thus, this evening is the *first time* he knows pleasure and loses his virginity (SYM. Initiation).

XLIX. THE VOICE

Italian music, an object well defined historically, culturally, mythically (Rousseau, Gluckists-and-Piccinists, Stendhal, etc.), connotes a "sensual" art, an art of the voice. An erotic substance, the Italian voice was produced *a contrario* (according to a strictly symbolic inversion) by singers without sex: this inversion is *logical* ("*That angelic voice, that delicate voice would be an anomaly, coming from any body but yours,*" Sarrasine says to La Zambinella in No. 445), as though, by selective hypertrophy, sexual density were obliged to abandon the rest of the body and lodge in the throat, thereby draining the organism of all that *connects* it. Thus, emitted by a castrated body, a wildly erotic frenzy is returned to that body: the star castrati are cheered by hysterical audiences, women fall in love with them, wear their portraits "one on each arm, one at the neck hanging from a gold chain, and two on the buckles of each slipper" (Stendhal). This music's erotic quality (attached to its *vocal nature*) is here defined: it is the power of *lubrication; connection* is a specific characteristic of the voice; the model of the lubricated is the organic, the "living," in short, seminal fluid (Italian music "floods with pleasure"); singing (a characteristic generally ignored in aesthetics) has something coenesthetic about it, it is connected less to an "impression" than to an internal, muscular, humoral sensuality. The voice is a diffusion, an insinuation, it passes over the entire surface of the body, the skin; and being a passage, an abolition of limitations, classes, names (*"His soul passed into his ears. He seemed to hear through every pore,"* No. 215), it possesses a special hallucinatory power. Music, therefore, has an effect utterly different from sight; it can effect orgasm, penetrating Sarrasine (No. 243); and when Sarrasine attempts to acclimatize himself (in order to repeat it at will) to the excessive pleasure he seeks on the sofa, his hearing is the first thing he will train; moreover, it is La Zambinella's voice that Sarrasine is in love with (No. 277): the voice, the direct product of castration, the complete, connected evidence of deficiency. The antonym of *lubricated* (already encountered a number of times) is discontinuous, divided, creaking, composite, bizarre: everything that is excluded from the liquid plenitude of pleasure, everything that is unable to unite with the *phrased*, a preciously ambiguous value, since it is both linguistic and musical, unites in the one plenitude both meaning and sex.

(214) *He remained speechless, motionless, not even feeling crowded by the two priests.* ★ ACT. "Discomfort": 2: to feel nothing.

(215) *His soul passed into his ears and eyes. He seemed to hear through every pore.* ★ ACT. "Seduction": 2: extraversion (the body's "passage" toward the object of its desire is prehallucinatory; the wall—of reality—is crossed).

(216) *Suddenly a burst of applause which shook the house greeted the prima donna's entrance* ★ ACT. "Theater": 6: entrance of the star. ★★ SEM. Star ("Stardom"). ★★★ HER. Enigma 6: thematization and snare (prima donna).

(217) *She came coquettishly to the front of the stage and greeted the audience with infinite grace. The lights, the general enthusiasm, the theatrical illusion, the glamour of a style of dress which in those days was quite attractive, all conspired in favor* ★ ACT. "Theater": 7: greeting of the star. ★★ SEM. Femininity. Here the discourse is not lying: of course, it treats La Zambinella as a woman, but it treats her femininity as an *impression*, the causes for which are indicated.

(218) *of this woman.* ★ However, the end of the sentence is a snare (the discourse need only have said "artist" to avoid lying); truthful at the outset, the sentence ends in a lie: in sum, *by the very continuity of its inflections,* the sentence is that nature which controls the mix of the voices, the *dissolve* of the origin (HER. Enigma 6: snare).

(219) *Sarrasine cried out with pleasure.* ★ ACT. "Seduction": 3: intense pleasure.

(220) *At that instant he marveled at the ideal beauty he had hitherto sought in life, seeking in one often unworthy model the roundness of a perfect leg; in another, the curve of a breast; in another, white shoulders; finally taking some girl's neck, some woman's hands, and some child's smooth knees,* ★ SYM. The body fragmented, reassembled.

L. THE REASSEMBLED BODY

Young Marianina's (vocal) perfection resulted from her combining in one body partial qualities usually shared among several singers (No. 20). The same is true of La Zambinella in

Sarrasine's eyes: the subject (aside from the insignificant Clotilde episode, XLV) knows the female body only as a division
and dissemination of partial objects: leg, breast, shoulder,
neck, hands.³ Fragmented Woman is the object offered to Sarrasine's love. Divided, anatomized, she is merely a kind of dictionary of fetish objects. This sundered, dissected body (we are
reminded of the boy's games at school) is reassembled by the
artist (and this is the meaning of his vocation) into a whole
body, the body of love descended from the heaven of art, in
which fetishism is abolished and by which Sarrasine is cured.
However, without the subject's realizing it as yet, and although
the finally reassembled woman is actually there before him,
near enough to touch, this redeeming body remains a fictive
one, through the very praises Sarrasine addresses to it: its
status is that of a *creation* (it is the work of Pygmalion *"come
down from its pedestal,"* No. 229), of an object whose *underneath*, whose *insides* will continue to arouse his concern, his
curiosity, and his aggression: undressing La Zambinella (by
drawing), questioning her and himself, and ultimately breaking the hollow statue, the sculptor will continue to whittle the
woman (just as he whittled his pew in church as a child),
thereby returning to its (fragmented) fetish condition a body
whose unity he supposed he had discovered in such amaze-
ment.

(221) *without ever having encountered under the cold Parisian
sky the rich, sweet creations of ancient Greece.* ★ REF. History of
Art: classical statuary (art alone can establish the total body).

(222) *La Zambinella displayed to him, united, living, and delicate,
those exquisite female forms he so ardently desired, of which a*

³ Jean Reboul was the first to note the presence of this Lacanian theme in
Sarrasine (cf. *supra*, p. 16).

sculptor is at once the severest and the most passionate judge. ★
SYM. The reassembled body. ★★ Psychology of Art (the Woman
and the Artist).

(223) *Her mouth was expressive, her eyes loving, her complexion
dazzlingly white.* ★ SYM. The fragmented body reassembled (beginning of the "inventory").

(224) *And along with these details, which would have enraptured
a painter,* ★ REF. Code of Art: Painting. There is a division of
labor: to the painter, eyes, mouth, face, in a word *soul, expression,*
i.e., inwardness to be portrayed on the surface; to the sculptor,
owner of volume, body, matter, sensuality.

(225) *were all the wonders of those images of Venus revered and
rendered by the chisels of the Greeks.* ★ REF. Code of Art: classical statuary.

(226) *The artist never wearied of admiring the inimitable grace
with which the arms were attached to the torso, the marvelous
roundness of the neck, the harmonious lines drawn by the eyebrows, the nose, and the perfect oval of the face, the purity of its
vivid contours and the effect of the thick, curved lashes which lined
her heavy and voluptuous eyelids.* ★ SEM. Femininity (heavy
curved lashes, voluptuous eyelids). ★★ SYM. The fragmented
body, reassembled (the "inventory" continued).

LI. THE BLAZON

The spitefulness of language: once reassembled, in order to
utter itself, the total body must revert to the dust of words,
to the listing of details, to a monotonous inventory of parts, to
crumbling: language undoes the body, returns it to the fetish.
This return is coded under the term *blazon.* The blazon consists of predicating a single subject, beauty, upon a certain
number of anatomical attributes: *she was beautiful for her*

arms, neck, eyebrows, nose, eyelashes, etc.: the adjective becomes subject and the substantive becomes predicate. Similarly with the striptease: an action, denudation, is predicated on the succession of its attributes (legs, arms, bosom, etc.). Striptease and blazon refer to the very destiny of the sentence (both are constructed like sentences), which consists in this (doomed thereto by its structure): the sentence can never constitute a *total*; meanings can be listed, not admixed: the total, the sum are for language the promised lands, glimpsed *at the end* of enumeration, but once this enumeration has been completed, no feature can reassemble it—or, if this feature is produced, it too can only be *added* to the others. Thus with beauty: it can only be tautological (affirmed under the very name of beauty) or analytic (if we run through its predicates), never synthetic. As a genre, the blazon expresses the belief that a *complete* inventory can reproduce a *total* body, as if the extremity of enumeration could devise a new category, that of totality: description is then subject to a kind of enumerative erethism: it accumulates in order to totalize, multiplies fetishes in order to obtain a total, defetishised body; thereby, description *represents* no beauty at all: no one can *see* La Zambinella, infinitely projected as a totality impossible because linguistic, *written*.

(227) *This was more than a woman, this was a masterpiece!* ★ SYM. Replication of bodies.

LII. THE MASTERPIECE

The Zambinellan body is a real body; but this real body is total (glorious, miraculous) only insofar as it descends from a body already written by statuary (Ancient Greece, Pygma-

114

lion); it too (like the other bodies in *Sarrasine*) is a replica, issuing from a code. This code is infinite since it is written. Yet the duplicative chain may assert its origin and the Code declare itself grounded, stopped, jammed. This grounding, this stoppage, this jamming of the Code, is the *masterpiece*. Presented at first as an unprecedented collection of separate parts, as a concept induced from a vast number of experiences, the masterpiece is actually, according to Sarrasinean aesthetics, what the living statue is descended from; by the masterpiece, the writing of bodies is finally endowed with a term which is at the same time its origin. To discover La Zambinella's body is therefore to put an end to the infinity of the codes, to find at last the origin (the original) of the copies, to ascertain the cultural starting point, to assign performances their supplement (*"more than a woman"*); in the Zambinellan body as masterpiece, the referent (this actual body to be copied, expressed, signified) and the Reference (the beginning which puts an end to the infinity of writing and consequently establishes it) theologically coincide.

(228) *In this unhoped-for creation could be found a love to enrapture any man and beauties worthy of satisfying a critic.* ★ REF. Psychology of the artist.

(229) *With his eyes, Sarrasine devoured Pygmalion's statue, come down from its pedestal.* ★ SYM. Pygmalion, replication of bodies.

(230) *When La Zambinella sang,* ★ ACT. "Theater": 8: the star's aria.

(231) *the effect was delirium.* ★ ACT. "Seduction": 4: delirium (the *delirium* is internalized, it is a coenesthetic state—cold/hot, whereas *madness*—No. 235—entails a minor *acting out*, which will be orgasm).

(232) *The artist felt cold;* ★ ACT. "Seduction": 5: Delirium: cold.

(233) *then he felt a heat which suddenly began to prickle in the innermost depth of his being, in what we call the heart, for lack of any other word!* ★ ACT. "Seduction": 6: Delirium: heat. ★★ REF. Euphemism ("Heart" can only designate the sexual organ: *"for lack of any other word"*: this word exists, but it is indecorous, taboo).

(234) *He did not applaud, he said nothing,* ★ ACT. "Seduction": 7: Delirium: silence. The *delirium* is broken down into three stages, three terms: thus in retrospect it becomes a generic word, the rhetorical statement of a subsequence, at once temporal and analytic (definitional).

(235) *he experienced an impulse of madness,* ★ Rhetorically, madness intensifies delirium; but whereas delirium is a (classic) moment of amorous rapture, madness here denotes one of the terms (the second) in a progression which will covertly lead Sarrasine, seated in close proximity to La Zambinella, to orgasm (which occurs in No. 244). *Madness* is to be cast in various terms which will be the conditions, gradually established or clarified, of pleasure. ACT. "Pleasure": 2: madness (condition of the *acting out*).

(236) *a kind of frenzy which overcomes us only when we are at the age when desire has something frightening and infernal about it.* ★ REF. Psychology of ages.

(237) *Sarrasine wanted to leap onto the stage and take possession of this woman: his strength, increased a hundredfold by a moral depression impossible to explain, since these phenomena occur in an area hidden from human observation, seemed to manifest itself with painful violence.* ★ ACT. "Pleasure": 3: tension (to want to leap, to hold oneself back). The tension is hallucinatory, it coincides with a collapse of moral restraint. The element of violence, aggressiveness, anger, present in this first desire, must be eradicated when subsequent desires are to be invoked voluntarily: a ritual will

satisfy these requirements (No. 270). ★★ REF. Passion and its depths.

(238) *Looking at him, one would have thought him a cold and senseless man.* ★ ACT. "Pleasure": 4: apparent immobility (the imminent *acting out* is secret).

(239) *Fame, knowledge, future, existence, laurels, everything collapsed.* ★ The act of choosing (love or death) is here preceded by a formal phase of mental purification; the "excessive" (radical, life-risking) decision presupposes putting other commitments, other connections in parenthesis (ACT. "To decide": 1: mental condition of the choice).

(240) *"To be loved by her, or to die!" Such was the decree Sarrasine passed upon himself.* ★ ACT. "To decide": 2: to propose an alternative. The "decision" stops at the alternative, whose two terms are diachronic (to be loved and *then*, if unsuccessful, to die); but the alternative itself, based on these two terms, opens a double sequence of features: the *will-to-love* and the *will-to-die*. ★★ The will-to-love (or *to be loved*) constitutes an enterprise whose principle is given here, but whose development is brought up short: to rent a box and gratify oneself by repeating the "first pleasure": what follows will no longer be based on the sequence (*"events took him by surprise . . ."* No. 263) (ACT. "Will-to-love": 1: proposal of the enterprise). ★★★ Undoubtedly, once La Zambinella is lost, Sarrasine will not choose to die; yet his death, prepared for by a series of hints, premonitions, and challenges, hailed by the victim himself (No. 540), is suicide, already implicit in the proposed alternative (ACT. "Will-to-die": 1: proposal of the project).

(241) *He was so utterly intoxicated that he no longer saw the theater, the spectators, the actors, or heard the music.* ★ ACT. "Pleasure": 5: isolation.

(242) *Moreover, the distance between himself and La Zambinella had ceased to exist, he possessed her, his eyes were riveted upon her, he took her for his own. An almost diabolical power enabled him to feel the breath of this voice, to smell the scented powder*

*covering her hair, to see the planes of her face, to count the blue
veins shadowing her satin skin.* ★ The proximity of La Zambinella
(prepared for by seating the subject close to the stage, No. 209) is
of an hallucinatory order: it is an abolition of the Wall, identification with the object; what is involved is an hallucinatory embrace:
thus, La Zambinella's features are no longer described according to
the aesthetic, rhetorical code, but according to the anatomical code
(veins, planes, hair) (ACT. "Pleasure": 6: embrace). ★★ SEM.
Diabolic (this seme has already been attached to Sarrasine, a transgressor; the "devil" is the name for the minor psychotic impulse
which overcomes the subject).

(243) *Last, this agile voice, fresh and silvery in timbre, supple as a
thread shaped by the slightest breath of air, rolling and unrolling,
cascading and scattering, this voice attacked his soul so vividly* ★
The voice is described by its power of penetration, insinuation,
flow; but here it is the man who is penetrated; like Endymion "re-
ceiving" the light of his beloved, he is visited by an active emanation of femininity, by a subtle force which "attacks" him, seizes
him, and fixes him in a situation of passivity (ACT. "Pleasure": 7:
to be penetrated).

(244) *that several times he gave vent to involuntary cries torn
from him by convulsive feelings of pleasure* ★ ACT. "Pleasure":
8: ejaculation. Ejaculation was achieved by chance, through a hallucinatory seizure; in the future, this "first" ejaculation is to be voluntarily repeated (so precious has it been for the subject, who,
sequestered from fulfilled sexuality, has never experienced it) by
(organized, albeit solitary) sessions on the sofa.

(245) *which are all too rarely vouchsafed by human passions.* ★
REF. Human passions.

(246) *He was presently obliged to leave the theater.* ★ ACT.
"Theater": 9: to leave.

(247) *His trembling legs almost refused to support him. He was
limp, weak as a sensitive man who has given way to overwhelming
anger. He had experienced such pleasure, or perhaps he had suf-*

118

fered so keenly, that his life had drained away like water from a broken vase. He felt empty inside, a prostration similar to the debilitation that overcomes those convalescing from a serious illness. ★ ACT. "Pleasure": 9: emptiness. ★★ REF. Code of illnesses.

(248) *Overcome by an inexplicable sadness,* ★ ACT. "Pleasure": 10: *"post coitum"* sadness.

(249) *he sat down on the steps of a church. There, leaning back against a pillar, he fell into a confused meditation, as in a dream. He had been smitten by passion.* ★ ACT. "Pleasure": 11: to recuperate. Recuperation can be read according to various codes: psychological (the mind regains control), Christian (sadness of the flesh, refuge near a church), psychoanalytical (return to the pillar-phallus), trivial (rest *post coitum*).

LIII. EUPHEMISM

Here is one story about Sarrasine: he goes into a theater; the beauty, voice, and art of the star enrapture him; he leaves the hall overcome, determined to recapture the enchantment of the first evening by renting a box near the stage for the entire season. Now here is another story about Sarrasine: he enters a theater by chance (206), by chance he is seated near the stage (209); the sensual music (213), the beauty of the prima donna (220) and her voice (231) fill him with desire; because of his proximity to the stage, he hallucinates, imagines he is possessing La Zambinella (242); penetrated by the artist's voice (243), he achieves orgasm (244); after which, drained (247), sad (248), he leaves, sits down and muses (249): this was in fact his first ejaculation; he decides to reexperience this solitary pleasure every evening, domesticating it to a point where he can experience it whenever he wishes. —A diagrammatic relationship exists between these two stories which assures their identity: it is the same story, because it is the same design, the same sequence: tension, seizure or possession, explosion, fatigue, conclusion. To read into this scene at the theater a solitary orgasm, to substitute an erotic story for the euphemistic version, this operation of reading is based not on a lexicon of symbols but on a systematic cohesion, a congruence of relationships. It follows that the meaning of a text lies not in this or that interpretation but in the diagrammatic totality of its readings, in their plural system. Some will say that the scene in the theater *"as told by the author"* has the privilege of literality and thus constitutes the "truth," the reality of the text; the reading of the orgasm would therefore be a symbolic reading in their eyes, an unwarranted elucubration. *"The text and nothing but the text"*: this proposition has little meaning except intimidation: the literality of the text is a system like any other: the literal in Balzac is, after all, nothing but the "transcription" of another literality, that of the symbol: euphemism is a language. In fact, the meaning of a text can be nothing but the plurality of its systems, its infinite (circular) "transcribability": one system transcribes another, but reciprocally as well: with regard to the text, there is no "primary," "natural," "national," "mother" critical language: from the outset, as it is created, the text is multilingual; there is no entrance language or exit language for the textual dictionary, since it is not the dictionary's (closed) definitional power that the text possesses, but its infinite structure.

(250) *Upon returning to his lodgings,* ★ ACT. "Theater": 10: to return home.

(251) *he fell into one of those frenzies of activity which disclose to us the presence of new elements in our lives. A prey to this first fever of love derived equally from both pleasure and pain, he tried to appease his impatience and his delirium by drawing La Zambi-*

nella from memory. It was a kind of embodied meditation. ★
REF. Love sickness. ★★ ACT. "Will-to-love": 2: to draw. Here,
the enterprise of love involves an erratic temporizing activity. ★★★
SYM. Replication of bodies: drawing. Drawing, an act which consists in recoding the human body by reintegrating it into a classification of styles, poses, stereotypes, is presented by the discourse
according to a rhetorical schema: a generic activity (drawing) will
be transformed into three species.

(252) *On one page, La Zambinella appeared in that apparently
calm and cool pose favored by Raphael, Giorgione, and every great
painter.* ★ SYM. Replication of bodies: drawing (1): academic
(unity is supported by a cultural code, by a Reference: the Book
of Art).

(253) *On another, she was delicately turning her head after having
finished a trill, and appeared to be listening to herself.* ★ SYM.
Replication of bodies: drawing (2): romantic (the most fleeting
moment of a gesture, copied from the Book of Life).

(254) *Sarrasine sketched his mistress in every pose: he drew her
unveiled, seated, standing, lying down, chaste or amorous, embodying through the delirium of his pencils every capricious notion that
can enter our heads when we think intently about a mistress.* ★
SYM. Replication of bodies: drawing (3): hallucinated. The
model is subjected "freely" (that is, in conformity with a code:
hallucination) to the manipulations of desire ("every capricious
notion," "in every pose"). In fact, the preceding drawings are already hallucinatory: to copy a pose of Raphael's, to imagine an
unusual gesture, is to indulge in controlled doodling, to manipulate
the desired body according to "fantasy" (hallucination). Following
the realist notion of art, all painting can be defined as an enormous
gallery of hallucinatory manipulation—wherein one does with bodies *as one wants,* so that gradually they fill every compartment of
desire (which is what happens bluntly, that is, exemplarily, in
Sade's *tableaux vivants*). ★★ REF. Code of Passion. ★★★ SYM.
Undressing (La Zambinella is imagined *unveiled*).

(255) *However, his fevered thoughts went beyond drawing.* ★
REF. Excess (aggressiveness). ★★ SYM. Undressing.

Continually undressing his model, the sculptor Sarrasine anticipates Freud, who (apropos of Leonardo) identifies sculpture with analysis: each is a *via di levare*, or clearing away. Returning to a gesture of his childhood (he whittled the pews in order to carve clumsy figures), the sculptor tears off La Zambinella's veils to get at what he believes to be the truth about her body; for his part, the subject Sarrasine, through repeated snares, proceeds ineluctably toward the real condition of the castrato, the void which is his center. This dual movement is that of the realist ambiguity. The Sarrasinean artist tries to undress appearance, tries always to get *beyond*, *behind*, according to the idealistic principle which identifies secrecy with truth: one must thus go *into* the model, *beneath* the statue, *behind* the canvas (this is what another Balzacian artist, Frenhofer, asks of the ideal canvas he dreams of). The same rule holds for the realist writer (and his critical posterity): he must go *behind* the paper, must know, for example, the exact relationship between Vautrin and Lucien de Rubempré (though what is behind the paper is not reality, the referent, but the Reference, the "subtle immensity of writings"). This impulse, which leads Sarrasine, the realistic artist, and the critic to turn over the model, the statue, the canvas, or the text in order to examine its back, its interior, leads to a failure—to Failure—of which *Sarrasine* is in a way the emblem: *behind* the canvas Frenhofer envisions there is still nothing but its surface, scribbled lines, an abstract, undecipherable writing, the unknown (unknowable) masterpiece which the inspired painter ends up with and which is in fact the signal of his death: *beneath* La Zambinella (and therefore inside her statue) there is the *nothingness* of castration, of which Sarrasine will die after having destroyed in his illusory statue the evidence of his failure: the envelope of things cannot be authenticated, the dilatory movement of the signifier cannot be stopped.

(256) *He saw La Zambinella, spoke to her, beseeched her, he passed a thousand years of life and happiness with her by placing her in every imaginable position;* ★ A very precise definition of hallucination: the hallucination is a scenario in which the object's positions are innumerable (*"every imaginable situation"*) but always related, as in voluptuous manipulation, to the subject, who is at the center of the scene (*"he saw, he spoke, beseeched, passed"*) (SYM. Hallucinatory scenario).

(257) *in short, by sampling the future with her.* ★ There is even a scenario for the *future*, the tense proper to hallucination (SYM. The hallucinatory future).

(258) *On the following day, he sent his valet to rent a box next to the stage for the entire season.* ★ REF. Chronology ("the following day"). ★★ ACT. "Will-to-love": 3: to rent a theater box. In Sarrasine's case, the amorous undertaking is based on pure impulse: what he plans is not the conquest of La Zambinella but the repetition of his first solitary pleasure; thus, once its beginning has been proclaimed (*"be loved by her or die"*), the sequence has only two dilatory terms: to draw, to contemplate; after which the progress of events is no longer in Sarrasine's hands, and it is his *will-to-die*, which is engaged. ★★★ Proximity to the stage—whose great advantages to pleasure the subject discovered by chance—is now deliberately sought, for this pleasure must now be repeated, organized every evening throughout the entire season (ACT. "Pleasure": 12: conditions for repetition).

(259) *Then, like all young people with lusty souls,* ★ REF. Psychology of ages.

(260) *he exaggerated to himself the difficulties of his undertaking and first fed his passion with the pleasure of being able to admire his mistress without obstruction.* ★ ACT. "Will-to-love": 4: to

pause. The pleasure the subject plans to take in his object is more hallucinatory than real; he therefore postpones the actual undertaking and first establishes conditions propitious to an hallucinatory manipulation, and as an excuse for this very purposeful impulsiveness he creates the obstacle of difficulties, which he exaggerates because they are useful to his "dream," which alone interests him and which the difficulties excuse.

(261) *This golden age of love, during which we take pleasure in our own feeling and in which we are happy almost by ourselves,* ★ REF. Code of the ages of love.

(262) *was not destined to last long in Sarrasine's case.* ★ REF. Chronology.

(263) *Nevertheless, events took him by surprise* ★ Sarrasine actively directs only his hallucination; anything from outside (from "reality") is therefore a surprise to him. The notation thus establishes the end of the "will-to-love"; however, since this notation is prospective (we must wait for some twenty more lexias before these "events" occur, namely the rendezvous with the duenna), the pause begun in No. 240 can still be turned into a series of hallucinatory terms (ACT. "Will-to-love": 5: interruption of the undertaking).

(264) *while he was still under the spell of this vernal hallucination, as naïve as it was voluptuous.* ★ The pause introduced into the amorous undertaking, although we have just been told it is over, will be filled with a number of occupations, actions, or impressions; these subsequent terms are here given their generic name: voluptuous hallucination (ACT. "Will-to-love": 6: indication of terms composing the interlude).

(265) *In a week he lived a lifetime, spending the mornings kneading the clay by which he would copy La Zambinella,* ★ REF. Chronology (eight days in the box, on the sofa: this places the meeting with the duenna, the event which "surprises" Sarrasine, on the twenty-fourth day of his stay in Rome—information congruent with his ignorance of Roman customs). ★★ ACT. "Will-to-love": 7: morning: to sculpt (the first item in voluptuous hallucination).

Kneading, mentioned in No. 163 as one of Sarrasine's adolescent activities, symbolically implies the same act as whittling; the hand must be thrust in, the envelope penetrated, to apprehend the interior of a volume, to seize the *underneath*, the *true*.

(266) *despite the veils, skirts, corsets, and ribbons which concealed her from him.* ★ SYM. Undressing.

(267) *In the evenings, installed in his box early, alone, lying on a sofa like a Turk under the influence of opium, he created for himself a pleasure as rich and varied as he wished it to be.* ★ ACT. "Will-to-love": 8: evening, the sofa (the second item in the hallucinatory pause). The connotations indicate the nature of this pleasure, ritually arranged and repeated by Sarrasine on the basis of the "first pleasure" he discovered one evening by chance: solitary, hallucinatory (no distance between subject and object), at will. As the deliberate, ritual production of a pleasure, it involves a kind of ascesis, of labor: it requires purifying pleasure of every element of roughness, suffering, violence, excess: whence a technique of gradual tempering, intended not to forgo but to control pleasure, freeing it from all disparate sensations. This pleasure on the sofa will in its turn be transformed into action.

(268) *First, he gradually familiarized himself with the overly vivid emotions his mistress's singing afforded him;* ★ ACT. "Will-to-love": 9: to accustom the ear.

(269) *he then trained his eyes to see her, and finally he could contemplate her* ★ ACT. "Will-to-love": 10: to train the eye.

(270) *without fearing an outburst of the wild frenzy which had seized him on the first day. As his passion became calmer, it grew deeper.* ★ The dual ascesis, of hearing and sight, produces a more profitable hallucination, freed of its first violence (No. 237: "*his strength . . . seemed to manifest itself with painful violence*") (ACT. "Will-to-love": 11: result of the two preceding operations).

(271) *For the rest, the unsociable sculptor did not allow his friends to intrude upon his solitude, which was peopled with images, adorned with fantasies of hope, and filled with happiness.* ★ ACT. "Will-to-love": 12: protection of the induced hallucination. —Sar-

rasine's deliberate solitude has a diegetic function: it "explains" how Sarrasine, isolated from any society, has managed to remain ignorant of the fact that in the Papal states, female singers are castrati; it performs the same function as the brevity of Sarrasine's residence in Rome, which the chronological code stresses on several occasions; all of which is congruent with the elderly Prince Chigi's exclamation: *"Where are you from?"* (No. 468).

(272) *His love was so strong, so naïve, that he experienced all the innocent scruples that assail us when we love for the first time.* ★ REF. Code of Passion.

(273) *As he began to realize that he would soon have to act, to plot, to inquire where La Zambinella lived, whether she had a mother, uncle, teacher, family, to ponder, in short, on ways to see her, speak to her, these great, ambitious thoughts made his heart swell so painfully that he put them off until later,* ★ ACT. "Will-to-love": 13: alibi for the pause and prorogation of the respite.

(274) *deriving as much satisfaction from his physical suffering as he did from his intellectual pleasures.* ★ SEM. Composite (we know Sarrasine's paradoxical nature, in which opposites unite).

(275) *"But," Mme de Rochefide interrupted me, "I still don't see anything about either Marianina or her little old man."*
"You are seeing nothing but him!" I cried impatiently, like an author who is being forced to spoil a theatrical effect. ★ Code of Authors (through a metalinguistic act, the narrator indicates the code of narrators). ★★ HER. Enigma 4 (who is the old man?): request for an answer. ★★★ The narrator's answer leads both to truth (Zambinella is the old man) and error (we might think that Sarrasine was the old man): it is an equivocation (HER. Enigma 4: equivocation).

LV. LANGUAGE AS NATURE

In practical terms, Sarrasine's adventure concerns only two characters: Sarrasine himself and La Zambinella. Thus, the old man is one of the two (*"You are seeing nothing but him"*). Truth and error are reduced to a simple alternative: the reader is getting "warm," since he need only consider—for a split second—each term of the alternative, and thus La Zambinella, for the soprano's identity to be revealed: to suspect a sex is to assign it a definitional class, that of anomaly: where sexual classification is concerned, doubt instantly turns into "doubtful." However, this is not what is read; the ambiguity, one might say, is certain only on the analytical level; at ordinary reading speed, the alternative's two elements (error/truth) are attached to a kind of swivel which neutralizes its revelatory power. This swivel is the sentence. Everything about it, the simplicity of its structure, its brevity, its speed (which seems borrowed, by metonymy, from the narrator's impatience) keeps the truth (dangerous to the story's interest) away from the reader. Elsewhere (a further example), it will be no more than a syntactical inflexion, both expeditious and elegant, a resource present in the language itself—the reduction of a structural contradiction to a simple concessional morpheme: *"despite the eloquence of a few mutual glances, he was astonished at the reserve La Zambinella maintained toward him"* (No. 351)—which softens, lightens, dissipates the articulations of the narrative structure. To put it another way, there is a force in the sentence (linguistic entity) that domesticates the artifice of the narrative, a meaning that denies the meaning. We might call this diacritical element (since it overhangs the articulation of the narrative units): *sentencing.* To put it still another way: the sentence is a *nature* whose function—or scope —is to justify the culture of the narrative. Superimposed on the narrative structure, forming it, guiding it, regulating its rhythm, imposing on it morphemes of a purely grammatical logic, the sentence serves as *evidence* for the narrative. For language (in this case, French), by the way it is learned (by children), by its historical weight, by the apparent universality of its conventions, in short, by its *anteriority*, seems to have every right over a contingent anecdote, one which has begun only some twenty pages back—whereas language has lasted forever. Whereby we see that denotation is not the truth of discourse: denotation is not outside structures, it has a structural function on a par with the others: that of *justifying* structure; it furnishes the codes with a kind of precious excipient, but, in a circular fashion, it is also a particular, specialized substance used by the other codes to smooth their articulation.

(276) *For several days, I resumed after a pause, Sarrasine had reappeared so faithfully in his box and his eyes had expressed such love* ★ REF. Chronology (from lexia 265 we know that these several days have been a week). ★★ ACT. "Will-to-love": 14: résumé of the pause.

LVI. THE TREE

Sometimes, as the utterance proceeds, the rhetorical code is superimposed on the proairetic code: the sequence lists its actions (*to choose/to draw/to rent a box/to pause/to break off the undertaking*), but the discourse expands by branching out logically: a nominal genus (*amorous hallucination*) is transformed into particular behavior (*evening/morning*), which together turn into result, alibi or résumé. Starting from the implicit nomination of the sequence ("will-to-love"), we thus arrive at a proairetic (often trellised) tree whose forks and new joints represent the incessant transformation of the sentence line into textual volume:

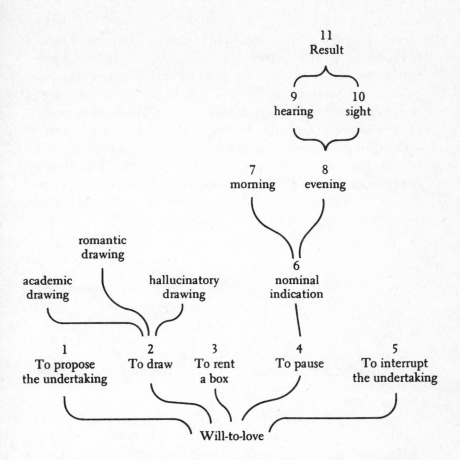

The rhetorical code, so powerful in the readerly text, produces offshoots at certain places in the sequence: the term becomes a knot; a noun caps off, to indicate or summarize, an enumeration which will be or which has been detailed: the pause by moments, the drawing by types, the hallucination by the organs affected. Through a structure which is strictly Aristotelian, discourse continually oscillates between the (nominal) genus and its (proairetic) species: as a system of generic and special names, the lexicon makes a basic contribution to structuring, indeed appropriates it, for meaning is a force: to name

is to subject, and the more generic the nomination, the stronger
the subjection. When discourse itself speaks of *hallucination*
(not to mention subsequently *producing* it), it commits the
same act of violence as the mathematician or logician who
says: *let us call P the object which . . . ; let us call P¹ the
image which . . .* etc. Readerly discourse is thus shot through
with pre-demonstrative nominations which ensure the text's
subjection—but which also, perhaps, provoke the nausea
brought on by any appropriative violence. We ourselves, by
naming the sequence ("will-to-love"), are only prolonging the
war of meaning, reversing the appropriation effected by the
text itself.

(277) *that his passion for La Zambinella's voice would have been
common knowledge throughout Paris, had this adventure happened there;* ★ SYM. The castrato's voice (what might pass for a
common synecdoche—Zambinella being designated by her voice—
should here be taken literally: it is with the castrato's voice, with
castration itself, that Sarrasine is in love). ★★ REF. Ethnic psychology: Paris.

(278) *however, in Italy, madame, everyone goes to the theater for
himself, with his own passions, and with a heartfelt interest which
precludes spying through opera glasses.* ★ REF. Ethnic psychology: Italy.

(279) *Nevertheless, the sculptor's enthusiasm did not escape the
attention of the singers for long.* ★ Enigma 6 (Who is La Zambinella?) is a loaded enigma, it is based on a stratagem. Thus each
time in Enigma 6 that the trick can be traced back to a machinating agent, we have a byte, a coherent sequence: Machination. However, La Zambinella's ruses will still be considered *snares*, relating
to Enigma 6 in general, and not to machination, in order to respect
the (possible) ambiguity of La Zambinella's own feelings (HER.
"Machination": 1: the machinating group).

(280) *One evening, the Frenchman saw that they were laughing at him in the wings.* ★ REF. Chronology ("One evening" continues "events took him by surprise," No. 263). ★★ HER. "Machination": 2: to laugh (motive of the stratagem). Laughter, the basis for the machination, will in No. 513 be exposed as castrating (*"Laugh! Laugh! You dared play with a man's feeling?"*).

(281) *It is hard to know what extreme actions he might not have taken* ★ SEM. Violence, excess.

(282) *had La Zambinella not come onto the stage. She gave Sarrasine one of those eloquent glances* ★ The "eloquent" glance of La Zambinella is a snare set by the agency of the machinating group and intended for its victim (HER. Enigma 6: snare, by La Zambinella, for Sarrasine).

LVII. THE LINES OF DESTINATION

One might call *idyllic* the communication which unites two partners sheltered from any "noise" (in the cybernetic sense of the word), linked by a simple destination, a single thread. Narrative communication is not idyllic; its lines of destination are multiple, so that any message in it can be properly defined only if it is specified whence it comes and where it is going. As regards Enigma 6 (Who is La Zambinella?), *Sarrasine* starts five lines of destination. The first goes from the machinating group (the singers, Vitagliani) to its victim (Sarrasine); the message is then traditionally constituted of lies, snares, stratagems, and, if it is equivocal, of jokes and hoaxes designed to amuse the gallery of accomplices. The second line of destination goes from La Zambinella to Sarrasine; here the message is a pretense, an imposture, or, if there is some equivocation, a stifled remorse, a pang of authenticity. The third line goes from Sarrasine to himself: it transmits alibis, prejudices, and fallacious evidence by which the sculptor misleads himself, because of his vital interest. The fourth line goes from the external world (Prince Chigi, the sculptor's friends) to Sarrasine; here what is transmitted is public knowledge, evidence, "reality" ("La Zambinella is a castrato disguised as a woman"). The fifth line of destination goes from the discourse to the reader; sometimes it transmits snares (in order not to reveal the secret of the enigma too soon), sometimes ambiguities (to arouse the reader's curiosity). What this multiplication has at stake is obviously *spectacle*, the text as spectacle. Idyllic communication denies all theater, it refuses any presence *in front of which* the destination can be achieved, it suppresses everything *other*, every subject. Narrative communication is the opposite: each destination is at one moment or another a spectacle for the other participants in the game: the messages that La Zambinella sends to Sarrasine or that Sarrasine sends to himself are heard by the machinating group; the snare, in which Sarrasine persists after the truth has been revealed to him, is divined by the reader, with the complicity of the discourse. Thus, like a telephone network gone haywire, the lines are simultaneously twisted and routed according to a whole new system of splicings, of which the reader is the ultimate beneficiary: over-all reception is never jammed, yet it is broken, refracted, caught up in a system of interferences; the various listeners (here we ought to be able to say *écouteur* as we say *voyeur*) seem to be located at every corner of the utterance, each waiting for an origin he reverses with a second gesture into the flux of the reading. Thus, in contrast to idyllic communication, to pure communication (which would be, for example, that of the formalized sciences), readerly writing stages a certain "noise," it is the writing of noise, of impure communication; but this noise is not confused, massive, unnameable; it is a clear noise made up of connections, not superpositions: it is of a distinct "cacography."

(283) *which often reveal much more than women intend them to.*
★ REF. Psychology of Women.

(284) *This glance was a total revelation. Sarrasine was loved!*
"*If it's only a caprice,*" *he thought, already accusing his mistress of excessive ardor,* "*she doesn't know what she is subjecting herself to. I am hoping her caprice will last my whole life.*" ★ SEM. Excess, violence, etc. ★★ HER. Enigma 6: snare (by Sarrasine, for himself). The snare involves not La Zambinella's feeling but her sex, since common opinion (*endoxa*) holds that only a woman can look at a man "eloquently."

(285) *At that moment, the artist's attention was distracted by three soft knocks on the door of his box.* ★ ACT. "Door II": 1: to knock (the three soft knocks connote a mystery without danger: complicity).

(286) *He opened it.* ★ ACT. "Door II": 2: to open.

(287) *An old woman entered with an air of mystery.* ★ ACT. "Door II": 3: to enter. If we want to make banality speak, we must compare this "Door" to the one we have already encountered (No. 125–27), when Marianina entrusted the old man to a servant. There we had: *to arrive/to knock/to appear/(to open).* Here we have: *to knock/to open/to enter.* Now, it is precisely the omission of the first term (*to arrive*) that defines the mystery: a door which is "knocked on" without anyone's having arrived at it.

(288) "*Young man,*" *she said,* "*if you want to be happy, be prudent. Put on a cape, wear a hat drawn down over your eyes; then, around ten in the evening, be in the Via del Corso in front of the Hotel di Spagna.*" ★ ACT. "Rendezvous": I: to arrange a rendezvous. ★★ REF. Mysterious and romantic Italy.

(289) "*I'll be there,*" *he replied,* ★ ACT. "Rendezvous": 2: to give assent to the messenger.

(290) *placing two louis in the duenna's wrinkled hand.* ★ ACT. "Rendezvous": 3: to thank, to tip.

(291) *He left his box* ★ ACT. "To leave": 1: a first locality.

(292) *after having given a signal to La Zambinella, who timidly lowered her heavy eyelids, like a woman pleased to be understood at last.* ★ ACT. "Rendezvous": 4: to give assent to the person offering the rendezvous. ★★ SEM. Femininity (heavy eyelids). ★★★ *Like a woman . . .*; here is a snare, since La Zambinella is not a woman; but by whom is the snare set, for whom is it intended? by Sarrasine for himself (if the utterance is indirect in style, reproducing Sarrasine's thought)? by the discourse for the reader (plausible, since the *like* gives a modality to La Zambinella's putative membership in the female species)? In other words, who is responsible for La Zambinella's gesture? The origin of the statement is indiscernable or, more precisely, indeterminable (HER. Enigma 6: snare).

(293) *Then he ran home to dress himself as seductively as he could.* ★ ACT. "Dress": 1: to want to dress.

(294) *As he was leaving the theater,* ★ ACT. "To leave": 2: a second locality. (Leaving is an action broken down into various localities: the box, the building.)

(295) *a strange man took his arm.*
"Be on your guard, Frenchman," he whispered in his ear. "This is a matter of life and death. Cardinal Cicognara is her protector and doesn't trifle." ★ ACT. "Warning": 1: to give a warning. ★★ ACT. "Murder": 1: designation of the future murderer ("this man is dangerous").

(296) *At that moment, had some demon set the pit of hell between Sarrasine and La Zambinella, he would have crossed it with one leap. Like the horses of the gods described by Homer, the sculptor's love had traversed vast distances in the twinkling of an eye.* ★ SEM. Energy, excess. ★★ REF. Literary history.

(297) *"If death itself were waiting for me outside the house, I would go even faster," he replied.* ★ ACT. "Warning": 2: to ignore it. ★★ ACT. "Will-to-die": 2: to flout a warning, to take a risk.

134

Sarrasine is free to heed or to reject the unknown man's warning. This alternative freedom is structural: it marks each term of a sequence and ensures the story's progress in "rebounds." No less structurally, however, Sarrasine is not free to reject the Italian's warning; if he were to heed it and to refrain from pursuing his adventure, there would be no story. In other words, *Sarrasine is forced by the discourse* to keep his rendezvous with La Zambinella: the character's freedom is dominated by the discourse's instinct for preservation. On one hand an alternative, on the other and simultaneously a constraint. Now, this conflict is organized as follows: the constraint of the discourse ("the story must go on") is modestly "forgotten"; the freedom of the alternative is nobly imputed to the free will of the character, who appears to have complete responsibility for choice rather than dying a *paper death* (the most terrible for a character in a novel), to which the discourse constrains him. This sleight of hand permits the novelistic high tragedy to get off the ground. For once posited *far from the paper*, in a referential utopia, the character's choice appears to be subject to internal determinations: Sarrasine chooses the rendezvous: (1) because he is naturally obstinate, (2) because his passion is the stronger element, (3) because it is his destiny to die. Overdetermination thereby serves a dual function: it appears to refer to a freedom of the character and of the story, since the action falls within a psychology of the person; and at the same time it masks by superposition the implacable constraint of the discourse. This game is an economic one: it is to the story's interest that Sarrasine ignore the stranger's dissuasion; he must *at all costs* keep the duenna's rendezvous. In other words, he keeps it to ensure the very survival of the anecdote, or, if one prefers, to protect an article of merchandise (the narrative) which has not yet been put on the reading market: the story's "interest" is the "interest" of its producer (or its consumer); as usual, however, the *price* of the narrative article is sublimated by an abundance of referential determinations (drawn from the world of the soul, *off the paper*), which form the noblest of images: the Destiny of the subject.

(298) "*Poverino!*" *the stranger cried as he disappeared.* ★ REF. Italianness (*poverino* and not *poor wretch!*).

(299) *Speaking of danger to a lover is tantamount to selling him pleasures, is it not?* ★ REF. Proverbial code.

(300) *Sarrasine's valet had never seen his master take so much care over his toilette* ★ ACT. "Dressing": 2: to dress (the sequence "Dressing" has an over-all value as a signifier of love, of hope). ★★ We recognize this theme: Sarrasine sequestered from sexuality, kept in a state of virginity by the mother's (Bouchardon's) vigilance. This state was destroyed when Sarrasine saw and heard La Zambinella. On that occasion, an expression signified the accession to sexuality, the end of virginity: *for the first time.* This *first time* is what reappears in Sarrasine's dressing: *the sculptor is dressing for the first time:* we recall that Clotilde was unable to dissuade him from his "untidy dress" (No. 194) (understood: was unable to dissuade him from his *aphanisis*), which moreover was the reason she left him (SYM. End of sexual exile).

(301) *His finest sword, a gift from Bouchardon, the sash Clotilde had given him, his embroidered coat, his silver-brocade waistcoat, his gold snuffbox, his jeweled watches, were all taken from their coffers,* ★ Bouchardon and Clotilde were linked to constraint, constriction, *aphanisis;* they therefore preside ritually, through their gifts, over Sarrasine's initiation: those who sequestered now consecrate what is released. The "deflowering" is accompanied by symbolic objects (a sash, a sword) given by the guardians of virginity (SYM. Initiation).

(302) *and he adorned himself like a girl about to appear before her first love.* ★ REF. Psychology of lovers. ★★ The hero dresses himself in the manner of a young girl: this inversion connotes Sarrasine's (already noted) Femininity (SEM. Femininity).

(303) *At the appointed hour, drunk with love and seething with hope,* ★ Here begins a long sequence articulated in three principal terms: *to hope/to be deceived/to compensate* (ACT. "Hope": 1: to hope).

(304) *Sarrasine, concealed in his cape, sped to the rendezvous the old woman had given him. The duenna was waiting for him.*
"You took a long time," she said. ★ ACT. "Rendezvous": 5: rendezvous kept (*You took a long time* is redundant in the light of Sarrasine's very careful dressing, No. 300).

(305) *"Come."*
She led the Frenchman along several back streets ★ ACT. "Route": 1: to set out ★★ ACT. "Route": 2: to walk along. ★★★ REF. Mysterious and romantic Italy (back streets).

(306) *and stopped before a rather handsome mansion.* ★ ACT. "Door III": 1: to stop at.

(307) *She knocked.* ★ ACT. "Door III": 2: to knock.

(308) *The door opened.* ★ ACT. "Door III": 3: to open. No more banal (expected) or seemingly more useless proairetism can be imagined; from the anecdotal viewpoint, the story would have been equally readerly had the discourse stated: *She led the Frenchman to a mansion and, having entered it, led him to a room . . .* The operative structure of the story would have remained intact. So what does the Door add? semantics itself: first, because every door is an object of some vague symbolism (a whole complex of death, pleasure, limit, secret, is bound up in it); and next, because this door which opens (without a subject) connotes an atmosphere of mystery; last, because the open door and the end of the route still remain uncertain, the suspense is prolonged, in other words heightened.

(309) *She led Sarrasine along a labyrinth of stairways, galleries, and rooms which were lit only by the feeble light of the moon, and soon came to a door* ★ ACT. "Route": 3: to penetrate. ★★ REF. Adventure, the Novelistic (labyrinth, stairways, darkness, the moon).

(310) *through whose cracks gleamed bright lights and from behind which came the joyful sounds of several voices.* ★ ACT. "Orgy": 1: precursory signs. The diegetic statement (interior to the story) must not be confused with the rhetorical statement, whereby the discourse merely names in advance what it will later on detail (here: diegetic statement).

(311) *When at a word from the old woman he was admitted to this mysterious room, Sarrasine was suddenly dazzled at finding himself in a salon as brilliantly lighted as it was sumptuously furnished, in the center of which stood a table laden with venerable bottles and flashing flagons sparkling with ruby facets.* ★ ACT. "Route": 4: to arrive. ★★ REF. Wine (sad/joyous/murderer/bad/loyal/tender/etc.). This code is accompanied by an implicitly literary code (Rabelais, etc.).

(312) *He recognized the singers from the theater,* ★ HER. "Machination": 3: the machinating group.

(313) *along with some charming women, all ready to begin an artists' orgy as soon as he was among them.* ★ ACT. "Orgy": 2: statement (Here the statement is more rhetorical than diegetic).

(314) *Sarrasine suppressed a feeling of disappointment* ★ ACT. "Hope": 2: to be disappointed.

(315) *and put on a good face.* ★ ACT. "Hope": 3: to compensate (This term is close to the proverbial code: to face misfortune bravely).

(316) *He had expected a dim room, his mistress seated by the fire, some jealous person nearby, death and love, an exchange of confidences in low voices, heart to heart, dangerous kisses and faces so close that La Zambinella's hair would have caressed his forehead*

throbbing with desire, feverish with happiness. ★ ACT. "Hope":
4: to hope (retrospective reprise). ★★ REF. Codes of Passion,
Fiction, Irony.

LIX. THREE CODES TOGETHER

The referential codes have a kind of emetic virtue, they bring
on nausea by the boredom, conformism, and disgust with repetition that establishes them. The classic remedy, more or less
employed according to the author, is to make them ironical,
i.e., to superimpose on the vomited code a second code which
expresses it at a distance (the limit of this procedure has been
stated, XXI); in other words, to engage a metalinguistic process (the *modern* problem is not to halt this process, not to span
the distance taken with respect to a language). In saying that
Sarrasine *"had expected a dim room, some jealous person,
death and love,"* etc., the discourse mingles three disconnected
codes (each absorbing the others) from three different sources.
The Code of Passion establishes what Sarrasine is supposed to
be feeling. The Novelistic Code transforms this "feeling" into
literature: it is the code of an author in good faith, an author
who has no doubt that the novelistic is a *just* (natural) expression of passion (who, contrary to Dante, does not know that
passion comes from books). The Ironic Code absorbs the "na-
ïveté" of the first two codes: as the novelist undertakes to speak
of the character (code 2), the ironist undertakes to speak of
the novelist (code 3): Sarrasine's "natural" (interior) language is spoken twice; it would suffice to produce, on the
model of this sentence 316, a pastiche of Balzac to back up
still further this terracing of the codes. What is the bearing of
this disconnection? Constantly exceeding the last span and
aspiring to infinity, it constitutes writing in all its power as a

game. Classic writing does not go so far: it is quickly winded, closes down, and signs its final code quite soon (for example, by displaying, as here, its irony). Flaubert, however (as has already been suggested), working with an irony impregnated with uncertainty, achieves a salutary discomfort of writing: he does not stop the play of codes (or stops it only partially), so that (and this is indubitably the *proof* of writing) *one never knows if he is responsible for what he writes* (if there is a subject *behind* his language); for the very being of writing (the meaning of the labor that constitutes it) is to keep the question *Who is speaking?* from ever being answered.

(317) "Vive la folie" *he cried.* "Signori e belle donne, *you will allow me to take my revenge later and to show you my gratitude for the way you have welcomed a poor sculptor.*" ★ ACT. "Hope": 5: to compensate (reprise). ★★ REF. Italianness.

(318) *Having been greeted warmly enough by most of those present, whom he knew by sight,* ★ HER. "Machination": 4: pretense ("Those present" are the agents of the machination against Sarrasine; their greeting is a part of this plot).

LX. THE CASUISTRY OF DISCOURSE

Sarrasine is greeted warmly *enough*—a curious qualifier: by reducing a possible *extremely* or *very*, it reduces the positive itself: these warm *enough* greetings are actually something less than warm, or, at least, warm with embarrassment and reticence. This reticence of the discourse is the result of a compromise: on the one hand, the singers must give Sarrasine a warm welcome in order to mislead him and to further the machination they have undertaken (whence warm greetings); on the other hand, this welcome is a pretense for which the discourse would prefer not to take responsibility—without, however, being able to assume its own detachment, which would be tantamount to a premature exposure of the lies of the machinators, and the story would lose its suspense (hence, the warmly *enough*). This shows us that the discourse is trying to lie *as little as possible:* just what is required to ensure the interests of reading, that is, its own survival. Caught up in a civilization of enigma, truth, and decipherment, the discourse reinvents on its own level the moral terms elaborated by that civilization: there is a casuistry of discourse.

(319) *he sought to approach the armchair on which La Zambinella* ★ ACT. "Conversation": 1: to approach.

(320) *was casually reclining.* ★ SEM. Femininity.

(321) *Ah! how his heart beat when he spied a delicate foot shod in one of those slippers which in those days, may I say, madame, gave women's feet such a coquettish and voluptuous look that I don't know how men were able to resist them. The well-fitting white stockings with green clocks, the short skirts, the slippers with pointed toes, and the high heels of Louis XV's reign may have contributed something to the demoralization of Europe and the clergy.*
"*Something?*" *the Marquise replied.* "*Have you read nothing?*" ★ SEM. Femininity. ★★ La Zambinella's entire costume is a trick played on Sarrasine; this trick succeeds because Sarrasine inevitably turns the imposture into proof (coquetry proves the Woman): here one might call it the proof by foot (HER. Enigma 6: snare, by Zambinella, for Sarrasine). ★★★ REF. The century of Louis XV. Furthermore, it cannot be a matter of indifference that the moment when the young woman resumes contact with the narrative (by interrupting it) is that of an erotic allusion; a brief mari-

vaudage (in which the Marquise suddenly shows herself to be emancipated, "knowing," almost vulgar) reactivates the contract which is in the process of being honored and which is of an amorous nature (the narrator is not deceived and answers the Marquise with a smile).

(322) *"La Zambinella,"* I continued, smiling, *"had impudently crossed her legs and was gently swinging the upper one with a certain attractive indolence which suited her capricious sort of beauty.* ★ La Zambinella's coquetry, signified very precisely by "crossed legs," a conspicuous gesture condemned by the code of Good Manners, is understood as a provocation: here, therefore, it has the value of a pretense (HER. Enigma 6: snare, by La Zambinella, for Sarrasine).

(323) *She had removed her costume and was wearing a bodice that accentuated her narrow waist and set off the satin panniers of her dress, which was embroidered with blue flowers.* ★ As long as La Zambinella was on stage, her woman's costume was somehow institutional; but in private life, the musician is deceptive in retaining the appearance of a woman: there is a deliberate pretense. Moreover, it is from clothing that Sarrasine will learn the truth (No. 466); for only the institution (clothing) teaches Sarrasine his reading of the sexes: if he did not believe clothing, Sarrasine would still be alive (HER. Enigma 6: snare, by La Zambinella, for Sarrasine).

(324) *Her bosom, the treasures of which were concealed, in an excess of coquetry, by a covering of lace, was dazzlingly white.* In order to analyze—and perhaps even to enjoy—the rather intricate ambiguity of this sentence, we must break it down into two parallel snares, of which only the lines of destination are slightly divergent. ★ La Zambinella conceals her bosom (the text's only allusion to an anatomical, and no longer cultural, femininity); along with her bosom, La Zambinella also conceals from Sarrasine the very reason for the concealment: what must be concealed is the fact that there is *nothing*: the perversity of the deficiency lies in the fact that it is concealed not by padding out (the vulgar falsehood of the artificial), but by the very thing which is usually used

142

to conceal the full bosom (lace): deficiency borrows from fullness not its appearance but its deception (HER. Enigma 6: snare, by La Zambinella, for Sarrasine). ★★ The discourse itself lies more crudely: it alleges fullness (*treasures*) as the only possible purpose for concealment, and because it provides a motive (coquetry) for this concealment, it makes its existence undeniable (by drawing attention to the cause, it avoids having to ascertain the fact) (HER. Enigma 6: snare, by the discourse, for the reader). ★★★ The deficiency is *dazzlingly white*, it is designated on the castrato's body as a source of light, an area of purity (SYM. Whiteness of deficiency).

(325) *Her hair arranged something like that of Mme du Barry, her face, though it was partially hidden under a full bonnet, appeared only the more delicate, and powder suited her.* ★ SEM. Femininity. ★★ REF. Historical code.

(326) *To see her thus was to adore her.* ★ REF. Code of Love.

LXI. NARCISSISTIC PROOF

A commonplace truism (a completely literary *endoxa* which "life" constantly disproves) maintains that there is an obligatory link between beauty and love (*to see her so lovely is to love her*). This link derives its power from the fact that (novelistic) love, which is itself a code, must be supported by a *secure* code: beauty provides this; not, as we have seen, because such a code can be based on any referential traits: beauty cannot be described (other than by lists and tautologies); it has no referent; yet it does not lack references (Venus, the Sultan's daughter, Raphael's Madonnas, etc.), and it is this abundance of authorities, this heritage of writings, this anteriority of models, which make beauty a secure code; consequently, the love established by this beauty is brought under the *natural* rules of culture: the codes meet, one rests on the other, there is a circularity: beauty obliges me to love, but also what I love is inevitably beautiful. By declaring La Zambinella adorable, Sarrasine establishes one of the three proofs (narcissistic, psychological, aesthetic) he will continually use in order to deceive himself about the castrato's sex: I am justified in loving her because she is beautiful, and if I love her (I who cannot be mistaken), it is because she is a woman.

(327) *She gave the sculptor a graceful smile.* ★ HER. Enigma 6: snare, by La Zambinella, for Sarrasine.

(328) *Unhappy at not being able to speak to her without witnesses present, Sarrasine* ★ ACT. "Hope": 6: to be disappointed (reprise).

(329) *politely sat down next to her and talked about music, praising her extraordinary talent;* ★ ACT. "Hope": 7: to compensate (reprise). ★★ ACT. "Conversation I": 2 and 3: to sit down and talk.

(330) *but his voice trembled with love, with fear and hope.* ★ ACT. "Hope": 8: to hope (reprise).

(331) *"What are you afraid of?" asked Vitagliani, the company's most famous singer. "Go ahead; you need fear no rivals here." Having said this, the tenor smiled without another word. This smile was repeated on the lips of all the guests,* ★ HER. "Machination": 5: index of machination (complicity of the machinating group). ★★ HER. Enigma 6: equivocation.

LXII. EQUIVOCATION I: DOUBLE UNDERSTANDING

The tenor says "*You have no rival,*" because: (1) you are loved (Sarrasine's understanding); (2) you are wooing a castrato (understanding of the accomplices and perhaps, already, of the reader). According to the first understanding, there is a snare; according to the second, a revelation. The braid of the two understandings creates an equivocation. And in fact the equivocation results from two voices, received on an equal basis: there is an interference of two lines of destination. Put another way, the *double understanding*, the basis for a play on words, cannot be analyzed in simple terms of signification (two signifieds for one signifier); for that there must be the distinction of two recipients; and if, contrary to what occurs here, both recipients are not given in the story, if the play on words seems to be addressed to one person only (for example, the reader), this person must be imagined as being divided into two subjects, two cultures, two languages, two zones of listening (whence the traditional affinity between puns and "folly" or madness: the Fool, dressed in motley, a divided costume, was once the purveyor of the *double understanding*). In relation to an ideally pure message (as in mathematics), the division of reception constitutes a "noise," it makes communication obscure, fallacious, hazardous: uncertain. Yet this noise, this uncertainty are emitted by the discourse with a view toward a communication: they are given to the reader so that he may feed on them: what the reader reads is a countercommunication; and if we grant that the *double understanding* far exceeds the limited case of the play on words or the equivocation and permeates, in various forms and densities, all classic writing (by very reason of its polysemic vocation), we see that literatures are in fact arts of "noise"; what the reader consumes is this defect in communication, this deficient message; what the whole structuration erects for him and offers him as the most precious nourishment is a *countercommunication*; the reader is an accomplice, not of this or that character, but of the discourse itself insofar as it plays on the division of reception, the impurity of communication: the discourse, and not one or another of its characters, is the only *positive* hero of the story.

145

(332) *whose attention contained a hidden malice a lover would not have noticed.* ★ On the one hand, Sarrasine is powerless to understand the stratagem because he is blinded by love: structurally, this is tantamount to his setting a snare for himself; on the other hand, in noting his blindness, the discourse presents the reader with the beginning of a solution, it proposes the stratagem openly (HER. Enigma 6: equivocation). ★★ REF. the lover (blindfolded).

(333) *Such openness was like a dagger thrust in Sarrasine's heart. Although endowed with a certain strength of character, and although nothing could change his love,* ★ Sarrasine takes the tenor's smile as an index not of malignity but of indiscretion; he deceives himself (HER. Enigma 6: snare, by Sarrasine, for himself). ★★ SEM. Energy.

(334) *it had perhaps not yet occurred to him that La Zambinella was virtually a courtesan,* ★ Sarrasine's forgetfulness (which echoes the *"ignorance of the facts of life"* in which Bouchardon had kept him) is a snare: to make La Zambinella a courtesan is to confirm her in her femininity; to doubt her social identity is to avoid doubting her sexual identity (HER. Enigma 6: snare, by Sarrasine, for himself).

(335) *and that he could not have both the pure pleasures that make a young girl's love so delicious and the tempestuous transports by which the hazardous possession of an actress must be purchased.* ★ REF. Paradigm of Women: young girl/courtesan.

(336) *He reflected and resigned himself.* ★ ACT. "Hope": 9: to compensate, to resign oneself (reprise).

(337) *Supper was served.* ★ ACT. "Orgy": 3: supper.

(338) *Sarrasine and La Zambinella sat down informally side by side.* ★ ACT. "Conversation II": 1: to sit side by side.

(339) *For the first half of the meal, the artists preserved some decorum,* ★ ACT. "Orgy": 4: initial calm.

(340) *and the sculptor was able to chat with the singer.* ★ ACT. "Conversation II": 2: to chat.

(341) *He found her witty, acute,* ★ SEM. Mental acuity. This seme, a kind of *hapax* in the account of La Zambinella's character, serves to correct, according to a euphemistic and conformist intention, what would be injurious in the image of a *retarded* woman.

(342) *but astonishingly ignorant,* ★ La Zambinella's ignorance is equivalent to her physical immaturity (SEM. Immaturity).

(343) *and she revealed herself to be weak and superstitious.* ★ Weakness and superstition are equivalent to pusillanimity (SEM. Pusillanimity).

(344) *The delicacy of her organs was reflected in her understanding.* ★ If one understands by La Zambinella's "organs" her vocal chords, nothing has been revealed; but if these organs are her sexual characteristics, everything has been suggested: thus there is a double understanding (HER. Enigma 6: equivocation). ★★ Psychophysiological code: physical deficiency and mental weakness.

(345) *When Vitagliani uncorked the first bottle of champagne,* ★ ACT. "Orgy": 5: Wines.

(346) *Sarrasine read in his companion's eyes a start of terror at the tiny explosion caused by the escaping gas.* ★ HER. Enigma 6: snare, by Sarrasine, for himself (timidity *proves* femininity: Sarrasine uses this psychological proof to deceive himself).

LXIII. PSYCHOLOGICAL PROOF

Champagne serves to prove La Zambinella's pusillanimity. La Zambinella's pusillanimity serves to prove her femininity. Thus, the Sarrasinean snare shifts from proof to proof. Some are inductive, based on that old rhetorical deity: the *exem-*

plum: from a narrative episode (champagne, later the snake), one induces a character trait (or, rather, one constructs the episode to signify the character). Others are deductive; these are enthymemes, imperfect syllogisms (defective, or incomplete, or simply probable): all women are timid; La Zambinella is timid; therefore La Zambinella is a woman. The two logical systems intermingle: the *exemplum* permits positing the minor premise of the syllogism: La Zambinella is frightened by a popping cork, thus La Zambinella is timid. As for the major premise, it derives from the narcissistic zone (woman is adorable), the psychological zone (woman is timid), the aesthetic zone (woman is beautiful); what establishes this major premise is, in conformity with the definition of the enthymeme, not a scientific truth but "common knowledge," an *endoxa*. Thus the snares Sarrasine sets for himself are based on the most social discourse: completely immersed in sociality, the subject takes from it his censures and his alibis, in short his blindness, or even: his own death—since he will die from having misled himself. Psychology—pure social discourse— thus appears as a murderous language which *conduces* (under this word we would like to put the inductive *exemplum* and the deductive syllogism) the subject to the final castration.

(347) *The love-stricken artist interpreted the involuntary shudder of this feminine constitution as the sign of an excessive sensitivity. The Frenchman was charmed by this weakness.* ★ SEM. Pusillanimity (timidity, femininity). ★★ *Feminine constitution* is a snare if taken literally and a decipherment if understood metaphorically (HER. Enigma 6: equivocation).

(348) *How much is protective in a man's love!*
"My strength your shield!" Is this not written at the heart of all declarations of love? ★ REF. Proverbial code: Love.

148

(349) *Too excited to shower the beautiful Italian with compliments, Sarrasine, like all lovers, was by turns serious, laughing, or reflective.* ★ REF. Psychology of Lovers.

(350) *Although he seemed to be listening to the other guests, he did not hear a word they were saying, so absorbed was he in the pleasure of finding himself beside her, touching her hand as he served her. He bathed in a secret joy.* ★ REF. Love: actions and feelings.

(351) *Despite the eloquence of a few mutual glances,* ★ *Mutual glances* are signs of reciprocal love. However, structurally, Sarrasine's feeling has no pertinence, since it has long been established in the discourse and has nothing uncertain about it; the only thing that counts here is the sign of agreement emitted by La Zambinella; this sign is a pretense (HER. Enigma 6: snare, by La Zambinella, for Sarrasine).

(352) *he was astonished at the reserve La Zambinella maintained toward him.* ★ Were Sarrasine to extend his "astonishment" a trifle, he might discover the truth; thus this "astonishment" is a decipherment Sarrasine performs incompletely in his own behalf (HER. Enigma 6: partial decipherment, by Sarrasine, for himself).

(353) *Indeed, she had begun by pressing his foot and teasing him with the flirtatiousness of a woman in love and free to show it;* ★ HER. Enigma 6: snare, by La Zambinella, for Sarrasine. ★★ REF. Typology of Women.

(354) *but she suddenly wrapped herself in the modesty of a young girl,* ★ REF. Typology of Women. ★★ All of La Zambinella's reserve, whatever its motive (fear or scruple), is a suspension of the stratagem and is tantamount to an initial decipherment; here, however, we cannot tell whether the message comes from La Zambinella or from the discourse, whether it proceeds toward Sarrasine or the reader: it is strictly *unsituated*: whereby we see once again that writing has this power of producing a veritable silence of destination: it is, literally, a countercommunication, a "cacography" (HER. Enigma 6: partial decipherment).

149

(355) *after hearing Sarrasine describe a trait which revealed the excessive violence of his character.* ★ SEM. Violence (excess). ★★ La Zambinella's pusillanimity (logical source of her femininity) is signified in several examples (champagne, snake), but also in certain of Sarrasine's offensives; the seme then assumes an operative value (even though these offensives are not initially directed against La Zambinella); it forms the conclusion of a long sequence ("Danger") laid down by the threats of which La Zambinella will increasingly be the object, until the moment when, the machination having been discovered, the singer is nearly killed by Sarrasine. These fears, following certain threats (however abstract), are harbingers of the final crisis (ACT. "Danger": 1: act of violence, sign of a dangerous character).

(356) *When the supper became an orgy,* ★ ACT. "Orgy": 6: nomination of the orgy (here a rhetorical, denominative statement: the discourse gives an over-all name to what it will detail).

(357) *the guests broke into song under the influence of the Peralta and the Pedro-Ximenes. There were ravishing duets, songs from Calabria, Spanish seguidillas, Neapolitan canzonettas.* ★ ACT. "Orgy": 7: to sing.

(358) *Intoxication was in every eye, in the music, in hearts and voices alike. Suddenly an enchanting vivacity welled up, a gay abandon, an Italian warmth of feeling* ★ ACT. "Orgy": 8: to abandon oneself (denominative statement).

(359) *inconceivable to those acquainted only with Parisian gatherings, London routs, or Viennese circles.* ★ REF. Worldly Europe.

(360) *Jokes and words of love flew like bullets in a battle through laughter, profanities, and invocations to the Holy Virgin or il Bambino.* ★ ACT. "Orgy": 9: to abandon oneself (1) unbridled talk. ★★ REF. Italianness (*il Bambino*).

(361) *Someone lay down on a sofa and fell asleep.* ★ ACT. "Orgy": 10: to let oneself go (2): to sleep.

(362) *A girl was listening to a declaration of love, unaware that she was spilling sherry on the tablecloth.* ★ ACT. "Orgy": 11: to abandon oneself (3): to spill wine (this gesture is not in conformity with the Code of the Young Girl and this incongruity reinforces the sign of disorder).

(363) *In the midst of this disorder,* ★ ACT. "Orgy": 12: to abandon oneself (denominative reprise). *Abandon,* a fragment of the orgy, is rhetorically constructed: a statement, three terms, a reprise.

(364) *La Zambinella remained thoughtful, as though terror-struck. She refused to drink,* ★ ACT. "Danger": 2: the victim's fear.

LXIV. THE VOICE OF THE READER

As though terror-struck: who is speaking here? It cannot be Sarrasine, even indirectly, since he interprets La Zambinella's fear as timidity. Above all, it cannot be the narrator, because he knows that La Zambinella really is terrified. The modalization (*as though*) expresses the interests of only one character, who is neither Sarrasine nor the narrator, but the reader: it is the reader who is concerned that the truth be simultaneously named and evaded, an ambiguity which the discourse nicely creates by *as though*, which indicates the truth and yet reduces it declaratively to a mere appearance. What we hear, therefore, is the *displaced* voice which the reader lends, by proxy, to the discourse: the discourse is speaking according to the reader's interests. Whereby we see that writing is not the communication of a message which starts from the author and proceeds to the reader; it is specifically the voice of reading itself: *in the text, only the reader speaks.* This inversion of our prejudices (which make reading a *reception* or, to put matters more clearly, a simple psychological participation in the adventure being related), this inversion can be illustrated by a linguistic image: in the Indo-European verb (for example, Greek), two diatheses (specifically: two *voices*) were set in opposition: the middle voice, according to which the agent performed the action for his own sake (*I sacrifice for myself*), and the active voice, according to which he performed this same action for another's benefit (as in the case of the priest who sacrificed on his client's behalf). In this accounting, writing is *active*, for it acts for the reader: it proceeds not from an author but from a *public scribe*, a notary institutionally responsible not for flattering his client's tastes but rather for registering at his dictation the summary of his interests, the operations by which, within an economy of disclosure, he manages this merchandise: the narrative.

(365) *perhaps she ate a bit too much; however, it is said that greediness in a woman is a charming quality.* ★ REF. Code of Women (they are greedy). ★★ Greediness *proves* the Woman, as does her timidity: this is a psychological proof (HER. Enigma 6: snare: by Sarrasine, for himself? by the discourse, for the reader?).

(366) *Admiring his mistress's modesty,* ★ Deceiving himself, Sarrasine transforms fear into modesty (HER. Enigma 6: snare, by Sarrasine, for himself).

(367) *Sarrasine thought seriously about the future.*
"She probably wants to be married," he thought. He then turned his thoughts to the delights of this marriage. His whole life seemed too short to exhaust the springs of happiness he found in the depths of his soul. ★ Sarrasine's self-deception, first concerned with a denomination of fact (*modesty* instead of *fright*), extends metonymically to motive, which is in turn placed under the authority of the Code governing bourgeois marriage (if a woman refuses to give herself, it is because she wants to be married) (HER.

Enigma 6: snare, by Sarrasine, for himself). ★★ REF. The Lover's imaginings.

(368) *Vitagliani, who was sitting next to him, refilled his glass so often that, toward three in the morning,* ★ ACT. "Machination": 6: the victim is made drunk.

(369) *without being totally drunk, Sarrasine could no longer control his delirium.* ★ Here begins a limited "Rape" which we will distinguish from the final "Abduction" (ACT. "Rape": 1: conditioning of the ravisher) (this rape is constructed as a "delirium," a minor *acting out*).

(370) *Impetuously, he picked up the woman,* ★ ACT. "Rape": 2: to carry off the victim.

(371) *escaping into a kind of boudoir next to the salon,* ★ ACT. "Rape": 3: to change locale.

(372) *toward the door of which he had glanced more than once.* ★ ACT. "Rape": 4: to have premeditated the abduction.

(373) *The Italian woman was armed with a dagger.*
"*If you come any closer,*" she said, "*I will be forced to plunge this weapon into your heart.* ★ ACT. "Rape": 5: the victim's armed defense. ★★ La Zambinella is defending not her virtue but her lie; thereby she designates the truth and her action is tantamount to an index. Sarrasine, however, attributes this action to a courtesan's wiles, he misleads himself: index and blindness create an equivocation (HER. Enigma 6: equivocation). ★★★ The discourse is on La Zambinella's side [in French, "I will be forced," *je serai forcée*, the past participle is feminine]; obliged by no more than orthography (agreement of the past participle), it has no option but to become an accomplice in the imposture (HER. Enigma 6: snare, discourse for reader). ★★★★ La Zambinella threatens Sarrasine with mutilation—which will moreover be carried out in the end: "*You have dragged me down to your level,*" No. 525 (SYM. Castration, the knife).

(374) *Let me go! You would despise me. I have conceived too much respect for your character to surrender in this fashion. I don't want to betray the feeling you have for me."* ★ HER. Enigma 6: equivocation (the reason La Zambinella gives can be either tactical or sincere). ★★ REF. Honor of Women, Esteem and not love, etc.

(375) *"Oh no!"* cried Sarrasine. *"You cannot stifle a passion by stimulating it!* ★ REF. Psychology and strategy of the passions.

(376) *Are you already so corrupt that, old in heart, you would act like a young courtesan who whets the emotions by which she plies her trade?"* ★ REF. Typology of Women (the courtesan). ★★ HER. Enigma 6: snare, by Sarrasine, for himself (Sarrasine misleads himself as to La Zambinella's motive).

LXV. THE "SCENE"

La Zambinella and Sarrasine exchange lines of dialogue. Each line is a snare, a misuse, and each misuse is justified by a code: Honor of Women corresponds to Typology of Women: codes are hurled back and forth, and this volley of codes is the "scene." Thereby appears the nature of meaning: it is a force which attempts to subjugate other forces, other meanings, other languages. The force of meaning depends on its degree of systematization: the strongest meaning is the one whose systematization includes a large number of elements, to the point where it appears to include everything noteworthy in the world: thus great ideological systems which battle each other with strokes of meaning. The model for this is always the "scene," the endless confrontation of two different codes communicating solely through their interlockings, the adjustment of their limits (dual replication, stychomythia). A society aware of the—in some sense—linguistic nature of the world, as was medieval society with its Trivium of the arts of speech, believing that it is not the truth which brings an end to the confrontation of languages, but merely the force of one of them, can then, in a ludic spirit, attempt to encode this force, to endow it with a protocol of results: this is the *disputatio*, the function of certain of whose terms was to close off, arbitrarily but necessarily, the infinite repetition of dialogue—"terminemes," in short, marks of abandonment that brought the interplay of languages to an end.

(377) *"But today is Friday," she replied,* ★ SEM. Superstition (pusillanimity, timorousness).

(378) *frightened at the Frenchman's violence.* ★ ACT. "Danger": 3: the victim's repeated fright.

(379) *Sarrasine, who was not devout, broke into laughter.* ★ SEM. Impiety. Sarrasine's impiety paradigmatically corresponds to La Zambinella's superstition; this paradigm is (will be) actually tragic: the pusillanimous being will draw the virile being into its deficiency, the symbolic figure will contaminate the strong mind.

(380) *La Zambinella jumped up like a young deer* ★ ACT. "Rape": 6: victim's flight.

(381) *and ran toward the salon.* ★ ACT. "Rape": 7: change of locale (symmetrical to and the inverse of No. 371).

(382) *When Sarrasine appeared in her pursuit,* ★ ACT. "Rape": 8: pursuit.

(383) *he was greeted by an infernal burst of laughter.* ★ HER. "Machination": 7: laughter, signaling success of the stratagem (collective laughter is the motive for the machination: *"I only agreed to trick you to please my friends, who wanted to laugh,"* No. 512).

(384) *He saw La Zambinella lying in a swoon upon a sofa. She was pale and drained by the extraordinary effort she had just made.* ★ SYM. Weakness, pusillanimity, timorousness, femininity.

(385) *Although Sarrasine knew little Italian,* ★ REF. Chronology (the notation refers to the number of days Sarrasine has been in Rome: three weeks, by the evening of the orgy).

LXVI. THE READERLY I: "EVERYTHING HOLDS TOGETHER"

It is necessary (likely) for Sarrasine to understand Italian, since his mistress's remark must confound him and end his delirium; however, it is no less necessary (likely) that he not know it well, since he has been in Italy only twenty-four days (as we know from the chronological code); he cannot have been there longer, since he must be unaware of the Roman custom of putting castrati on the stage; he must be unaware of the custom, since he has to mistake La Zambinella's identity, etc. In other words, the discourse scrupulously keeps within a circle of *solidarities*, and this circle, in which "everything holds together," is that of the readerly. As we might expect, the readerly is controlled by the principle of non-contradiction, but by multiplying solidarities, by stressing at every opportunity the *compatible* nature of circumstances, by attaching narrated events together with a kind of logical "paste," the discourse carries this principle to the point of obsession; it assumes the careful and suspicious mien of an individual afraid of being caught in some flagrant contradiction; it is always on the lookout and always, just in case, preparing its defense against the enemy that may force it to acknowledge the scandal of some illogicality, some disturbance of "common sense." The solidarity of notations thus appears to be a kind of defensive weapon, it says in its way that meaning is a force, that it is devised within an economy of forces.

156

(386) *he heard his mistress saying in a low voice to Vitagliani:* *"But he will kill me!"* ★ HER. "Machination": 8: indication of complicity between the instigator and the agent of the machination. ★★ ACT. "Danger": 4: victim's premonitory fear.

(387) *The sculptor was utterly confounded by this strange scene. He regained his senses. At first he stood motionless; then he found his voice, sat down next to his mistress, and assured her of his respect. He was able to divert his passion by addressing the most high-minded phrases to this woman; and in depicting his love, he used all the resources* ★ ACT. "Abduction": 9: failure of the rape, return to order.

(388) *of that magical eloquence, that inspired intermediary* ★ REF. Code of passion.

(389) *which women rarely refuse to believe.* ★ REF. Psychology of Women.

(390) *When the guests were surprised by the first gleams of morning light, a woman suggested they go to Frascati.* ★ ACT. "Excursion": 1: proposal. ★★ ACT. "Orgy": 13: end (dawn).

LXVII. HOW AN ORGY IS CREATED

Someone, not the reader but a character (Sarrasine, in this instance), gradually approaches the scene of an orgy; it is announced to him by the sound of voices, by bright lights glimpsed through cracks of a door: this is an announcement interior to the story, analogous to the physical indices that enable us to decipher in advance a tempest, an earthquake: we are in a natural history of the orgy. Then the orgy is announced interior to the discourse: it is named, which supposes that like a denominative résumé (a chapter title, for example) we are going to analyze it, give its moments, the signifieds which compose it: we are in a rhetoric of the orgy. These parts of the orgy are stereotyped items of behavior, created by a repetition of experiences (supper, uncorking champagne, singing, licentiousness): we are in an empirical knowledge of the orgy. Further, a certain moment of this orgy, given under its generic name, *abandonment,* can no longer be analyzed like the orgy itself, but *illustrated* by certain typical items of behavior (sleeping, spilling wine): we are in an inductive logic of the orgy (based on *exempla*). Finally, the orgy dies down, ends: we are in a physics of the orgy. What we have called the proairetic code is thus itself made up of other diverse codes based on different disciplines. The series of actions, natural, logical, linear as it may appear, is not controlled by a single rule of order; not only can it "divagate," accommodating endless expansions (as here, with the failed rape of La Zambinella), it refracts different disciplines, orders, codes: it is a perspective space: the materiality of the discourse is the point of view; the codes are the vanishing points; the referent (the orgy) is the framed image.

(391) *Everyone enthusiastically fell in with the idea of spending the day at the Villa Ludovisi.* ★ ACT. "Excursion": 2: general agreement.

(392) *Vitagliani went down to hire some carriages.* ★ ACT. "Excursion": 3: hiring of carriages.

(393) *Sarrasine had the pleasure of leading La Zambinella to a phaeton.* ★ ACT. "Amorous outing": 1: to get into the same carriage.

(394) *Once outside Rome, the gaiety which had been momentarily repressed by each person's battle with sleepiness suddenly revived. Men and women alike seemed used to this strange life, these ceaseless pleasures, this artist's impulsiveness which turns life into a*

perpetual party at which one laughed unreservedly. ★ ACT. "Excursion": 4: collective gaiety. ★★ Artist's Life.

(395) *The sculptor's companion was the only one who seemed downcast.*
   "Are you ill?" Sarrasine asked her. "Would you rather go home?"
   "I'm not strong enough to stand all these excesses," she replied.
"I must be very careful; ★ ACT. "Danger": 5: persistent fear.
★★ Sarrasine continues to mislead himself: after having taken La Zambinella's resistance for modesty or flirtatiousness, he attributes her depression to illness (HER. Enigma 6: snare, by Sarrasine, for himself). ★★★ La Zambinella's response is a snare if the fatigue she alleges is due to the orgy; it is truthful if her illness results from fear, it is a snare if her pusillanimity is attributed to her femininity; it is truthful if it is due to "her" castration: there is a double understanding (HER. Enigma 6: equivocation). ★★★★ ACT. "Amorous Outing": 2: tête-à-tête conversation.

(396) *but with you I feel so well! Had it not been for you, I would never have stayed for supper;* ★ Two likelihoods make their voices heard here, thereby producing a double understanding: (1) the operative likelihood will say that La Zambinella is offering Sarrasine a discourse which is, if not amorous, at least amical, in order to allay any suspicion of the stratagem in which he is caught; it will then be a snare; (2) the "psychological" likelihood which considers logical the "contradictions of the human heart" will see in La Zambinella's confidence an impulse of sincerity, the fugitive suspension of the fraud (HER. Enigma 6: equivocation). ★★ The request for protection signifies: *everything but sex;* but thereby the very deficiency of sex is designated (SYM. Asexual protection: the theme will reappear).

(397) *a sleepless night and I lose whatever bloom I have."*
   "You are so delicate," Sarrasine said, looking at the charming creature's pretty face.
   "Orgies ruin the voice." ★ SEM. Femininity.

(398) *"Now that we're alone," the artist cried, "and you no longer need fear the outbursts of my passion, tell me that you love me."* ★ ACT. "Declaration of love": 1: request for an avowal.

At this point in the narrative (it could be at another) several actions are still underway at the same time: the "danger" run by La Zambinella, the hero's "will-to-die," his "declaration of love" to his mistress, their "amorous outing," the group's "machination" and "excursion" are still in process, suspended and interwoven. The text, while it is being produced, is like a piece of Valenciennes lace created before us under the lacemaker's fingers: each sequence undertaken hangs like the temporarily inactive bobbin waiting while its neighbor works; then, when its turn comes, the hand takes up the thread again, brings it back to the frame; and as the pattern is filled out, the progress of each thread is marked with a pin which holds it and is gradually moved forward: thus the terms of the sequence: they are positions held and then left behind in the course of a gradual invasion of meaning. This process is valid for the entire text. The grouping of codes, as they enter into the work, into the movement of the reading, constitute a braid (*text, fabric, braid*: the same thing); each thread, each code, is a voice; these braided—or braiding—voices form the writing: when it is alone, the voice does no labor, transforms nothing: it *expresses*; but as soon as the hand intervenes to gather and intertwine the inert threads, there is labor, there is transformation. We know the symbolism of the braid: Freud, considering the origin of weaving, saw it as the labor of a woman braiding her pubic hairs to form the absent penis. The text, in short, is a fetish; and to reduce it to the unity of meaning, by a deceptively univocal reading, is to *cut the braid*, to sketch the castrating gesture.

(399) *"Why?" she replied. "What would be the use?* ★ ACT. "Declaration": 2: to elude the requested avowal. ★★ Like every *embarrassed* attitude, La Zambinella's reply designates the truth by

eluding it (or at least says that there is an enigma) (HER. Enigma
6: equivocation).

(400) *I seemed pretty to you. But you are French and your feelings will pass.* ★ HER. Enigma 6: snare, by La Zambinella, for
Sarrasine (You will stop loving me because you are fickle; therefore I am truly a woman). ★★ "Declaration": 3: first basis for declining an offer of love (love is fickle). ★★★ REF. Amorous typology of nationalities: the fickle French. ★★★★ HER. Enigma 6:
snare (by the discourse: *I seemed pretty [jolie] to you* puts *jolie* in
the feminine, cf. No. 373).

(401) *Ah, you would not love me as I long to be loved."*
  "How can you say that?"
  "Not to satisfy any vulgar passion; purely. ★ ACT. "Declaration": 4: second basis for declining an offer of love (impossibility
of a suitable feeling). ★★ SYM. Asexual protection. ★★★ SYM.
Alibi of castration: the Misunderstood Woman. Sincere or not (to
decide that, one would have to go *behind the paper*), La Zambinella sublimates the condition of castration (or of exclusion) beneath a noble and plaintive theme: that of the Misunderstood
Woman. This theme will be taken up again by Mme de Rochefide
when the narrator's story has drawn her into castration: *"No one
will have known me, I am proud of that!"* No. 560. ★★★★ *"Not to
satisfy any vulgar passion; purely"* is an equivocation; for either
exile from sex is a physical deficiency (the truth) or it is a sublime
release granted, by the ideal, to the flesh (snare) (HER. Enigma
6; equivocation).

(402) *I abhor men perhaps even more than I hate women.* ★
SYM. The neuter (*ne-uter*) of the castrato.

(403) *I need to seek refuge in friendship.* ★ SYM. Asexual protection. ★★ HER. Enigma 6: equivocation (a sincere feeling or
an evasion determined by the toils of the machination).

(404) *For me, the world is a desert. I am an accursed creature,
condemned to understand happiness, to feel it, to desire it, and,
like many others, forced to see it flee from me continually.* ★
ACT. "Declaration": 5: third basis for declining an offer of love

(excluded from normal affections). ★★ SYM. Exclusion, curse (in the untenable position of a *ne-uter*, the castrato is a creature belonging nowhere: he is excluded from difference, from antithesis: he transgresses, not the sexes, but classification). ★★★ SYM. Euphemistic definition of the castrato: unfulfilled desire. ★★★★ REF. Code of acquired wisdom (happiness flees from man).

(405) *Remember, sir, that I will not have deceived you.* ★ The future perfect refers to the moment when the machination will be uncovered; a predictive and exorcising term (HER. "Machination": 9: prediction and exorcism of the outcome). ★★ HER. Enigma 6: equivocation. The equivocation arises because La Zambinella's "frankness" takes the form of a statement general enough to include the truth, but too general, in fact, to designate it.

LXIX. EQUIVOCATION II: METONYMIC FALSEHOOD

Equivocation (often) consists in disclosing genus (*I am an excluded creature*) and silencing species (*I am a castrato*): one says the whole for the part, a synechdoche, but in the ambivalence, metonymy is in a sense caught in the act, as statement and no longer as thing stated; for the discourse (or, by proxy, the character) on the one hand advances, discloses, and on the other holds back, conceals; it undertakes to impregnate the void of what it silences by the plenitude of what it says, to identify two different truths, the truth of speech and the truth of silence; of the two species of the genus *Excluded* (on one hand the Inaccessible Woman, on the other the undesirable castrato), the discourse implies one, the receiver the other; here again there is a divided reception. As we might expect, this metonymic falsehood (since by stating the whole for the part, it induces error or at least masks the truth, hides vacuum under plenitude) has a strategic function: as the difference between species and genus, it is La Zambinella's *specificity* which is silenced: now this *specificity* is both operationally decisive (it controls the disclosure of the enigma) and symbolically vital (it is castration itself).

(406) *I forbid you to love me.* ★ ACT. "Declaration": 6: to forbid to love.

(407) *I can be your devoted friend, for I admire your strength and your character. I need a brother, a protector. Be all that for me,* ★ ACT. "Declaration": 7: reduction of love to friendship. ★★ SYM. Asexual protection (the alibi conceals sexual deficiency). ★★★ Can La Zambinella be a friend (*un ami,* masculine)? Since there is a feminine form (*une amie*), a choice exists, and the use of the masculine reveals the transvestite. Yet this disclosure has no real effect on the reading: the giveaway word is carried along in the commonplace generality of the sentence, covered by its similarity to a stereotyped phrase (*to be a devoted friend*) and thereby blurred (HER. Enigma 6: disclosure, by La Zambinella to Sarrasine).

(408) *but no more."* ★ Throughout the story, the excedent is obviously the sexual organ (SYM. Asexual protection).

(409) *"Not love you!" Sarrasine cried. "But my dearest angel, you are my life, my happiness!"* ★ ACT. "Declaration": 8: protestation of love. ★★ REF. Rhetoric of love (*dear angel, my life*).

(410) *"If I were to say one word, you would repulse me with horror."* ★ If one word can alter a situation, it is because it has revelatory power, and thus *there is an enigma* (HER. Enigma 6: proposal). ★★ SYM. Mark, curse, exclusion. ★★★ SYM. Taboo on the word *castrato.*

LXX. BEING-CASTRATED AND CASTRATION

To make *being-castrated,* an anecdotal condition, coincide with *castration,* a symbolic structure, is the task successfully carried out by the performer (Balzac), since the former does not necessarily entail the latter: witness many anecdotal narratives about *castrati* (Casanova, Président De Brosses, Sade, Stendhal). This success hinges on a structural artifice: identifying the symbolic and the hermeneutic, making the search for truth (hermeneutic structure) into the search for castration (symbolic structure), making the truth be *anecdotally* (and no longer symbolically) the absent phallus. The coincidence of the two paths is effected (structurally) by keeping one or the other from ever being determined upon (indeterminacy is a "proof" of writing): aphasia concerning the word *castrato* has a double value, whose duplicity is insoluble: on the symbolic level, there is a taboo; on the operative level, the disclosure is delayed: the truth is suspended *both* by censorship and by machination. The *readerly* structure of the text is thereby raised to the level of an analytical investigation; however, we can also, and more justifiably, say that, by becoming anecdotal, the psychoanalytical progression of the subject (perfused throughout: through Sarrasine, the narrator, the author, and the reader) becomes unnecessary: the symbolic is in *excess*, useless (what we have here called *symbolic* does not derive from psychoanalytic knowledge). Which accounts for this story's perhaps unique value: "illustrating" castration by being-castrated, like with like, it mocks the notion of illustration, it abolishes both sides of the equivalence (letter and symbol) without advantage to either one; the latent here occupies the line of the manifest from the start, the sign is flattened out: there is no longer any "representation."

(411) *"Coquette!* ★ HER. Enigma 6: snare, by Sarrasine, for himself. Sarrasine persists in *reversing* the partial clues La Zambinella, either sincere or wary, offers him: he denies his partner's disclaimers. This second disclaimer is made in actual semantic terms:

of La Zambinella's messages, Sarrasine retains only the connotation associated with them by the cultural code of amorous pretense (here: coquetry).

(412) *Nothing can frighten me.* ★ SEM. Stubbornness. ★★ The disclaimer of danger designates precisely the place where fate will strike (or rather: fate is the very thing being denied) (ACT. "Will-to-die": 3: to accept any risk).

(413) *Tell me you will cost my future, that I will die in two months, that I will be damned merely for having kissed you."* ★ ACT. "Will-to-die": 4: predictive term (*I will die*) in the form of a provocation of fate. ★★ ACT. "Declaration": 9: gift of life (purchase of the desired object).

(414) *He kissed her,* ★ ACT. "Amorous Outing": 3: to want to kiss.

LXXI. THE TRANSPOSED KISS

A second reading, the reading which places behind the transparency of suspense (placed on the text by the first avid and ignorant reader) the anticipated knowledge of what is to come in the story, this further reading—unjustly condemned by the commercial imperatives of our society, which compels us to squander the book, to discard it as though it were deflowered, in order to buy a new one—this retrospective reading bestows upon Sarrasine's kiss a precious enormity: Sarrasine passionately kisses a castrato (or a boy in drag); the castration is transposed onto Sarrasine's own body and we ourselves, second readers, receive the shock. Thus it would be wrong to say that if we undertake to reread the text we do so for some intellectual advantage (to understand better, to analyze on good grounds): it is actually and invariably for a ludic advantage: to multiply the signifiers, not to reach some ultimate signified.

(415) *despite La Zambinella's efforts to resist this passionate embrace.* ★ ACT. "Amorous Outing": 4: to resist.

(416) *"Tell me you are a devil, that you want my money, my name, all my fame! Do you want me to give up being a sculptor? Tell me."* ★ ACT. "Declaration": 10: gift of one's most precious possession (Art).

(417) *"And if I were not a woman?"* ★ HER. Enigma 6: disclosure, La Zambinella to Sarrasine. ★★ The impossibilities of loving which La Zambinella has heretofore alleged (400, 401, 404) were all of a psychological order. What is now advanced is a physical limit. There is a shift from the banal contestation of feelings based on certain psychological attributes (*You are fickle, I am demanding, excluded*), each of which was nonetheless deemed a sufficient motive for refusal when it was presented, to the radical contestation of being (*I am not a woman*): we will admit this is an unusual term in the banal "Declaration of love" sequence: a term whose content is anomalous, scandalous, but whose form (*impossibility of loving*) leaves the sequence all its readerliness (ACT. "Declaration": 11: physical impediment).

(418) *La Zambinella asked in a soft, silvery voice.* ★ SEM. Femininity. ★★ (Connoted) femininity denies its own (denoted) disclaimer, the sign is more powerful than the message, associated meaning than literal meaning (this will of course be seized upon by Sarrasine, great devourer of connotations as he is, who understands in a sentence not what it asserts but what it suggests) (HER. Enigma 6: snare, by La Zambinella, for Sarrasine).

(419) *"What a joke!" Sarrasine cried. "Do you think you can deceive an artist's eye?* ★ ACT. "Declaration": 12: disclaimer of the disclaimer. ★★ REF. Anatomical knowledge of the realistic artist. ★★★ HER. Enigma 6: snare, by Sarrasine, for himself: aesthetic proof: artists are infallible.

To ensnare himself (a task upon which he lavishes a vigilant energy), Sarrasine employs three enthymemes: narcissistic proof (*I love her, therefore she is a woman*), psychological proof (*women are weak, La Zambinella is weak*, etc.), and aesthetic proof (*beauty is solely the province of woman, therefore . . .*). These false syllogisms can unite and reinforce their errors, can form a kind of sorites (or abridged syllogism): *beauty is feminine; only an artist can know beauty; I am an artist; therefore I know beauty and therefore I know woman*, etc. A "realistic" reader might ask Sarrasine why, even if it is to triumph over it in the end, he shows no surprise, no shock at his partner's incredible remark (*"if I were not a woman?"*); why he immediately accepts an (ill-founded) rationalization against this appeal, however timid, however interrogative, to "reality" (we have already noted that to suspect a sex is definitively to deny it). The answer is: because the "realistic" artist never places "reality" at the origin of his discourse, but only and always, as far back as can be traced, an already written real, a prospective code, along which we discern, as far as the eye can see, only a succession of copies. In this case, the code is that of plastic art: it is the code which sustains beauty and love, as reflected in the Pygmalion myth, under whose authority Sarrasine is placed (No. 229). By immediately advancing an artist's reason in refutation of La Zambinella's avowal, the sculptor is merely citing the supreme code, the basis for all reality, which is art, whence flow truths and facts alike: the artist is infallible not by the sureness of his performance (he is not merely a good copyist of "reality") but by the authority of his competence; it is he who knows the code, the origin, the basis, and thus he becomes the guarantor, the witness, the author (*auctor*) of reality: he has the right to determine the difference between the sexes, against the very protestation of the interested parties, who, confronted by the original and ultimate authority of Art, live in the contingency of phenomena.

(420) *Haven't I spent ten days devouring, scrutinizing, admiring your perfection?* ★ REF. Chronology (this datum is just about exact: one evening at the theater, eight days on the sofa, then right afterwards the duenna's rendezvous, the orgy, the outing). ★★ Sarrasine defines the nature—or the origin—of his admiration for La Zambinella in relation to a seme which has already been applied to him (162), his taste for whittling, for kneading, for what, in order to grasp the form of this action, we would have to call *drilling,* the urge to pierce, a kind of endoscopic energy which, removing veils, garments, will probe the object for its internal essence. To *scrutinize* means, literally, *to excavate, to probe, to visit, to explore:* in scrutinizing La Zambinella (for ten days), Sarrasine has exercised a triple function: neurotic, since he repeats a childhood act (No. 162); aesthetic (i.e., for him, the basis of existence), since the artist, and specifically the sculptor, authenticates the copy of appearance by his knowledge of its interior, its *underneath;* and last, symbolic—or inevitable, or even: absurd—since this excavation whose triumphant product (La Zambinella's femininity) Sarrasine reveals would, if carried further, definitively bring to light the *nothing* which constitutes the castrato, so that once this *nothing* was discovered, the artist's very knowledge would be voided and the statue destroyed (SEM. Whittling).

(421) *Only a woman could have this round, soft arm, these elegant curves.* ★ Aesthetic proof rests on an enthymeme with a false premise (*only women are beautful*), since at least castrati can be as beautiful (HER. Enigma 6: snare, by Sarrasine, for himself).

(422) *Oh, you want compliments."* ★ HER. Enigma 6: snare, by Sarrasine, for himself (psychological proof: coquetry).

(423) *She smiled at him sadly, and raising her eyes heavenward, she murmured: "Fatal beauty!"* ★ Derived from a complex picto-

168

rial code, La Zambinella here achieves her final incarnation, or reveals her ultimate origin: *the Madonna with Raised Eyes*. This is a powerful stereotype, a major element in the Code of Pathos (Raphael, El Greco, Racine's Junie and Esther, etc.). The image is sadistic (we understand it as giving rise to Sarrasine's *dumb rage* in No. 430): it describes the pure, pious, sublime, passive victim (Sade's Justine) whose eyes raised heavenward are saying quite clearly: see what I will not see, do as you like with my body, I am disinterested, pursue your interest (REF. Code of Pathos).

(424) *At that moment her gaze had an indescribable expression of horror, so powerful and vivid that Sarrasine shuddered.* ★ SYM. The curse, exclusion ("horror"). ★★ La Zambinella clearly reveals to Sarrasine the essence of her condition, which is horror (the curse, the mark)—through the kind of alethic hierarchy of signs in which sounds (a cry, an exclamation) are more trustworthy than words, aspect more than sounds, and expression (the *nec plus ultra* of sincerity) than aspect. Sarrasine receives the message: he shudders (led to the verge of truth); but he is distracted from the signified (from its formulation, from its accession to language, which is the only thing that would count) by a sadistic impulse: the signifier (*eyes raised heavenward*) leads him not to the castrato's truth but to his own, which is to destroy La Zambinella, whatever her sex (HER. Enigma 6: disclosure, La Zambinella to Sarrasine).

(425) *"Frenchman," she went on, "forget this moment of madness forever.* ★ ACT. "Declaration": 13: command to forget.

(426) *I respect you,* ★ Three meanings are mingled here: refusal of sex (in the Code of Love, *respect* is the euphemism which permits rejecting the partner's desire without inflicting too deep a narcissistic wound); sincerity (led on for the sake of fun into a trick at your expense, I have come to know you and respect you); prudence (when you learn the truth, without having lost everything, you will forgo your violence and thus we will end this adventure at the least cost to me). These meanings are possible, i.e., indiscernible (HER. Enigma 6: equivocation).

(427) *but as for love, do not ask it of me; that feeling is smothered in my heart. I have no heart!" she cried, weeping. "The stage where*

you saw me, that applause, that music, that fame I am condemned to, such is my life, I have no other. ★ La Zambinella reverts again to the definition of being-castrated. By a euphemism already employed, the "heart" designates the very thing removed from the castrato. A deficient creature, he is condemned to an exterior existence, mutilated at his core, in his plenitude, in that *underneath* which, for Sarrasine, defines in one impulse art, truth, and life. This definition draws its support (by citing it) from a cultural code: the actor is condemned to exteriority (the tragedy of the clown, etc.) (SYM. Castrato's condition).

(428) *In a few hours you will not see me in the same way, the woman you love will be dead."* ★ HER. "Machination": 10: anticipation of the end. ★★ The woman will be dead: (1) because I will die; (2) because you will no longer love me; (3) because the false envelope of femininity will fall away, etc. This ambivalence is based on what we have called the metonymic falsehood: Woman sometimes designates the total person, sometimes the sex, sometimes the imaginary object created by a sentiment of love; the pretense consists in playing on relations of identity between the whole and the parts (HER. Enigma 6: equivocation).

(429) *The sculptor made no reply.* ★ The speeches of the Declaration here involve a significant blank, since it is in this silent "answer" that Sarrasine's sadism is located (ACT. "Declaration": 14: to remain silent).

(430) *He was overcome with a dumb rage which oppressed his heart. He could only gaze with enflamed, burning eyes at this extraordinary woman. La Zambinella's weak voice, her manner, her movements and gestures marked with sorrow, melancholy, and discouragement, awakened all the wealth of passion in his soul. Each word was a goad.* ★ This sadistic configuration has two purposes here: on the one hand, for a short while, it allows the subject to ignore the truth his partner is offering him and dispenses him from responding to the rejection he has been given; on the other, it fulfills in the situation the seme of violence, aggressiveness, assigned to Sarrasine at the outset; meaning shifts to action (SEM. Violence, excess).

(431) *At that moment they reached Frascati.* ★ ACT. "Amorous outing": 5: to come to an end. ★★ "Excursion": 5: to arrive at the destination.

(432) *As the artist offered his mistress his arm to assist her in alighting,* ★ ACT. "Amorous outing": 6: to assist in alighting from the carriage (corresponds to No. 393: to get into the same carriage).

(433) *he felt her shiver.*
"What is wrong? You would kill me," he cried, seeing her grow pale, "if I were even an innocent cause of your slightest unhappiness."
"A snake," she said, pointing to a grass snake which was gliding along a ditch. "I am afraid of those horrid creatures." Sarrasine crushed the snake's head with his heel. ★ The episode of the snake is the element of a proof (a *probatio*) whose enthymeme (albeit defective) we know: Women are timid; La Zambinella is timid; La Zambinella is a woman. The snake episode serves as a minor *exemplum* (SEM. Pusillanimity, timidity).

LXXIII. THE SIGNIFIED AS CONCLUSION

The snake episode is both an *exemplum* (inductive weapon of the old rhetoric) and a signifier (referring to a character seme attached in this case to the castrato). In the classic system, semantic proof is indistinguishable from a logical process: one must simultaneously work up from signifier to signified and work down from the example to the generality that can be induced from it. Between the signifier (to be frightened of a snake) and the signified (to be impressionable as a woman) there is the same distance as between an endoxal premise (timid people are afraid of snakes) and its abridged conclusion (La Zambinella is timid). Semic space is glued to hermeneutic space: the point is always to locate in the perspective of the classic text a profound or final truth (the profound is what is discovered *at the end*).

(434) *"How can you be so brave?" La Zambinella continued, looking with visible horror at the dead reptile.* ★ SEM. "Timidity." Timidity permits a recurrence of "protection," an alibi of love "minus sex."

(435) *"Ah," the artist replied, smiling, "now do you dare deny you are a woman?"* ★ The form of the sentence *"Do you dare deny"* attests the arrogant triumph of a fact. But this fact is merely the conclusion of a defective enthymeme (You are timid, therefore you are a woman) (HER. Enigma 6: snare, by Sarrasine, for himself: psychological proof of femininity).

(436) *They rejoined their companions and strolled through the woods of the Villa Ludovisi, which in those days belonged to Cardinal Cicognara.* ★ ACT. "Excursion": 6: to stroll in the woods. Strictly speaking, the allusion to Cardinal Cicognara is insignificant (has no functional importance); however, in addition to introducing an effect of reality, it enables the name of La Zambinella's protector and Sarrasine's murderer to be reintroduced: this is the "glue" of the readerly.

(437) *That morning fled too quickly for the enamored sculptor,* ★ REF. Love and Time Passing.

(438) *but it was filled with a host of incidents which revealed to him the coquetry, the weakness, and the delicacy of this soft and enervated being.* ★ SEM. Pusillanimity, Femininity.

(439) *This was woman herself, with her sudden fears, her irrational whims, her instinctive worries, her impetuous boldness, her fussings, and her delicious sensibility.* ★ SEM. Femininity. The source of the sentence cannot be discerned. Who is speaking? Is it Sarrasine? the narrator? the author? Balzac-the-author? Balzac-the-

man? romanticism? bourgeoisie? universal wisdom? The intersecting of all these origins creates the writing.

(440) *It happened that as they were wandering in the open countryside, the little group of merry singers saw in the distance some heavily armed men whose manner of dress was far from reassuring. Someone said, "They must be highwaymen," and everyone quickened his pace toward the refuge of the Cardinal's grounds. At this critical moment, Sarrasine saw from La Zambinella's pallor that she no longer had the strength to walk; he took her up in his arms and carried her for a while, running. When he came to a nearby arbor, he put her down.* ★ The episode of the highwaymen is an *exemplum* (SEM. Pusillanimity, Timidity, Femininity).

LXXIV. THE MASTERY OF MEANING

A classic narrative always gives this impression: the author first conceives the signified (or the generality) and then finds for it, according to the chance of his imagination, "good" signifiers, probative examples; the classic author is like an artisan bent over the workbench of meaning and selecting the best *expressions* for the concept he has already formed. For instance, *timidity*: one selects the sound of a champagne cork, a story of a snake, a story of highwaymen. However, the signifying imagination is even more profitable if it fills a double function; it then endeavors to produce doubly articulated signs, committed to that solidarity of notations which defines the readerly; for instance, *impiety*: one could be content to represent the subject playing games in church, but it is a greater art to link impiety to the child's vocation (by showing Sarrasine whittling licentious pieces during Mass) or to contrast it with La Zambinella's superstition (which makes Sarrasine laugh); for sculpture and pusillanimity belong to different narrative networks, and the closer and better calculated the anastomosis

173

of the signifiers, the more the text is regarded as "well written." In the old rhetoric, the choice of *exempla* and demonstrative premises constituted a vast department: *inventio*: beginning with the very end of the demonstration (what one wished to prove), one endeavored to marshal arguments and direct them appropriately; certain rules helped in doing so (notably the topic). Similarly, the classic author becomes a performer at the moment he evidences his power of *conducing* meaning (a marvelously ambiguous, semantic, and directional verb). Indeed, it is the *direction* of meaning which determines the two major management functions of the classic text: the *author* is always supposed to go from signified to signifier, from content to form, from idea to text, from passion to expression; and, in contrast, the *critic* goes in the other direction, works back from signifiers to signified. The *mastery of meaning*, a veritable semiurgism, is a divine attribute, once this meaning is defined as the discharge, the emanation, the spiritual effluvium overflowing from the signified toward the signifier: the *author* is a god (his place of origin is the signified); as for the critic, he is the priest whose task is to decipher the Writing of the god.

(441) *"Explain to me,"* he said, *"how this extreme weakness, which I would find hideous in any other woman, which would displease me and whose slightest indication would be almost enough to choke my love, pleases and charms me in you?* ★ From the symbolic point of view, it is now the subject's turn to advance in avowal; he attempts to define *that thing* he loves in La Zambinella, and *that thing* is deficiency, *non-being*, castration. Nevertheless, however far Sarrasine goes in this kind of self-analysis, he persists in misleading himself by continuing to employ a language of double understanding: for if the *extremity* of weakness is the superlative term of a hierarchy, pusillanimity connotes a superlative woman, a reinforced essence, a Super-Woman; if, on the other

174

hand, *extremity* is defined as the lowest depth, it designates, in the Zambinellian body, its center, which is absence. These are, in a sense, the two extremities that are superimposed, or that set up an interference, in Sarrasine's statement: social language, saturated with prejudices, *endoxai*, syllogisms, cultural references (this language infallibly decides in favor of La Zambinella's femininity), and symbolic language, which persists in stating the agreement between Sarrasine and castration (SYM. Desire for Castration).

(442) *Ah, how I love you," he went on. "All your faults, your terrors, your resentments, add an indefinable grace to your soul.* ★ Deficiency (*faults, terrors, resentments,* all the characteristic products of castration)is a *supplement* by which La Zambinella differs: (1) from other women (snare of Sarrasine based on an *originality* in La Zambinella), (2) from women (truth of Sarrasine who loves the castrato in La Zambinella) (SYM. Supplement of deficiency).

(443) *I think I would detest a strong woman, a Sappho, a courageous creature full of energy and passion.* ★ Sarrasine could hardly identify more clearly the woman he fears: the castrating woman, defined by the inverted place she occupies on the sexual axis (*a Sappho*). We recall that the text has already presented several images of this active woman: Mme de Lanty, the young woman the narrator loves, and substitutively Bouchardon, a possessive mother who has kept her child sequestered from sex. Now, if *destiny* is indeed that precise and "designated" action which causes two *exactly* opposite events suddenly to overlap and become identified, Sarrasine here states his destiny (or what is *fatal* in his adventure): for in order to flee Sappho, the castrating woman, he seeks refuge with the castrated being whose very deficiency reassures him; however, this being will lay hands on him more certainly than the redoubtable Sappho, and will drag him into its own emptiness: it is for having fled castration that Sarrasine will be castrated: thus the figure familiar from dream and story is fulfilled: to seek refuge in the arms of the murderer who is seeking you (SYM. Fear of castration).

(444) *Oh, soft, frail creature, how could you be otherwise?* ★ La Zambinella's *difference* (that deficiency which is an absolutely precious supplement, since it is the very essence of the adorable) is

175

necessary: everything is justified, both the castrato and desire for the castrato (SYM. Inevitability of castration).

(445) *That angelic voice, that delicate voice would be an anomaly, coming from any body but yours."* ★ The difference, an essential, adorable difference, is here given a specific site: the body. If Sarrasine were reading what he says, he could no longer pretend his pleasure in the castrato was a mistake or a sublimation; he himself formulates the *truth*, the truth of the enigma, of La Zambinella, of himself. The symbolic terms are here restated in their proper order: to public opinion, to mythic language, to the cultural code under which the castrato is a *counterfeit* of woman and the pleasure he can create an *anomaly*, Sarrasine replies that the union of the adorable voice and the castrated body is *right*: the body produces the voice and the voice justifies the body; to love La Zambinella's voice, as it is, is to love the body from which it proceeds, as it is (SYM. Love of the castrato).

(446) *"I cannot give you any hope,"* she said. ★ ACT. "Declaration": 15: command to give up.

(447) *"Stop speaking to me in this way,* ★ "Declaration": 16: command to be silent.

(448) *because they will make a fool of you.* ★ HER. "Machination": 11: equivocation. La Zambinella's warning is equivocal: on the one hand she refers to the true purpose of the plot, laughter, and on the other she speaks of a risk, whereas the damage has already been done.

(449) *I cannot stop you from coming to the theater; but if you love me or if you are wise, you will come there no more.* ★ ACT. "Declaration": 17: final dismissal.

LXXV. THE DECLARATION OF LOVE

The declaration of love (a banal, *already written* sequence, if ever there was one) merely alternates an assertion (*I love you*) and a disclaimer (*do not love me*); formally, therefore, it is both subject to variation (in the musical sense) and infinite. Variation results from the poverty of terms (there are only two), which requires finding for each of them a whole list of different signifiers; here these signifiers are *reasons* (*to love or to reject*); however, in other cases (in lyric poetry, for example) they can be metaphorical substitutes. Only a historical inventory of the forms of the language of love could exploit these variations and reveal to us the meaning of "Parlez-moi d'amour," whether this meaning has evolved, etc. Infinitude, on the other hand, results from repetition: repetition is, very precisely, the fact that there is no reason to stop. By these two characteristics (variation and infinitude) we already see that the declaration of love (accepted or rejected) is a contestant discourse, like the "scene" (LXIV): two languages with different vanishing points (metaphorical perspectives) are placed back to back; all they have in common is their participation in the same paradigm, that of *yes/no*, which is ultimately the pure form of any paradigm, so that the contestation (or the declaration) appears as a kind of obsessive game of meaning, a *litany*, comparable to the child's game of alternatives in Freud, or to the game of the Hindu god who eternally alternates the creation and destruction of the world, thereby making that world, our world, a mere plaything, and the *repeated* difference the game itself, meaning as a superior game.

(450) *Listen, monsieur,*" *she said in a low voice.* ★ HER. Enigma 6: disclosure, imminent and delayed.

(451) "*Oh, be still,*" *the impassioned artist said.* ★ The naming of the castrato has been interrupted (for that is what La Zambinella was finally prepared to do, *in a low voice*) (SYM. Taboo on the word castrato). ★★ HER. Enigma 6: snare, by Sarrasine, for

himself. The subject's vital interest is not to hear the truth, just as the vital interest of the discourse is to continue to suspend the answer to the enigma.

LXXVI. CHARACTER AND DISCOURSE

Sarrasine interrupts La Zambinella and thereby arrests the appearance of the truth. If we have a realistic view of *character*, if we believe that Sarrasine has a life off the page, we will look for motives for this interruption (enthusiasm, unconscious denial of the truth, etc.). If we have a realistic view of *discourse*, if we consider the story being told as a mechanism which must function until the end, we will say that since the law of narrative decrees that it continue, it was necessary that the word *castrato* not be spoken. Now these two views, although derived from different likelihoods and in principle independent (even opposed), support each other: a common sentence is produced which unexpectedly contains elements of various languages: Sarrasine is impassioned because the discourse must not end; the discourse can continue because Sarrasine, impassioned, talks without listening. Both circuits are necessarily undecidable. Good narrative writing is of this very undecidability. From a critical point of view, therefore, it is as wrong to suppress the character as it is to take him off the page in order to turn him into a psychological character (endowed with possible motives): *the character and the discourse are each other's accomplices*: the discourse creates in the character its own accomplice: a form of theurgical detachment by which, mythically, God has given himself a subject, man a helpmate, etc., whose relative independence, once they have been created, allows for *playing*. Such is discourse: if it creates characters, it is not to make them play among themselves before us but to play with them, to obtain from them a complicity which assures the uninterrupted exchange of the codes: the characters are types of discourse and, conversely, the discourse is a character like the others.

(452) *"Obstacles make my love more ardent."* ★ REF. Dynamics of passion.

(453) *La Zambinella's graceful and modest attitude did not change, but she fell silent as though a terrible thought had revealed some misfortune to her.* ★ ACT. "Danger": 6: premonition of misfortune.

(454) *When it came time to return to Rome, she got into the four-seated coach, ordering the sculptor with imperious cruelty to return to Rome alone in the carriage.* ★ ACT. "Excursion": 7: return. ★★ ACT. "Amorous Outing": 7: separate return.

(455) *During the journey, Sarrasine resolved to kidnap La Zambinella. He spent the entire day making plans, each more outrageous than the other.* ★ REF. Chronology: the excursion and the kidnapping are separated by one day (however, a mere period separates the "Excursion" from the "Kidnapping"). ★★ ACT. "Kidnapping": 1: decision and plans.

(456) *At nightfall, as he was going out to inquire where his mistress's palazzo was located,* ★ ACT. "Kidnapping": 2: preliminary information.

(457) *he met one of his friends on the threshold.*
   "My dear fellow," he said, *"our ambassador has asked me to invite you to his house tonight. He is giving a magnificent concert,* ★ ACT. "Concert": 1: invitation.

(458) *and when I tell you that Zambinella will be there . . . "* ★ Italian normally calls for the article before a proper name. This rule, elsewhere insignificant, here has consequences of a hermeneu-

tic order, owing to the enigma of Zambinella's sex: for a French and English reader, the article (*La*) emphasizes the feminine of the name it precedes (it is a common way of establishing the femininity of transvestites), and the discourse, with an eye to supporting the sexual pretense of which Sarrasine is the victim, has heretofore (with one or two exceptions) stated: La Zambinella. Any loss of the article therefore has a hermeneutic decoding function, shifting the soprano from feminine to masculine (*Zambinella*). Whence a considerable play on this article, present or absent according to the speaker's situation in relation to the castrato's secret. Here Sarrasine's friend, aware of Roman customs and speaking French to a French person, defeminizes the singer (HER. Enigma 6: decipherment, common knowledge to Sarrasine).

(459) *"Zambinella,"* cried Sarrasine, intoxicated by the name, *"I'm mad about her!"*
"You're like everyone else," his friend replied. ★ When Sarrasine repeats Zambinella's name without the article, he does so with an entirely different inflection; first from the viewpoint of verisimilitude (that is, a certain psychological congruence of data), Sarrasine, with a poor knowledge of Italian (as the chronological code has informed us) grants no pertinence to the article's presence or absence; in addition, from the stylistic viewpoint, the exclamation point puts the name at "degree zero," for it appears here in its essence, anterior to any morphological treatment (this was earlier the case with the shout by which acclaim, in No. 205, informed Sarrasine of La Zambinella's existence). His friend's word informs Sarrasine of the artist's masculinity no more than the masculine he himself employs signifies the least awareness on his part of Zambinella's secret (HER. Enigma 6: snare, by Sarrasine, for himself).
★★ The two lines of dialogue (458 and 459) establish a further ambivalence in the discourse: the friend is aesthetically mad about Zambinella; Sarrasine is erotically mad about La Zambinella (HER. Enigma 6: equivocation).

(460) *"If you are my friends, you, Vien, Lauterbourg, and Allegrain, will you help me do something after the party?"* Sarrasine asked.
"It's not some cardinal to be killed? . . . not . . . ?"

"No, no," Sarrasine said, "I'm not asking you to do anything an honest person couldn't do." ★ ACT. "Kidnapping": 3: recruiting accomplices. ★★ By copying later on, as Adonis, the statue of La Zambinella, Vien, introduced here, will ensure the continuity of the chain of duplication (SYM. Replication of bodies).

(461) *In a short time, the sculptor had arranged everything for the success of his undertaking.* ★ ACT. "Kidnapping": 4: arrangements made.

(462) *He was one of the last to arrive at the ambassador's,* ★ ACT. "Concert": 2: to arrive late. In a banal sequence (to go to a concert) this equally banal term (to arrive late) can have immense operative force: is it not because he arrives late at the Princess de Guermantes's concert that Proust's narrator is vouchsafed the reminiscences on which the work is based?

LXXVII. THE READERLY II: DETERMINED/DETERMINANT

We have discussed the law of solidarity which governs the readerly: everything holds together, everything must hold together as well as possible (LXVI). Vien is both Sarrasine's accomplice and his heir (he will transmit La Zambinella's image to posterity); these two functions are separated in the sequence of the discourse, so that on the one hand Vien seems to appear in the story for the first time by pure contingency, without our knowing at the time whether he will "re-serve" some purpose (Vien's syntagmatic companions, Lauterbourg and Allegrain, no sooner brought into the discourse, disappear from it forever), and on the other hand, reappearing later on (No. 546) to copy the statue of La Zambinella, Vien is then *recognized*, a recognition which must afford logical satisfaction: is it not fitting that Vien copy the statue Sarrasine has created, since he was his friend? The moral law, the law of value of the readerly, is to *fill in* the chains of causality; for thus each determinant must be, insofar as possible, determined, so that every notation is intermediary, doubly oriented, caught up in an ultimate progression: the old man's deafness determines the narrator to let it be known that he knows his identity (No. 70), but the deafness itself is determined by his great age. So here: Sarrasine arrives late at the ambassador's concert: this is *explained* (preparation for the kidnapping has been time-consuming) and it *explains*: Zambinella is already singing, she will falter in public, Cicognara will notice it and issue the order to have her watched and then to have Sarrasine murdered. Sarrasine's lateness therefore is a crossroad term: determined and determinant, it allows for a *natural* anasto-mosis between the Kidnapping and the Murder. This is the narrative fabric: seemingly subject to the discontinuity of mes-sages, each of which, when it comes into play, is received as a useless supplement (whose very gratuitousness serves to au-thenticate the fiction by what we have called the *reality ef-fect*), but is in fact saturated with pseudo-logical links, relays, doubly oriented terms: in short, it is *calculation* which effects the plenitude of this literature: here dissemination is not the random scattering of meanings toward the infinity of the lan-guage but a simple—temporary—suspension of affinitive, al-ready magnetized elements, before they are summoned to-gether to take their place, economically, in the same *package*.

(463) *but he had come in a traveling carriage drawn by powerful horses and driven by one of the most enterprising* vetturini *of Rome.* ★ ACT. "Kidnapping": 5: rapid means of escape. ★★ REF. Italianness (*vetturini*).

(464) *The ambassador's palazzo was crowded;* ★ ACT. "Con-cert": 3: large audience. ★★ SEM. Star (the crowd is an index of La Zambinella's popularity; this popularity is functional, since it will justify the soprano's and consequently the Lantys' immense fortune.

(465) *not without some difficulty, the sculptor, who was a stranger to everyone present, made his way to the salon where Zambinella was singing at that very moment.* ★ ACT. "Concert": 4: to reach the music room. It takes Sarrasine some time to reach the salon, not only *because* there is a crowd; it is *so that*, retroactively, it can be stated that Zambinella is famous. ★★ REF. Chronology. Sarrasine is a stranger to those present because he has not been in Rome very long (basis for his ignorance): "everything holds together." ★★★ In its turn, after Sarrasine's friend, the discourse adopts the masculine, even though the truth has not yet been revealed either to Sarrasine or to the reader; in fact, the (realistic) discourse adheres mythically to an expressive function: it pretends to believe in the prior existence of a referent (a reality) that it must register, copy, communicate; now, at this point in the story, the referent, i.e., the soprano, is already bodily *before the eyes of the discourse*: the discourse is in the salon, it already sees La Zambinella dressed as a man: it would be carrying the lie a moment too far to continue to refer to a character in the feminine (HER. Enigma 6: decipherment, discourse to the reader).

(466) *"Is it out of consideration for the cardinals, bishops, and abbés present,"* Sarrasine asked, *"that she is dressed like a man, that she is wearing a snood, kinky hair, and a sword?"* ★ The enigma of La Zambinella is situated wholly between two modes of dress: as a woman (No. 323) and as man (here). Clothing appears (or would appear) to be the peremptory proof of sex: yet Sarrasine, determined to preserve his snare at any cost, hopes to destroy fact by disputing motivation (HER. Enigma 6: snare, by Sarrasine, for himself). ★★ From now on, La Zambinella's femininity is "cited" (*she*): it would seem that no one can assume it any longer. However, the origin of this citation is enigmatic: is the discourse italicizing it? Is Sarrasine emphasizing it in speaking the pronoun? (HER. Enigma 6: decipherment). ★★★ *"Kinky hair"*: this is a "realistic" detail, not because it is precise, but because it evokes the image of a Neapolitan *ragazzo* and because this image, in conformity with the historical code of castrati, helps to unmask the boy, decipher the enigma, more surely than the sword or mode of dress (HER. Enigma 6: decipherment, and REF. Historical code of castrati).

183

(467) *"She? What she?" asked the old nobleman to whom Sar-*
rasine had been speaking. "La Zambinella." "La Zambinella!" the
Roman prince replied. "Are you joking? ★ HER. Enigma 6: disclosure, by the collectivity, to Sarrasine. The disclosure occurs by
means of a kind of exclamatory and interrogatory agitation of the
snare; however, since the snare concerns sex, every contestation is
alternative and immediately discloses the *other* term.

(468) *Where are you from?* ★ Every chronological reference
tended to persuade us, "objectively," that Sarrasine's Italian experience was of short duration; this chronological line culminates here
in a diegetic function: Sarrasine's innocence explains the snare in
which he has lived and from which the elderly Prince Chigi is
awakening him (HER. Enigma 6: disclosure: indirect explanation
of the snare).

(469) *Has there ever been a woman on the Roman stage? And*
don't you know about the creatures who sing female roles in the
Papal States? ★ HER. Enigma 6: disclosure (although euphemistic, stated in generalities, and without the word being spoken, the
truth could not be better put: Zambinella is a castrato). ★★ REF.
History of music in the Papal States.

LXXVIII. TO DIE OF IGNORANCE

Résumés of common knowledge, the cultural codes provide
the syllogisms in the narrative (there are many, as we have
seen) with their major premise, based always on public opinion ("probable," as the old logic said), on an endoxal truth, in
short, on the discourse of others. Sarrasine, who has persisted
in proving to himself La Zambinella's false femininity by these
enthymemes, will die because of an inaccurate and inconclu-
sive reasoning: it is from the discourse of others, from its super-
fluity of reasons that he dies. But it is also, inversely and
complementarily, a defect in this discourse which kills him: all
the cultural codes, taken up from citation to citation, together

form an oddly joined miniature version of encyclopedic knowledge, a farrago: this farrago forms the everyday "reality" in relation to which the subject adapts himself, lives. One defect in this encyclopedia, one hole in this cultural fabric, and death can result. Ignorant of the code of Papal customs, Sarrasine dies from a gap in knowledge (*"Don't you know . . ."*), from a blank in the discourse of others. It is significant that this discourse finally succeeds (too late, but it would always have been too late) in reaching Sarrasine through the voice of an old, "realistic" (didn't he try to realize a good investment with his *ragazzo's* voice?) courtier, a spokesman for that vital knowledge on which "reality" is based. What is harshly contrasted to the complex constructions of the symbol (which have taken up the entire story), what is rightfully called upon to triumph over them, is social truth, the code of institutions—the principle of reality.

(470) *I am the one, monsieur, who gave Zambinella his voice. I paid for everything that scamp ever had, even his singing teacher. Well, he has so little gratitude for the service I rendered him that he has never consented to set foot in my house.* ★ Evoking the boy instead of the woman or the castrato, *that scamp* reestablishes (if only fleetingly) a normal—if one can use the word—axis of the sexes (garbled throughout the story by the castrato's uncertain situation, sometimes the essence of femininity, sometimes the disclaimer of all sexuality) (SYM. Axis of the sexes). ★★ SYM. Before castration.

LXXIX. BEFORE CASTRATION

Beyond denoting the truth, Chigi's little speech is fatal in two other ways, according to the images it releases. First, it denominates the boy in Zambinella, forces Sarrasine to retreat from the superlative Woman to the scamp (the Neapolitan boy with kinky hair): he produces in the subject what we might call a *paradigmatic fall*: two diametrically opposed terms (on the one hand the Super-Woman, end and foundation of Art, and on the other a dirty, tattered Neapolitan street boy) are suddenly brought together in one person: the *impossible conjunction* (to use Machiavelli's phrase) occurs; meaning, statutorily based on difference, is abolished: there is no more meaning, and this subversion is fatal. Further, by evoking the time prior to Zambinella's castration (this is not speculation on our part but merely a development of the connotation), Chigi releases a scene, a whole little anterior novel: the *ragazzo* taken in and kept by the old man who takes charge of both his operation (*I paid for everything*) and his education, the ingratitude of the protégé on his way to stardom, cynically taking a richer, more powerful, and visibly more amorous protector (the Cardinal). The image clearly has a sadistic function: it forces Sarrasine to read his beloved as a boy (the only touch of pederasty in the entire story); it vulgarizes castration, situated as a perfectly real surgical operation (dated, endowed with a *before* and an *after*); last, it exposes Chigi as the literal castrator (the one who paid for the operation); now it is this same Chigi who leads Sarrasine to castration and death through the insignificant froth of his prattle: a colorless mediator, lacking symbolic scale, engulfed in contingency, a self-assured upholder of the endoxal Law, but one who, precisely because situated outside meaning, is the very figure of "fate." This is the aggressive function of *chatter* (Proust and James would say: *gossip*), the essence of the discourse of others, and thereby the deadliest language imaginable.

(471) *And yet, if he makes a fortune, he will owe it all to me"* ★
In a hypothetical form, Zambinella's enormous success is predicted. We must here recall that in the eighteenth century a cas-

186

trato could occupy the position and amass the fortune of a great international star. Caffarelli bought a duchy (San Donato), became a duke, and built himself a magnificent palace. Farinelli (*"Il ragazzo"*) left England (where he had triumphed over Handel) covered with gold; proceeding to Spain, he cured the mystic lethargy of Philip V by singing to him daily (moreover, always the same song); and for ten years received from the King an annual pension of 14 million old francs; discharged by Charles III, he built himself a superb palace in Bologna. These facts show the fortune possible for a successful castrato like La Zambinella: the operation paid for by old Chigi could be profitable, and in alluding to this kind of quite financial interest (aside from the fact that money is never symbolically neuter), the discourse connects the Lanty fortune (the initial theme in a chain of enigmas and the "subject" of this "scene from Parisian Life") to a sordid origin: a castration operation, paid for by a Roman prince (for profit or debauch), performed on a young Neapolitan boy who later "threw him over" (SEM. Star).

(472) *Prince Chigi may well have gone on talking for some time; Sarrasine was not listening to him. A horrid truth had crept into his soul. It was as though he had been struck by lightning. He stood motionless, his eyes fixed* ★ HER. Enigma 6: disclosure confirmed. The complete disclosure is accomplished in three stages: (1) agitation of the snare, (2) explanation, (3) its effect.

LXXX. DÉNOUEMENT AND DISCLOSURE

In what Brecht calls dramatic theater, there is a passionate interest in the dénouement; in epic theater, in the development. Sarrasine is a dramatic story (what will happen to the hero? how will he "end up"?), but the dénouement is compromised in a disclosure: what happens, what constitutes the dénouement, is the truth. This truth can have different names, according to likelihoods (critical pertinences): for the anecdote, the truth is a referent (a real object): *Zambinella is a castrato.* For psychology, it is a misfortune: *I have loved a castrato*. For the symbol, it is an enlightenment: *in Zambinella, it is the castrato whom I have loved*. For the narrative, it is a prediction: *having been touched by castration, I must die*. In any event, truth is the predicate at last discovered, the subject at last provided with its complement; since the character, if we grasped it merely on the level of the story's *development*, i.e., from an epic viewpoint, would always appear incomplete, unsaturated, a subject wandering in search of its final predicate: nothing is shown during this wandering but snares, mistakes: the enigma is this predicative lack; disclosing, the discourse completes the logical formula and it is this recovered plenitude which affords the dénouement of the drama: the subject must ultimately be supplied with (own) an attribute, and the mother cell of the entire Occident (subject and predicate) must be saturated. This temporary wandering of the predicate can be described in terms of a game. The dramatic narrative is a game with two players: the snare and the truth. At first a tremendous indetermination rules their encounters, the wandering is wide of the mark; gradually, however, the two networks move closer together, co-penetrate, determination is completed and with it the subject; disclosure is then the final stroke by which the initial "probable" shifts to the "necessary": the game is ended, the drama has its dénouement, the subject correctly "predicated" (fixed): the discourse can do nothing more than fall silent. Contrary to what occurs in the epic work (as Brecht conceived it), nothing *has been* shown (offered an immediate critique by the reader): what is shown is shown in one stroke, and at the end: it is the end which is shown.

(473) *on the false singer.* ★ Enigmatic formulation (*le prétendu chanteur*); we would expect instead the feminine (*la prétendue*

188

chanteuse), for in La Zambinella, it is not the singing which is false but the sex, and since the sex here is masculine (the only gender the language possesses for castrato (*le castrat*), it cannot be "false"; but perhaps it is Zambinella's entire person which is affected by pretension, falseness, imposture, whatever his appearance; in order for this appearance not to be "false," La Zambinella would have to be dressed as a castrato, a costume that Papal society had not provided for (HER. Enigma 6: disclosure).

(474) *His fiery gaze exerted a sort of magnetic influence on Zambinella,* ★ ACT. "Incident" (at a concert, a performance): 1: gaining the attention of the artist on stage.

(475) *for the* musico *finally turned to look at Sarrasine,* ★ ACT. "Incident": 2: attention gained. ★★ REF. Italianness (henceforth the discourse no longer refers to Zambinella in the feminine).

(476) *and at that moment his heavenly voice faltered. He trembled!* ★ ACT. "Incident": 3: artist's difficulty. ★★ ACT. "Danger" (for La Zambinella): 7: reaction of fright.

(477) *An involuntary murmur escaping from the audience he had kept hanging on his lips completed his discomfiture;* ★ ACT. "Incident": 4: collective discomfiture.

(478) *he sat down and cut short his aria.* ★ ACT. "Incident": 5: interruption of the song, of the performance.

(479) *Cardinal Cicognara, who had glanced out the corner of his eye to see what had attracted his protégé's attention, then saw the Frenchman:* ★ ACT. "Murder": 2: indication of the victim. The "Murder" sequence develops on the basis of the Concert Incident, which is thereby justified functionally: without the incident (which itself is due to Sarrasine's delay), there would be no greeting for Zambinella, no murder for Sarrasine.

(480) *he leaned over to one of his ecclesiastical aides-de-camp and appeared to be asking the sculptor's name.* ★ ACT. "Murder": 5: request for information.

(481) *Having obtained the answer he sought,* ★ ACT. "Murder": 4: information received.

(482) *he regarded the artist with great attention* ★ ACT. "Murder": 5: evaluation and interior decision.

(483) *and gave an order to an abbé, who quickly disappeared.* ★ ACT. "Murder": 6: secret order. This portion of the sequence has a semic as well as an operative function: it establishes a "shadowy" atmosphere (occult power of the Church, forbidden loves, secret orders, etc.), the very one which, ironically, Sarrasine had been disappointed not to find when confronted with a carousing theater party instead of a lover's tryst (No. 316).

(484) *During this time, Zambinella, having recovered himself,* ★ ACT. "Incident": 6: to recover oneself.

(485) *once more began the piece* ★ ACT. "Incident": 7: recommence singing.

(486) *he had so capriciously interrupted;* ★ SEM. Star.

LXXXI. VOICE OF THE PERSON

The end approaches, the end of our transcription as well. We must therefore reexamine one by one each of the Voices (each of the codes) whose grid has formed the text. Here is one of the very last semes. What is it then that we have learned from the inventory of these semes? The seme (or the signified of connotation, strictly speaking) is a connotator of persons, places, objects, of which the signified is a *character*. Character is an adjective, an attribute, a predicate (for example: *unnatural, shadowy, star, composite, excessive, impious,* etc.). Even though the connotation may be clear, the nomination of its signified is uncertain, approximative, unstable: to fasten a name to this signified depends in large part on the critical pertinence to which we adhere: the seme is only a *departure*, an avenue of meaning. These avenues can be arranged to form various landscapes: these are thematics (we have done no such arranging here, we have only given a list of these characters, without putting them in any particular order). If we set aside the semes of objects or atmospheres, actually rather rare (here, at least), what is constant is that the seme is linked to an ideology of the person (to inventory the semes in a classic text is therefore merely to observe this ideology): the person is no more than a collection of semes (inversely, however, semes can migrate from one figure in the text to another, if we descend to a certain symbolic depth, where there is no longer any respect of persons: Sarrasine and the narrator have semes in common). Thus, from a classic viewpoint (more psychological than symbolic), Sarrasine is the sum, the point of convergence, of: *turbulence, artistic gift, independence, excess, femininity, ugliness, composite nature, impiety, love of whittling, will*, etc.). What gives the illusion that the sum is supplemented by a precious remainder (something like *individuality*, in that, qualitative and ineffable, it may escape the vulgar bookkeeping of compositional characters) is the Proper Name, the difference completed by what is *proper* to it. The proper name enables the person to exist outside the semes, whose sum nonetheless constitutes it entirely. As soon as a Name exists (even a pronoun) to flow toward and fasten onto, the semes become predicates, inductors of truth, and the Name becomes a subject: we can say that what is proper to narrative is not action but the character as Proper Name: the semic raw material (corresponding to a certain moment of our history of the narrative) *completes* what is proper to being, *fills* the name with adjectives. The inventory and structuration of semes, the reception of this Voice of the person, can be of great service to psychological criticism, of minor service to thematic criticism, of minor service to psychoanalytical criticism: everything depends on the level where we halt the nomination of the seme.

(487) *but he sang it badly,* ★ The remaining disturbance no longer refers to the concert incident but to Zambinella's awareness of the danger threatening him (ACT. "Danger": 8: feeling of threat).

(488) *and despite all the requests made to him, he refused to sing anything else.* ★ ACT. "Incident": 8: refusal to prolong the concert, the performance.

(489) *This was the first time he displayed that capricious tyranny for which he would later be as celebrated as for his talent* ★ SEM. Star. Here we see clearly the nature of the connotative seme: the "capricious" character of stars is not accounted for in any dictionary unless it be a dictionary of Accepted Ideas—which would be a dictionary of customary connotations. ★★ Articulated around the "Danger" run by Zambinella, a new sequence will shortly develop around the very precise threat the sculptor will bring to bear on the castrato during his kidnapping; the outcome of this sequence is already suggested here: the future (*later*) assures us that Zambinella will survive Sarrasine's aggression (ACT. "Threat": 1: prediction of outcome).

(490) *and his vast fortune, due, as they said, no less to his voice than to his beauty.* ★ The chain of enigmas is almost reconstituted. As soon as we know that the aged Zambinella is Mme de Lanty's uncle, already aware from this lexia of the castrato's fortune, we shall know the source of the Lanty fortune (HER. Enigma 2: the Lanty fortune: theme recalled). That Zambinella's beauty counts for something in his vast fortune can only refer to the amorous "protection" afforded him by the Cardinal: therefore, the origin of the Lanty fortune is "impure" (deriving from a "prostitution").

(491) *"It is a woman," Sarrasine said, believing himself alone. "There is some hidden intrigue here. Cardinal Cicognara is deceiv-*

ing the Pope and the whole city of Rome!" ★ HER. Enigma 6: snare, by Sarrasine, for himself. The reflexive snare (Sarrasine for Sarrasine) survives the disclosure: we know that the sculptor prefers the evidence of codes to the evidence of facts. ★★ REF. Machiavellian code (a fictional network of secret intrigues, shadowy impostures, subtle and preposterous deceptions: realm of paranoia and the code of Florentine and Papal Italy).

(492) *The sculptor thereupon left the salon,* ★ ACT. "Concert": 5: to leave the music room.

(493) *gathered his friends together,* ★ ACT. "Kidnapping": 6: gathering of the accomplices.

(494) *and posted them out of sight in the courtyard of the palazzo.* ★ ACT. "Kidnapping": 7: ambush.

(495) *When Zambinella was confident that Sarrasine had departed, he appeared to regain his composure.* ★ ACT. "Danger": 9: to become calm again.

(496) *Around midnight, having wandered through the rooms like a man seeking some enemy,* ★ REF. Chronology (*around midnight*, i.e., the evening of the concert). ★★ ACT. "Danger": 10: continued uneasiness. The "Danger" sequence will henceforth yield to the "Threat" sequence, which will take place in the studio where Sarrasine holds Zambinella prisoner. Although these two proaireticisms are very close, they are not of the same order. Danger here consists of a series of premonitions or of reactions to repeated incidents; Threat is a sequence constructed according to the design of a crisis; Danger may be an open, infinite series; Threat is a closed structure, requiring an end. Nevertheless, the two are structurally related: the dispersal of the terms of Danger serves to *mark* the object of the threat; long since designated as the victim, Zambinella can then enter the crisis of the Threat.

(497) *the* musico *departed.* ★ ACT. "Kidnapping": 8: the victim's innocent departure.

(498) *As soon as he crossed the threshold of the palazzo, he was adroitly seized by men who gagged him with a handkerchief and*

drew him into the carriage Sarrasine had hired. ★ ACT. "Kidnapping": 9: the act itself. This Kidnapping is structurally perfect: the accomplices were recruited in No. 460, gathered together in No. 493, stationed in ambush in No. 494, the (fast) carriage was brought in No. 463.

(499) *Frozen with horror, Zambinella remained in a corner, not daring to move. He saw before him the terrible face of the artist, who was silent as death.* ★ ACT. "Threat": 2: terrorized victim.

(500) *The journey was brief.* ★ ACT. "Kidnapping": 10: journey. In other narratives, this term is open to an infinite catalysis that lasts for an entire novel, an entire film.

(501) *Carried in Sarrasine's arms, Zambinella soon found himself in a dark, empty studio.* ★ ACT. "Kidnapping": 11: arrival at the hide-out.

(502) *Half dead, the singer remained in a chair,* ★ ACT. "Threat": 3: immobilized victim.

(503) *without daring to examine the statue of a woman in which he recognized his own features.* Another, more logical version of the text has: *"in which he had recognized his own features."* ★ ACT. "Statue": 1: thematization of the object which will centralize a certain number of actions. ★★ SYM. Replication of bodies: the statue is one link in that long chain which duplicates the bodies of the Essential Woman, from La Zambinella to Girodet's Endymion.

(504) *He made no attempt to speak, but his teeth chattered.* ★ ACT. "Threat": 4: mute victim.

(505) *Sarrasine paced up and down the room. Suddenly he stopped in front of Zambinella. "Tell me the truth,"* he pleaded ★ HER. Enigma 6: disclosure: equivocation. The disclosure has been made, but the subject is still uncertain. *Tell me the truth* implies: (1) that Sarrasine continues to doubt and hope; (2) that he already regards Zambinella as a "scamp" with whom he can

employ the familiar form of address (Sarrasine has heretofore addressed Zambinella as *"tu"* only twice, 444 and 445, but then as a sublime being, deserving of the high lyric apostrophe).

(506) *in a low, altered voice.* ★ The low sound (coming from the muffled depths of the body) is (in the West) supposed to connote the interiority—and thus the truth—of an emotion: Sarrasine *knows* Zambinella is not a woman (HER. Enigma 6: decipherment, Sarrasine for himself).

(507) *"You are a woman?* ★ HER. Enigma 6: equivocation (the snare implied by the statement is corrected by its interrogative form).

(508) *Cardinal Cicognara . . ."* ★ HER. Enigma 6: snare, by Sarrasine, for himself (Sarrasine returns to the notion of some Roman intrigue [No. 491], an explanation that preserves Zambinella's femininity). ★★ REF. Machiavellian code.

(509) *Zambinella fell to his knees, and in reply lowered his head.* ★ HER. Enigma 6: disclosure, Zambinella to Sarrasine.

(510) *"Ah, you are a woman," the artist cried in a delirium, "for even a . . ." He broke off. "No," he continued, "he would not be so cowardly."* ★ HER. Enigma 6: snare, by Sarrasine, for himself. Psychological proof furnishes Sarrasine his last snare, and provides delirium its last refuge. This proof bases femininity on the weakness of woman. Faced with this proof, which he has often employed, Sarrasine is nonetheless encumbered with a new term, the castrato, which he must situate in the moral hierarchy of biological creatures; since he needs to locate absolute, ultimate weakness in Woman, he gives the castrato an intermediate position (*"even a castrato would not be so cowardly"*); the enthymeme, on which all proof is based, is organized as follows: woman occupies the last stage of pusillanimity; Zambinella, by his submissive posture, the cowardliness of his behavior, attains this last stage; thus Zambinella is really a woman. ★★ SYM. Taboo on the word castrato. ★★★ SYM. Graphological mark of the neuter: the underlined, cited *he*, whose masculinity is suspect.

(511) *"Ah, do not kill me,"* cried Zambinella, *bursting into tears.* ★ ACT. "Threat": 5: first plea for mercy. Pleas for mercy do not necessarily follow on an explicit threat, but a diffuse threat, connoted by the situation and by Sarrasine's *delirium.*

(512) *"I only agreed to trick you to please my friends, who wanted to laugh."* ★ HER. "Machination": 12: disclosure of the motive for the machination (we know that Laughter is a substitute castrator).

(513) *"Laugh!" the sculptor replied in an infernal tone. "Laugh! Laugh! You dared play with a man's feelings, you?"* The castrating role of Laughter is confirmed here by the virile protest, linked to the threat of castration, which Sarrasine offers in opposition to it. We know that Adler had first suggested the phrase *male protest* for the rejection of all passive attitudes toward other men, and that it has subsequently been suggested that this protest be more explicitly defined as a *repudiation of femininity.* Sarrasine is in fact repudiating a femininity of which he himself bears traces; the "paradox" emphasized by Sarrasine himself is that his virility should have been contested, under the castrating tool of Laughter, by a creature whose very definition was that he had been stripped of his virility (SYM. Virile protest).

(514) *"Oh, have mercy!" Zambinella replied.* ★ ACT. "Threat": 6: second plea for mercy.

(515) *"I ought to kill you," Sarrasine cried, drawing his sword with a violent gesture.* ★ ACT. "Threat": 7: first threat of death (the conditional already indicates the suspension of the threat).

(516) *"However," he went on, in cold disdain,* ★ ACT. "Threat": 8: threat withdrawn.

(517) *were I to scour your body with this blade, would I find there one feeling to stifle, one vengeance to satisfy? You are nothing. If you were a man or a woman, I would kill you,* ★ SYM. The *nothingness* of the castrato. The reasoning is as follows: "You wanted to lure me into castration. In order to avenge myself and

punish you, I should castrate you too [*to scour your body with this blade*], but I cannot, since you are already castrated." The loss of desire puts the castrato beyond life or death, *outside all classification*: how to kill what is not classified? How to reach what transgresses, not the internal order of the sexual paradigm (a transvestite would have inverted this order but not destroyed it: *If you were a man, I would kill you*), but the very existence of difference which generates life and meaning; the ultimate horror is not death but that the classification of death and life should be broken off.

(518) *but . . ."*
  Sarrasine made a gesture of disgust ★ SYM. Taboo on the word castrato. ★★ SYM. Horror, curse, exclusion.

(519) *which forced him to turn away, whereupon he saw the statue.* ★ ACT. "Statue": 2: to see the object previously thematized.

LXXXII. GLISSANDO

Two codes set side by side in the same sentence: this operation, a common device of the readerly, is not indifferent: poured into the same linguistic unit, the two codes here form an apparently *natural* link; this *nature* (which is simply that of age-old syntax) is fulfilled each time the discourse can produce an *elegant* relation (in the mathematical sense: *an elegant solution*) between two codes. This elegance is associated with a kind of causal *glissando* which allows the symbolic fact to join the proairetic facts, for example, in the continuity of a single sentence. Thus, we articulate disgust for the castrato (symbolic term) and destruction of the statue (proairetic term) by a whole chain of tiny causalities strung close together, like beads sliding on an apparently smooth thread: (1) Sarrasine is disgusted at the sight of the castrato; (2) disgust makes him avert his eyes from this sight; (3) averting his eyes makes him turn his head; (4) as he turns, his eyes fall upon the statue, etc.: a whole marquetry of articulations that enable us to pass, as if from lock to lock, from the symbolic to the operative across the great naturalness of the sentence (*"Sarrasine made a gesture of disgust which forced him to turn away, where-upon he saw the statue."*) Brought to the surface of the discourse, the codal citation there loses its identity, it receives like a new garment the syntactical form deriving from the "eternal" sentence, that form justifies it and enthrones it in the vast nature of *ordinary* language.

(520) *"And it's an illusion," he cried.* ★ ACT. "Statue": 3: to be deceived (by the falsehood, the void, of the thematized object). ★★ HER. Enigma 6: disclosure, Sarrasine to himself.

(521) *Then, turning to Zambinella: "A woman's heart was a refuge for me, a home. Have you any sisters who resemble you?* ★ SYM. Replication of bodies. ★★ Zambinella's sisters permit a fleeting image of a female castrato, a corrected, cured castrato (SYM. The rectified castrato).

LXXXIII. PANDEMIA

Castration is contagious, it touches everything it approaches (it will touch Sarrasine, the narrator, the young woman, the narrative, the money): this is one of the "demonstrations" of *Sarrasine.* So with the statue: if it is an "illusion," this is not because by artificial means it copies a real object whose materiality it cannot possess (banal proposition) but because this object (La Zambinella) is empty. The "realist" work must be guaranteed by the integral truth of the model which the copying artist must know to its innermost depths (we know the function of undressing with regard to the sculptor Sarrasine); in the case of La Zambinella, the internal hollowness of any statue (which doubtless attracts many lovers of statuary and provides iconoclasm with its entire symbolic context) reproduces the central deficiency of the castrato: the statue is ironically true, dramatically unworthy: the emptiness of the model has invaded the copy, communicating to it its sense of horror: the statue has been touched by the metonymic force of castration. It is understandable that the subject should oppose this contagion with the dream of an inverse, *favorable,* saving metonymy: that of the essence of Femininity. The hoped-for sisters permit imagining a rectified, re-sexualized, cured castrato who would slough off his mutilation like some hideous envelope, retaining only his correct femininity. In the *mores* of certain peoples, society prescribes marrying not a person but a kind of family essence (sorority, sororal polygyny, levirate); similarly, Sarrasine is pursuing, far beyond the slough of castration the castrato leaves in his hands, a Zambinellan essence —which later on, moreover, will flourish anew in Marianina and Filippo.

(522) *Then die!* ★ ACT. "Threat": 9: second threat of death.

(523) *But no, you shall live. Isn't leaving you alive condemning you to something worse than death?* ★ ACT. "Threat": 10: withdrawal of the threat. ★★ SYM. The castrato outside any system. Death itself is touched, corrupted, is disnamed (*disfigured,* as the expression goes) by castration. There is a real death, an active death, a *classified* death which is part of the system of life: being outside the system, the castrato no longer even has access to this death.

(524) *It is neither my blood nor my existence that I regret, but the future and my heart's fortune. Your feeble hand has destroyed my happiness.* ★ Sarrasine comments on his death, which he has therefore accepted (ACT. "Will-to-die": 5: to comment on one's death in advance). ★★ SYM. Contagion of castration.

(525) *What hope can I strip from you for all those you have blighted? You have dragged me down to your level. To love, to be loved! are henceforth meaningless words for me, as they are for you.* ★ SYM. Contagion of castration: Sarrasine castrated.

LXXXIV. LITERATURE REPLETE

The Zambinellan disease has overtaken Sarrasine ("*You have dragged me down to your level*"). Here the contagious force of castration explodes. Its metonymic power is irreversible: touched by its void, not only is sex eradicated, but art too is broken (the statue is destroyed), language dies ("*to love, to be loved! are henceforth meaningless words for me*"): by which we can see that according to Sarrasinean metaphysics, meaning, art, and sex form a single sustitutive chain: that of the *replete*. As the product of an art (that of narration), the mobilization of a polysemic system (that of the classical text) and a thematics of sex, the story itself is an emblem of plenitude (though what it *represents*, as we shall soon state more clearly, is the catastrophic confusion of this plenitude): the text is replete with multiple, discontinuous, accumulated meanings, and yet burnished, smoothed by the "natural" movement of its sentences: it is an egg-text. A Renaissance author (Pierre Fabri) once wrote a treatise entitled *Le grand et vrai art de pleine rhétorique*. In like manner, we can say that any classic (readerly) text is implicitly an art of Replete Literature: literature that is replete: like a cupboard where meanings are shelved, stacked, safeguarded (in this text nothing is ever lost: meaning recuperates everything); like a pregnant female, replete with signifieds which criticism will not fail to deliver; like the sea, replete with depths and movements which give it its appearance of infinity, its vast meditative surface; like the sun, replete with the glory it sheds over those who write it, or finally, acknowledged as an established and recognized art: institutional. This Replete Literature, readerly literature, can no longer be written: symbolic plenitude (culminating in romantic art) is the last avatar of our culture.

(526) *I shall forever think of this imaginary woman when I see a real woman." He indicated the statue with a gesture of despair.* ★ The statue, the imaginary (superlative) woman, and the real woman are links in the duplicative chain of bodies, catastrophically broken by the castrato's deficiency (SYM. Replication of bodies). ★★ ACT. "Statue": 4: despair aroused by the thematized object.

(527) *"I shall always have the memory of a celestial harpy who thrusts its talons into all my manly feelings, and who will stamp all other women with a seal of imperfection!* ★ SYM. Contagion of castration. The image of the Harpies connotes both castration (the creature with talons) and guilt (the theme of the Furies). The code of female bodies, a written code if ever there was one, since it is the code of art, of culture, will henceforth be *stamped* by deficiency.

(528) *Monster!* ★ Here the apostrophe has its literal plenitude: the monster is outside nature, outside any classification, any meaning (this seme has already been attached to the old man) (SEM. Outside nature).

(529) *You who can give life to nothing.* ★ SYM. Replication of bodies.

LXXXV. INTERRUPTED REPLICATION

As an "imaginary" woman—imaginary, that is, in the modern sense, i.e., evoked in Sarrasine by the misreading of his unconscious—La Zambinella served as a relay between contingent, fragmented speech (real women: so many fetishes) and the code establishing all beauty, the masterpiece, both goal and point of departure. Once this relay is defective (it is empty), the entire system of transmission collapses: we have the Sarrasinean de-ception, dis-connection of the entire circuit of bodies. The banal definition of being-castrated (*"You who can give life to nothing"*) thus has a structural bearing, it concerns not merely the aesthetic duplication of bodies (the "copy" of realist art) but also the metonymic force in its generality: the fundamental crime or disaster (*"Monster!"*) is in fact to interrupt the circulation of (aesthetic or biological) copies, to disturb the controlled permeability of meanings, their *concatenation*, which is classification and repetition, as with language. Itself metonymic (and with what power!), castration jams all metonymy: the chains of art and life are broken, as in a moment will be the statue, emblem of the glorious transmission of bodies (but it will be saved, and something will be transmitted to the Adonis, to the Endymion, to the Lantys, to the narrator, to the reader).

(530) *For me, you have wiped women from the earth."* ★ SYM. Pandemic castration. ★★ The hero's physical death is preceded by three partial deaths: to women, to pleasures, to art (ACT. "Will-to-die": 6: to die to women).

(531) *Sarrasine sat down before the terrified singer. Two huge tears welled from his dry eyes, rolled down his manly cheeks, and fell to the ground: two tears of rage, two bitter and burning tears.* ★ REF. Code of Tears. The code of the hero allows a man to cry

within the very strict limits of a certain ritual, itself strongly historical: Michelet complimented and envied St. Louis for having had the "gift of tears," audiences cried abundantly at Racine's tragedies, etc., whereas in Japan, in the Bushido, a code inherited from the Samurai, any physical sign of emotion is forbidden. Sarrasine has the right to cry for four reasons (or on four conditions): because his dream as an artist, a lover, has been destroyed; because he is about to die (it would not be fitting for him to survive his tears); because he is alone (the castrato being nothing); because the very contrast between virility and tears inspires pathos. Further, his tears are few (two) and burning (they do not participate in the unworthy humidity associated with femininity, but in fire, dryness, virility).

(532) *"No more love! I am dead to all pleasure, to every human emotion."* ★ SYM. Contagion of castration. ★★ ACT. "Will-to-die": 7: to die to pleasure, to feeling.

(533) *So saying, he seized a hammer and hurled it at the statue with such extraordinary force* ★ ACT. "Will-to-die": 8: to die to Art. ★★ "Statue": 5: destructive act.

(534) *that he missed it. He thought he had destroyed this monument to his folly,* ★ ACT. "Statue": 6: statue spared. ★★ SYM. Replication of bodies: the chain, *in extremis*, is saved.

(535) *and then took up his sword and brandished it to kill the singer.* ★ ACT. "Threat": 11: third threat of death.

(536) *Zambinella uttered piercing screams.* ★ ACT. "Threat": 12: to call for help. The victim's call for help will allow the two sequences "Threat" and "Murder" to combine: the victim will be saved because his attacker will be killed: the rescuers of the former will be the murderers of the latter.

LXXXVI. THE EMPIRIC VOICE

Soon all the proairetic sequences will be closed. The narrative will die. What do we know about them? That they are born of a certain power of the reading, which tries to give a sufficiently transcendent name to a series of actions, themselves deriving from a patrimonial hoard of human experiences; that the typology of these proaireticisms seems uncertain or that at least they can be assigned no logic other than that of the probable, of empirics, of the "already-done" or "already-written," for the number and the order of their terms vary, some deriving from a practical reservoir of trivial everyday acts (*to knock at a door, to arrange a rendezvous*) and others from a written corpus of novelistic models (*the Abduction, the Declaration of Love, the Murder*); that such sequences are generally open to catalysis, to branching, and can form "trees"; that when subjected to a logico-temporal order, they constitute the strongest armature of the readerly; that by their typically sequential nature, simultaneously syntagmatic and organized, they can form the favored raw material for a certain structural analysis of narrative.

(537) *At that moment, three men entered* ★ ACT. "Threat": 13: arrival of the rescuers. ★★ ACT. "Murder: 7: entrance of the murderers.

(538) *and at once the sculptor fell, stabbed by three stiletto thrusts.* ★ ACT. "Threat": 14: elimination of the aggressor. ★★ ACT. "Murder": 8: murder of the hero. The weapons are coded: the sword is the phallic weapon of honor, of thwarted passion, of virile protest (with which Sarrasine tried first to charm La Zambinella, 301, and then to kill the castrato, 535); the stiletto (little phallus) is the contemptible weapon of hired killers, the weapon fit for the henceforth castrated hero.

(539) *"On behalf of Cardinal Cicognara,"* one of them said. ★ ACT. "Murder": 9: signature of the murder.

(540) *"It is a good deed worthy of a Christian,"* replied the Frenchman *as he died.* ★ Despite the ironic allusion to the murderer's
religion, the victim's blessing turns the murder into a suicide: the
subject assumes his death, in accord with the pact he had made
with himself (No. 240) and with the symbolic fate to which contact with castration has committed him (ACT. "Will-to-die": 9:
to assume one's death).

(541) *These sinister messengers* ★ REF. Novelistic mystery (cf.
below, *the closed carriage*).

LXXXVII. THE VOICE OF SCIENCE

The cultural codes, from which the Sarrasinean text has drawn
so many references, will also be extinguished (or at least will
emigrate to other texts; there is no lack of hosts): one might
say that it is the major voice of minor science that is departing
in this fashion. In fact, these citations are extracted from a
body of knowledge, from an anonymous Book whose best
model is doubtless the School Manual. For, on the one hand,
this anterior Book is both a book of science (of empirical observation) and a book of wisdom, and on the other hand, the
didactic material mobilized in the text (often, as we have
noted, as a basis for reasoning or to lend its written authority
to emotions) generally corresponds to the set of seven or eight
handbooks accessible to a diligent student in the classical bourgeois educational system: a History of Literature (Byron, *The
Thousand and One Nights*, Ann Radcliffe, Homer), a History
of Art (Michelangelo, Raphael, the Greek miracle), a History
of Europe (the age of Louis XV), an Outline of Practical
Medicine (disease, convalescence, old age, etc.), a Treatise on
Psychology (erotic, ethnic, etc.), an Ethics (Christian or Stoic:
themes from Latin translations), a Logic (for syllogisms), a

Rhetoric, and an anthology of maxims and proverbs about life, death, suffering, love, women, ages of man, etc. Although entirely derived from books, these codes, by a swivel characteristic of bourgeois ideology, which turns culture into nature, appear to establish reality, "Life." "Life" then, in the classic text, becomes a nauseating mixture of common opinions, a smothering layer of received ideas: in fact, it is in these cultural codes that what is outmoded in Balzac, the essence of what, in Balzac, cannot be (re)written, is concentrated. What is outmoded, of course, is not a defect in performance, a personal inability of the author to afford opportunities in his work for what will be modern, but rather a fatal condition of Replete Literature, mortally stalked by the army of stereotypes it contains. Thus, a critique of the references (the cultural codes) has never been tenable except through trickery, on the very limits of Replete Literature, where it is possible (but at the cost of what acrobatics and with what uncertainty) to criticize the stereotype (to vomit it up) without recourse to a new stereotype: that of irony. Perhaps this is what Flaubert did (we shall say it once again), particularly in *Bouvard et Pécuchet*, where the two copyists of scholastic codes are themselves "represented" in an uncertain status, the author using no metalanguage (or a suspended metalanguage) in their regard. In fact, the cultural code occupies the same position as stupidity: how can stupidity be pinned down without declaring onself intelligent? How can one code be superior to another without abusively closing off the plurality of codes? Only writing, by assuming the largest possible plural in its own task, can oppose without appeal to force the imperialism of each language.

(542) *informed Zambinella of the concern of his protector, who was waiting at the door in a closed carriage, to take him away as*

soon as he had been rescued. ★ ACT. "Threat": 15: to return with the rescuers. ★★ ACT. "Murder": 10: final explanation.

(543) *"But," Mme de Rochefide asked me, "what connection is there between this story and the little old man we saw at the Lantys'?"* ★ HER. Enigma 4 (Who is the old man?): formulation.

(544) *"Madame, Cardinal Cicognara took possession of Zambinella's statue and had it executed in marble; today it is in the Albani Museum.* ★ ACT. "Statue": 7: the statue (aimed at and missed) rediscovered. ★★ Yet another link in the duplicative chain of bodies: the statue was copied in marble. Desire is once again the agent of this duplicative energy: Cicognara, who has no scruples about appropriating his victim's work and contemplating his favorite's effigy through his rival's eyes, *passes,* as in a game of "button-button," his desire and the castration which is in this case attached to it, on to posterity: this desire will continue to impregnate Vien's Adonis (desired by Mme de Rochefide) and Girodet's Endymion visited by the moon (SYM. Replication of bodies).

(545) *There, in 1791, the Lanty family found it* ★ REF. Chronology. In fact, the item is a dead end, it cannot be connected with any other information (nor is it incompatible with any other: the life of Vien, for example, who died in 1809); it is a pure effect of "reality": nothing is more "real," we think, than a date. ★★ HER. Enigma 3 (Who are the Lantys?): beginning of an answer (there is a connection between the Lantys and the statue).

(546) *and asked Vien to copy it.* ★ SYM. Replication of bodies.

LXXXVIII. FROM SCULPTURE TO PAINTING

Sarrasine dead, La Zambinella emigrates from statue to canvas: something *dangerous* has been contained, exorcised, pacified. In passing from volume to plane surface, the copy loses or at least attenuates the burning problematics the story has continually evoked. Free-standing, penetrable, in short *profound*, the statue invites visitation, exploration, penetration: it implies ideally the plenitude and truth of the *inside* (which is why it is a tragedy that this inside is empty, castrated); according to Sarrasine, the perfect statue would have been an envelope containing a real woman (supposing she herself were a *masterpiece*), whose essence as reality would have verified, guaranteed the marble skin applied to her (this relation, in the opposite direction, gives us the Pygmalion myth: a real woman is born from the statue). The painting, by contrast, may have a back, but it has no inside: it cannot provoke the *indiscreet* act by which one might try to find out what there is *behind* the canvas (except, as we have seen, in Frenhofer's dream; he wanted us to be able to move *within* the picture, as though in three-dimensional space, to walk around the flesh of painted bodies, so as to test their authenticity). The Sarrasinean aesthetic of the statue is tragic, it risks the fall of desired plenitude into castrated emptiness, of meaning in outside-meaning; the aesthetic of the canvas—less emblematic, more indifferent—is more easily satisfied: a statue breaks; a canvas, more simply, blurs (as happens, in its self-destruction, to the "unknown masterpiece"). Passed down along the duplicative chain in the paintings of Vien and Girodet, the sinister story of La Zambinella grows distant, no longer exists save as a vague, moon-struck enigma, mysterious without being offensive (although the mere sight of the painted Adonis will reactivate the castrating metonymy: it is because she is seduced by it that the young woman provokes the narrator to the narrative that will castrate both of them). As for the final avatar, the passage of the canvas to written "representation," it recuperates all the preceding copies, but writing extenuates still further the hallucination of the *inside*, for it has no other substance than the interstice.

(547) *The portrait in which you saw Zambinella at twenty, a second after having seen him at one hundred, later served for Girodet's* Endymion; *you will have recognized its type in the Adonis."*
★ REF. Chronology (Zambinella is twenty in 1758; if he is actually one hundred at the time of the Lanty party, then this must occur in 1838, eight years after Balzac wrote it, cf. No. 55). ★★ HER. Enigma 4 (Who is the old man?): partial disclosure (the disclosure concerns the old man's public identity: he is La Zambinella; it remains to disclose his family identity, his relationship to the Lantys). ★★★ SYM. Replication of bodies. ★★★★ HER. Enigma 5 (Who is the Adonis?): disclosure (La Zambinella at twenty).

(548) *"But this Zambinella—he or she?"*
"He, madame, is none other than Marianina's great-uncle. ★ HER. Enigma 4: complete disclosure (the old man's family identity). ★★ HER. Enigma 3: disclosure (Who are the Lantys?— relatives of La Zambinella). ★★★ What grammatical gender to apply to the castrato? The neuter, probably, but French has none; thus this alternative he/she, the oscillation of which, as in physics, produces a kind of average sex, equidistant from masculine and feminine (SYM. Neuter).

(549) *Now you can readily see what interest Mme de Lanty has in hiding the source of a fortune which comes from—"* ★ HER. Enigma 2 (source of the Lanty fortune): disclosure.

LXXXIX. VOICE OF TRUTH

All the enigmas are now disclosed, the vast hermeneutic sentence is closed (all that will continue a little longer is what we might call the metonymic vibration of castration, whose last waves will disturb the young woman and the narrator). We now know the morphemes (or the "hermeneutemes") of this hermeneutic sentence, this *period* of truth (in the rhetorical sense). They are: (1) *thematization,* or an emphasizing of the subject which will be the object of the enigma; (2) *proposal*, a metalinguistic index which, by signaling in a thousand different ways that an enigma exists, designates the hermeneutic (or enigmatic) *genus*; (3) *formulation* of the enigma; (4) *promise of an answer* (or *request for an answer*); (5) *snare*, a pretense which must be defined, if possible, by its circuit of destination (by one character for another, for himself, by the discourse for the reader); (6) *equivocation*, or double understanding, the mixture in a single statement of a snare and a truth; (7) *jamming*, acknowledgment of the insolubility of the enigma; (8) *suspended answer* (after having been begun); (9) *partial answer*, which consists in stating only one of the features whose total will form the complete identification of the truth; (10) *disclosure*, *decipherment*, which is, in the pure enigma (whose model is always the Sphinx's question to Oedipus), a final nomination, the discovery and uttering of the irreversible word.

(550) *"Enough!" she said, gesturing to me imperiously. We sat for a moment plunged in the deepest silence.* ★ SYM. Taboo on castration. ★★ SYM. Horror of castration. The disgust attached to the Lanty fortune (the theme of this "scene from Parisian life") has several sources: it is a fortune tainted by prostitution (the *ragazzo* kept by old Chigi and later by Cardinal Cicognara), by blood (Sarrasine's murder), but especially imbued with the horror consubstantial with castration.

(551) *"Well?" I said to her.*
"Ah," she exclaimed, standing up and pacing up and down the room. She looked at me and spoke in an altered voice. ★ Castration reaches the young woman: she shows symptoms of illness (agitation, confusion) (SYM. Contagion of castration).

(552) *"You have given me a disgust for life and for passions that will last a long time.* ★ SYM. Contagion of castration. ★★ Cas-

tration has arrived by the bearer of the narrative (ACT. "To narrate": 13: castrating effect of the narration).

XC. THE BALZACIAN TEXT

A *long time?* Hardly. Béatrix, Countess Arthur de Rochefide, born in 1808, married in 1828, and very quickly weary of her husband, taken to the Lantys' ball by the narrator around 1830—and stricken then, she says, by a mortal castration—will nevertheless three years later run off to Italy with the tenor Conti, will have a celebrated affair with Calyste du Guénic to spite her friend and rival Félicité des Touches, will later become the mistress of La Palférine, etc.: castration is obviously not a mortal disease, one can be cured of it. However, to be cured we must leave *Sarrasine* and emigrate to other texts (*Béatrix, Modeste Mignon, Une Fille d'Eve, Autre Etude de Femme, Les Secrets de la Princesse de Cadignan,* etc.). These texts form the Balzacian text. There is no reason not to include the Sarrasinean text within the Balzacian text (we could have done so had we wanted to continue, to develop this game of the plural): by degrees, a text can come into contact with any other system: the inter-text is subject to no law but the infinitude of its reprises. The Author himself—that somewhat decrepit deity of the old criticism—can or could some day become a text like any other: he has only to avoid making his person the subject, the impulse, the origin, the authority, the Father, whence his work would proceed, by a channel of *expression*; he has only to see himself as a being on paper and his life as a *bio-graphy* (in the etymological sense of the word), a writing without referent, substance of a *connection* and not of a *filiation*: the critical undertaking (if we can still speak of criticism) will then consist in *returning* the documentary figure of the author into a novelistic, irretrievable, irresponsible figure, caught up in the plural of its own text: a task whose adventure has already been recounted, not by critics, but by authors themselves, a Proust, a Jean Genet.

(553) *Excepting for monsters, don't all human feelings come down to the same thing, to horrible disappointments? Mothers, our children kill us either by their bad behavior or by their lack of affection. Wives, we are deceived. Mistresses, we are forsaken, abandoned. Does friendship even exist?* ★ Engaged, under the narrative action in a labor of auto-castration, the young woman immediately elaborates the sublime version of her disease; she dresses up this retreat from sex, dignifies it by putting it under the comforting and ennobling authority of a high moral code (SYM. Alibi of castration). ★★ This code is the code of universal pessimism, of the vanity of the world and of the ungrateful, stoic, and admirable role of noble victims, mothers, wives, mistresses, and friends (REF. V*anitas vanitatum*).

(554) *I would become a nun tomorrow did I not know that I can remain unmoved as a rock amid the storms of life.* ★ SYM. Alibi of castration: Virtue (cultural code).

(555) *If the Christian's future is also an illusion, at least it is not destroyed until after death.* ★ REF. Christian code.

(556) *Leave me."*
"*Ah,*" I said, "*you know how to punish.*" ★ Touched by castration, the young woman breaks the contract with the narrator, withdraws from the bargain and dismisses her partner (ACT. "To narrate": 14: breaking of contract). ★★ SYM. The narrator drawn into castration (he is punished for having "told").

XCI. MODIFICATION

A man in love, taking advantage of the curiosity evidenced by his mistress about an enigmatic old man and a mysterious portrait, offers her a contract: the truth in exchange for a night of love, a narrative in exchange for a body. After having attempted to bargain her way out of it, the young woman agrees: the narrative begins; but it turns out to be the story of a terrible disease animated by an irresistible contagious strength; carried by the narrative itself, this disease ends by contaminating the lovely listener and, withdrawing her from love, keeps her from honoring the contract. Caught in his own trap, the lover is rebuffed: a story about castration is not told with impunity. —This fable teaches us that narration (object) modifies narration (action): the message is parametrically linked with its performance; there is no question of an utterance on the one hand and on the other its uttering. Telling is a responsible and commercial act (are these not the same thing? in both cases, a matter of *weighing?*) whose outcome (the virtuality of transformation) is "indexed" on the price of the merchandise, on the object of the narrative. This object, therefore, is not final, it is not the goal, the term, the end of the narration (*Sarrasine* is not a "story about a castrato"): as meaning, the subject of the anecdote harbors a recurrent force which reacts on language and demystifies, ravages the innocence of its utterance: what is told is the "telling." Ultimately, the narrative has no *object*: the narrative concerns only itself: *the narrative tells itself.*

(557) *"Am I wrong?"*

"Yes," I replied, with a kind of courage. "In telling this story, which is fairly well known in Italy, I have been able to give you a fine example of the progress made by civilization today. They no longer create these unfortunate creatures." ★ In a final effort—obviously doomed to failure, which is why he needs "a kind of courage"—the narrator attempts to set up against the terror of an all-powerful castration, which taints everything and of which he is the final victim, the dam of historical motive and positive fact: let us dismiss the symbol, he is saying, let us return to earth, to "reality," to history: there are no more castrati: *the disease has been*

213

wiped out, it has disappeared from Europe like the plague, like leprosy; petty proposition, insecure dam, absurd argument against the torrential force of the symbolic which has just swept away the entire personnel of *Sarrasine* (SYM. Denial of the contagion of castration). ★★ SYM. Rationality, asymbolism (this seme had already been attached to the narrator). ★★★ REF. History of castrati. The historical code to which the narrator refers informs us that the last two famous castrati were Crescentini, who was given the Order of the Iron Crown after Napoleon heard him in Vienna in 1805 and brought him to Paris, and who died in 1846, and Velluti, who sang his final performance in London in 1826 and died in 1861.

(558) *"Paris is a very hospitable place,"* she said. *"It accepts everything, shameful fortunes and bloodstained fortunes. Crime and infamy can find asylum here;* ★ REF. Paris, Gold, immorality of the new society, etc.

(559) *only virtue has no altars here. Yes, pure souls have their home in heaven!* ★ SYM. Sublime alibi for castration (heaven will justify the castrati we have become). ★★ REF. Moral code (virtue is not of this world).

(560) *No one will have known me. I am proud of that!"* ★ Like La Zambinella, whose condition she has symbolically come to share, the Marquise turns exclusion into "misunderstanding." The Misunderstood Woman, a replete figure, an ennobled role, an image fraught with imaginary meanings, an object of language ("*I am proud of that*"), profitably substitutes for the horrid emptiness of the castrato, who is the one about whom there is nothing to say (who can say nothing about himself: who cannot *imagine* himself) (SYM. Alibi of castration: the Misunderstood Woman).

XCII. THE THREE POINTS OF ENTRY

The symbolic field is occupied by a single object from which it derives its unity (and from which we have derived a certain right to name it, some pleasure in describing it, and what may pass for a privilege granted the symbolic system, the symbolic adventure of the hero, sculptor or narrator). This object is the human body. *Sarrasine* recounts the topological transgressions of this body. The antithesis of *inner* and *outer*: abolished. The *underneath*: empty. The chain of copies: interrupted. The contract of desire: falsified. Now we can enter this symbolic field by three routes, no one of which is privileged: provided with equal points of entry, the textual network, on its symbolic level, is reversible. The rhetorical route discovers the transgression of the Antithesis, the passage through the wall of opposites, the abolition of difference. The route of castration, strictly speaking, discovers the pandemic void of desire, the collapse of the creative chain (bodies and works). The economic route discovers the disappearance of all fake currency, empty Gold, without origin or odor, no longer an index but a sign, a narrative corroded by the story it bears. These three routes are all conducive to stating the same disturbance in classification: it is fatal, the text says, to remove the dividing line, the paradigmatic slash mark which permits meaning to function (the wall of the Antithesis), life to reproduce (the opposition of the sexes), property to be protected (rule of contract). In short, the story *represents* (we are in a readerly art) a generalized collapse of economies: the economy of language, usually protected by the separation of opposites, the economy of genders (the neuter must not lay claim to the human), the economy of the body (its parts cannot be interchanged, the sexes cannot be equivalent), the economy of money (Parisian Gold produced by the new social class, speculative and no longer land-based—such gold is without origin, it has repudiated every circulatory code, every rule of exchange, every line of propriety—in French, a justly ambiguous word *propriété*, since it indicates both the correction of meaning and the separation of possessions). This catastrophic collapse always takes the same form: that of an unrestrained metonymy. By abolishing the paradigmatic barriers, this metonymy abolishes the power of *legal substitution* on which meaning is based: it is then no longer possible regularly to contrast opposites, sexes, possessions; it is no longer possible to safeguard an order of just equivalence; in a word, it is no longer possible to *represent*, to make things *representative*, individuated, separate, assigned; *Sarrasine* represents the very confusion of representation, the unbridled (pandemic) circulation of signs, of sexes, of fortunes.

(561) *And the Marquise remained pensive.* ★ Pensive, the Marquise can think of many of the things that have happened or that will happen, but about which we shall never know anything: the infinite openness of the pensive (and this is precisely its structural function) removes this final lexia from any classification.

XCIII. THE PENSIVE TEXT

Like the Marquise, the classic text is pensive: replete with meaning (as we have seen), it still seems to be keeping in reserve some ultimate meaning, one it does not express but whose place it keeps free and signifying: this zero degree of meaning (which is not its annulment, but on the contrary its recognition), this supplementary, unexpected meaning which is the theatrical sign of the implicit, is pensiveness: the pensive (in faces, in texts) is the signifier of the inexpressible, not of the unexpressed. For if the classic text has nothing more to say than what it says, at least it attempts to "let it be understood" that it does not say everything; this *allusion* is coded by pensiveness, which is a sign of nothing but itself: as though, having filled the text but obsessively fearing that it is not *incontestably* filled, the discourse insisted on supplementing it with an *et cetera* of plenitudes. Just as the pensiveness of a face signals that this head is heavy with unspoken language, so the (classic) text inscribes within its system of signs the signature of its plenitude: like the face, the text becomes *expressive* (let us say that it signifies its expressivity), endowed with an interiority whose supposed depth compensates for the parsimony of its plural. At its discreet urging, we want to ask the classic text: *What are you thinking about?* but the text, wilier than all those who try to escape by answering: *about nothing*, does not reply, giving meaning its last closure: suspension.

Appendices

I

Honoré de Balzac

¹SARRASINE

²I was deep in one of those daydreams ³which overtake even the shallowest of men, in the midst of the most tumultuous parties. ⁴Midnight had just sounded from the clock of the Elysée-Bourbon. ⁵Seated in a window recess ⁶and hidden behind the sinuous folds of a silk curtain, ⁷I could contemplate at my leisure the garden of the mansion where I was spending the evening. ⁸The trees, partially covered with snow, stood out dimly against the grayish background of a cloudy sky, barely whitened by the moon. Seen amid these fantastic surroundings, they vaguely resembled ghosts half out of their shrouds, a gigantic representation of the famous Dance of the Dead. ⁹Then, turning in the other direction, ¹⁰I could admire the Dance of the Living! ¹¹a splendid salon decorated in silver and gold, with glittering chandeliers, sparkling with candles. There, milling about, whirling around, flitting here and there, were the most beautiful women of Paris, the richest, the noblest, dazzling, stately, resplendent with diamonds, flowers in their hair, on their bosoms, on their heads, strewn over dresses or in garlands at their feet. Light, rustling movements, voluptuous steps, made the laces, the silk brocades, the gauzes, float around their delicate forms. Here and there, some overly animated glances darted forth, eclipsing the lights, the

fire of the diamonds, and stimulated anew some too-ardent hearts. One might also catch movements of the head meaningful to lovers, and negative gestures for husbands. The sudden outbursts of the gamblers' voices at each unexpected turn of the dice, the clink of gold, mingled with the music and the murmur of conversation, and to complete the giddiness of this mass of people intoxicated by everything seductive the world can hold, a haze of perfume and general inebriation played upon the fevered mind. [12]*Thus, on my right, the dark and silent image of death; on my left, the seemly bacchanalias of life: here, cold nature, dull, in mourning; there, human beings enjoying themselves.* [13]*On the borderline between these two so different scenes, which, a thousand times repeated in various guises, make Paris the world's most amusing and most philosophical city, I was making for myself a moral macédoine, half pleasant, half funereal. With my left foot I beat time, and I felt as though the other were in the grave. My leg was in fact chilled by one of those insidious drafts which freeze half our bodies while the other half feels the humid heat of rooms, an occurrence rather frequent at balls.*

[14]*"Monsieur de Lanty hasn't owned this house for very long, has he?"*

"Oh yes. Maréchal Carigliano sold it to him nearly ten years ago."

"Ah!"

"These people must have a huge fortune."

"They must have."

"What a party! It's shockingly elegant."

"Do you think they're as rich as M. de Nucingen or M. de Gondreville?"

[15]*"You mean you don't know?"* . . .

I stuck my head out and recognized the two speakers as members of that strange race which, in Paris, deals exclusively with "whys" and "hows," with "Where did they come from?" "What's happening?" "What has she done?" They lowered their voices and walked off to talk in greater comfort on some isolated sofa. Never had a richer vein been offered to seekers after mystery. [16]*Nobody knew what country the Lanty family came from,* [17]*or from what business, what plunder, what piratical activity, or what inheritance derived a fortune estimated at several millions.* [18] *All the members of the family spoke Italian, French, Spanish, English, and German perfectly enough to create the belief that they must have spent a long time among these various peoples. Were they gypsies? Were they freebooters?*

[19] *"Even if it's the devil," some young politicians said, "they give a marvelous party."*

"Even if the Count de Lanty had robbed a bank, I'd marry his daughter any time!" cried a philosopher.

[20] *Who wouldn't have married Marianina, a girl of sixteen whose beauty embodied the fabled imaginings of the Eastern poets! Like the sultan's daughter, in the story of the Magic Lamp, she should have been kept veiled. Her singing put into the shade the partial talents of Malibran, Sontag, and Fodor, in whom one dominant quality has always excluded over-all perfection; whereas Marianina was able to bring to the same level purity of sound, sensibility, rightness of movement and pitch, soul and science, correctness and feeling. This girl was the embodiment of that secret poetry, the common bond among all the arts, which always eludes those who search for it. Sweet and modest, educated and witty, no one could eclipse Marianina, save her mother.*

[21] *Have you ever encountered one of those women whose striking beauty defies the inroads of age and who seem at thirty-six more desirable than they could have been fifteen years earlier? Their visage is a vibrant soul, it glows; each feature sparkles with intelligence; each pore has a special brilliance, especially in artificial light. Their seductive eyes refuse, attract, speak or remain silent; their walk is innocently knowledgeable; their voices employ the melodious wealth of the most coquettishly soft and tender notes. Based on comparisons, their praises flatter the self-love of the most sentient. A movement of their eyebrows, the least glance, their pursed lips, fill with a kind of terror those whose life and happiness depend upon them. Inexperienced in love and influenced by words, a young girl can be seduced; for this kind of woman, however, a man must know, like M. de Jaucourt, not to cry out when he is hiding in a closet and the maid breaks two of his fingers as she shuts the*

door on them. In loving these powerful sirens, one gambles with one's life. And this, perhaps, is why we love them so passionately. Such was the Countess de Lanty.

²²Filippo, Marianina's brother, shared with his sister in the Countess's marvelous beauty. To be brief, this young man was a living image of Antinous, even more slender. Yet how well these thin, delicate proportions are suited to young people when an olive complexion, strongly defined eyebrows, and the fire of velvet eyes give promise of future male passion, of brave thoughts! If Filippo resided in every girl's heart as an ideal, he also resided in the memory of every mother as the best catch in France.

²³The beauty, the fortune, the wit, the charms of these two children, came solely from their mother. ²⁴The Count de Lanty was small, ugly, and pock-marked; dark as a Spaniard, dull as a banker. However, he was taken to be a deep politician, perhaps because he rarely laughed, and was always quoting Metternich or Wellington.

²⁵This mysterious family had all the appeal of one of Lord Byron's poems, whose difficulties each person in the fashionable world interpreted in a different way: an obscure and sublime song in every strophe. ²⁶The reserve maintained by M. and Mme de Lanty about their origin, their past life, and their relationship with the four corners of the globe had not lasted long as a subject of astonishment in Paris. Nowhere perhaps is Vespasian's axiom better understood. There, even bloodstained or filthy money betrays nothing and stands for everything. So long as high society knows the amount of your fortune, you are classed among those having an equal amount, and no one asks to see your family tree, because everyone knows how much it cost. In a city where social problems are solved like algebraic equations, adventurers have every opportunity in their favor. Even supposing this family were of gypsy origin, it was so wealthy, so attractive, that society had no trouble in forgiving its little secrets. ²⁷Unfortunately, however, the mystery of the Lantys presented a continuing source of curiosity, rather like that contained in the novels of Ann Radcliffe.

²⁸Observers, people who make it a point to know in what shop you buy your candlesticks, or who ask the amount of your rent when they find your apartment attractive, had noticed, now and

then, in the midst of the Countess's parties, concerts, balls, and routs, the appearance of a strange personage. [29]It was a man. [30]The first time he had appeared in the mansion was during a concert, when he seemed to have been drawn to the salon by Marianina's enchanting voice.

[31]"All of a sudden, I'm cold," a lady had said who was standing with a friend by the door.

The stranger, who was standing next to the women, went away.

"That's odd! I'm warm now," she said, after the stranger had gone. "And you'll say I'm mad, but I can't help thinking that my neighbor, the man dressed in black who just left, was the cause of my chill."

[32]Before long, the exaggeration native to those in high society gave birth to and accumulated the most amusing ideas, the most outrageous expressions, the most ridiculous anecdotes about this mysterious personage. [33]Although not a vampire, a ghoul, or an artificial man, a kind of Faust or Robin Goodfellow, people fond of fantasy said he had something of all these anthropomorphic natures about him. [34]Here and there, one came across some Germans who accepted as fact these clever witticisms of Parisian scandalmongering. [35]The stranger was merely an old man. [36]Many of the young men who were in the habit of settling the future of Europe every morning in a few elegant phrases would have liked to see in this stranger some great criminal, the possessor of vast wealth. Some storytellers recounted the life of this old man and provided really curious details about the atrocities he had committed while in the service of the Maharaja of Mysore. Some bankers, more positive by nature, invented a fable about money. "Bah," they said, shrugging their shoulders in pity, "this poor old man is a tête génoise!"

[37]"Sir, without being indiscreet, could you please tell me what you mean by a tête génoise?"

"A man, sir, with an enormous lifetime capital and whose family's income doubtless depends on his good health."

[38]I remember having heard at Mme d'Espard's a hypnotist proving on highly suspect historical data that this old man, preserved under glass, was the famous Balsamo, known as Cagliostro. Accord-

225

ing to this contemporary alchemist, the Sicilian adventurer had escaped death and passed his time fabricating gold for his grandchildren. Last, the bailiff of Ferette maintained that he had recognized this odd personage as the Count of Saint-Germain. [39]These stupidities, spoken in witty accents, with the mocking air characteristic of atheistic society in our day, kept alive vague suspicions about the Lanty family. [40]Finally, through a strange combination of circumstances, the members of this family justified everyone's conjectures by behaving somewhat mysteriously toward this old man, whose life was somehow hidden from all investigation.

[41]Whenever this person crossed the threshold of the room he was supposed to inhabit in the Lanty mansion, his appearance always created a great sensation among the family. One might have called it an event of great importance. Filippo, Marianina, Mme de Lanty, and an old servant were the only persons privileged to assist the old man in walking, arising, sitting down. Each of them watched over his slightest movement. [42]It seemed that he was an enchanted being upon whom depended the happiness, the life, or the fortune of them all. [43]Was it affection or fear? Those in society were unable to discover any clue to help them solve this problem. [44]Hidden for whole months in the depths of a secret sanctuary, this family genie would suddenly come forth, unexpectedly, and would appear in the midst of the salons like those fairies of bygone days who descended from flying dragons to interrupt the rites to which they had not been invited. [45]Only the most avid onlookers were then able to perceive the uneasiness of the heads of the house, who could conceal their feelings with unusual skill. [46]Sometimes, however, while dancing a quadrille, Marianina, naïve as she was, would cast a terrified glance at the old man when she spied him among the crowd. Or else Filippo would slip quickly through the throng to his side and would stay near him, tender and attentive, as though contact with others or the slightest breath would destroy this strange creature. The Countess would make a point of drawing near, without seeming to have any intention of joining them; then, assuming a manner and expression of servitude mixed with tenderness, submission, and power, she would say a few words, to which the old man nearly always deferred, and he would disappear, led off, or, more

precisely, carried off, by her. ⁴⁷*If Mme de Lanty were not present, the Count used a thousand stratagems to reach his side; however, he seemed to have difficulty making himself heard, and treated him like a spoiled child whose mother gives in to his whims in order to avoid a scene.* ⁴⁸*Some bolder persons having thoughtlessly ventured to question the Count de Lanty, this cold, reserved man had appeared never to understand them. And so, after many tries, all futile because of the circumspection of the entire family, everyone stopped trying to fathom such a well-kept secret. Weary of trying, the companionable spies, the idly curious, and the politic all gave up bothering about this mystery.*

⁴⁹However, even now perhaps in these glittering salons there were some philosophers who, while eating an ice or a sherbet, or placing their empty punch glass on a side table, were saying to each other: "It wouldn't surprise me to learn that those people are crooks. The old man who hides and only makes his appearance on the first day of spring or winter, or at the solstices, looks to me like a killer . . ."

"Or a confidence man . . ."

"It's almost the same thing. Killing a man's fortune is sometimes worse than killing the man."

⁵⁰"Sir, I have bet twenty louis, I should get back forty."

"But, sir, there are only thirty on the table."

"Ah well, you see how mixed the crowd is, here. It's impossible to play."

"True . . . But it's now nearly six months since we've seen the Spirit. Do you think he's really alive?"

"Hah! at best . . ."

These last words were spoken near me by people I did not know, as they were moving off, ⁵¹and as I was resuming, in an afterthought, my mixed thoughts of white and black, life and death. My vivid imagination as well as my eyes looked back and forth from the party, which had reached the height of its splendor, and the somber scene in the gardens. ⁵²I do not know how long I meditated on these two faces of the human coin; ⁵³ but all at once I was awakened by the stifled laugh of a young woman. ⁵⁴I was stunned by the appearance of the image which arose before me. ⁵⁵By one of those tricks of nature, the half-mournful thought turning in my mind had emerged, and it appeared living before me, it had sprung like Minerva from the head of Jove, tall and strong, it was at once a hundred years old and twenty-two years old; it was alive and dead. [56]Escaped from his room like a lunatic from his cell, the little old man had obviously slipped behind a hedge of people who were listening to Marianina's voice, finishing the cavatina from Tancredi. [57]He seemed to have come out from underground, impelled by some piece of stage machinery. [58]Motionless and somber, he stood for a moment gazing at the party, the noises of which had perhaps reached his ears. His almost somnambulatory preoccupation was so concentrated on things that he was in the world without seeing it. [59]He had unceremoniously sprung up next to one of the most ravishing women in Paris, [60]a young and elegant dancer, delicately formed, with one of those faces as fresh as that of a child, pink and white, so frail and transparent that a man's glance seems to penetrate it like a ray of sunlight going through ice. [61]They were both there before me, together, united, and so close that the stranger brushed against her, her gauzy dress, her garlands of flowers, her softly curled hair, her floating sash.

[62]I had brought this young woman to Mme de Lanty's ball. Since this was her first visit to the house, I forgave her her stifled laugh, but I quickly gave her a signal which completely silenced her and filled her with awe for her neighbor. [63]She sat down next to me. [64]The old man did not want to leave this lovely creature, to whom he had attached himself with that silent and seemingly baseless stubbornness to which the extremely old are prone, and which makes them appear childish. [65]In order to sit near her, he had to take a folding chair. His slightest movements were full of that cold heaviness, the stupid indecision, characteristic of the gestures of a paralytic. He sat slowly down on his seat, with circumspection, [66]muttering some unintelligible words. His worn-out voice was like the sound made by a stone falling down a well. [67]The young woman held my hand tightly, as if seeking protection on some precipice, and she shivered when this man at whom she was looking [68]turned upon her two eyes without warmth, glaucous eyes which could only be compared to dull mother-of-pearl.

[69]"I'm afraid," she said, leaning toward my ear.

[70]"You can talk," I answered. "He is very hard of hearing."

"Do you know him?"

"Yes."

[71]Thereupon, she gathered up enough courage to look for a moment at this creature for which the human language had no name, a form without substance, a being without life, or a life without action. [72]She was under the spell of that timorous curiosity which leads women to seek out dangerous emotions, to go see chained tigers, to look at boa constrictors, frightening themselves because they are separated from them only by weak fences. [73]Although the little old man's back was stooped like a laborer's, one could easily tell that he must have had at one time a normal shape. His excessive thinness, the delicacy of his limbs, proved that he had always been slender. [74]He was dressed in black silk trousers which fell about his bony thighs in folds, like an empty sail. [75]An anatomist would have promptly recognized the symptoms of galloping consumption by looking at the skinny legs supporting this strange body. [76]You would have said they were two bones crossed on a tombstone.

[77]A feeling of profound horror for mankind gripped the heart when one saw the marks that decrepitude had left on this fragile machine. [78]The stranger was wearing an old-fashioned gold-embroidered white waistcoat, and his linen was dazzlingly white. A frill of somewhat yellowed lace, rich enough for a queen's envy, fell into ruffles on his breast. On him, however, this lace seemed more like a rag than like an ornament. Centered on it was a fabulous diamond which glittered like the sun. [79]This outmoded luxury, this particular and tasteless jewel, made the strange creature's face even more striking. [80]The setting was worthy of the portrait. This dark face was angular and all sunk in. The chin was sunken, the temples were sunken; the eyes were lost in yellowish sockets. The jawbones stood out because of his indescribable thinness, creating cavities in the center of each cheek. [81]These deformations, more or less illuminated by the candles, produced shadows and strange reflections which succeeded in erasing any human characteristics from his face. [82]And the years had glued the thin, yellow skin of his

face so closely to his skull that it was covered all over with a multitude of circular wrinkles, like the ripples on a pond into which a child has thrown a pebble, or star-shaped, like a cracked window-pane, but everywhere deep and close-set as the edges of pages in a closed book. [83]*Some old people have presented more hideous portraits; what contributed the most, however, in lending the appearance of an artificial creature to the specter which had risen up before us was the red and white with which he glistened. The eyebrows of his mask took from the light a luster which revealed that they were painted on. Fortunately for the eye depressed by the sight of such ruin, his cadaverous skull was covered by a blond wig whose innumerable curls were evidence of an extraordinary pretension.* [84]*For the rest, the feminine coquetry of this phantasmagorical personage was rather strongly emphasized by the gold ornaments hanging from his ears, by the rings whose fine stones glittered on his bony fingers, and by a watch chain which shimmered like the brilliants of a choker around a woman's neck.* [85]*Finally, this sort of Japanese idol* [86]*had on his bluish lips a fixed and frozen smile, implacable and mocking, like a skull.* [87]*Silent and motionless as a statue, it exuded the musty odor of old clothes which the heirs of some duchess take out for inventory.* [88]*Although the old man turned his eyes toward the crowd, it seemed that the movements of those orbs, incapable of sight, were accomplished only by means of some imperceptible artifice; and when the eyes came to rest on something, anyone looking at them would have concluded that they had not moved at all.* [89]*To see, next to this human wreckage, a young woman* [90]*whose neck, bosom, and arms were bare and white, whose figure was in the full bloom of its beauty, whose hair rose from her alabaster forehead and inspired love, whose eyes did not receive but gave off light, who was soft, fresh, and whose floating curls and sweet breath seemed too heavy, too hard, too powerful for this shadow, for this man of dust:* [91]*ah! here were death and life indeed, I thought, in a fantastic arabesque, half hideous chimera, divinely feminine from the waist up.*

"Yet there are marriages like that often enough in the world," I said to myself.

[92]"He smells like a graveyard," cried the terrified young woman,

[93]*pressing against me for protection, and whose uneasy movements told me she was frightened.* [94]*"What a horrible sight," she went on. "I can't stay here any longer. If I look at him again, I shall believe that death itself has come looking for me. Is he alive?"*

[95]*She reached out to the phenomenon* [96]*with that boldness women can summon up out of the strength of their desires;* [97]*but she broke into a cold sweat, for no sooner had she touched the old man than she heard a cry like a rattle. This sharp voice, if voice it was, issued from a nearly dried up throat.* [98]*Then the sound was quickly followed by a little, convulsive, childish cough of a peculiar sonorousness.* [99]*At this sound, Marianina, Filippo, and Mme de Lanty looked in our direction, and their glances were like bolts of lightning. The young woman wished she were at the bottom of the Seine.* [100]*She took my arm and led me into a side room. Men, women, everyone made way for us. At the end of the public rooms, we came into a small, semicircular chamber.* [101]*My companion threw herself onto a divan, trembling with fright, oblivious to her surroundings.*

[102]*"Madame, you are mad," I said to her.*

[103]*"But," she replied, after a moment's silence, during which I gazed at her in admiration,* [104]*"is it my fault? Why does Mme de Lanty allow ghosts to wander about in her house?"*

[105]*"Come," I replied, "you are being ridiculous, taking a little old man for a ghost."*

[106]*"Be still," she said, with that forceful and mocking air all women so easily assume when they want to be in the right.* [107]*"What a pretty room!" she cried, looking around. "Blue satin always makes such wonderful wall hangings. How refreshing it is!* [108]*Oh! what a beautiful painting!" she went on, getting up and going to stand before a painting in a magnificent frame.*

We stood for a moment in contemplation of this marvel, [109]*which seemed to have been painted by some supernatural brush.* [110]*The picture was of Adonis lying on a lion's skin.* [111]*The lamp hanging from the ceiling of the room in an alabaster globe illuminated this canvas with a soft glow which enabled us to make out all the beauties of the painting.*

[112]*"Does such a perfect creature exist?" she asked me,* [113]*after*

having, with a soft smile of contentment, examined the exquisite grace of the contours, the pose, the color, the hair; in short, the entire picture.

[114]"He is too beautiful for a man," she added, after an examination such as she might have made of some rival.

[115]Oh! how jealous I then felt: something [116] in which a poet had vainly tried to make me believe, the jealousy of engravings, of pictures, wherein artists exaggerate human beauty according to the doctrine which leads them to idealize everything.

[117]"It's a portrait," I replied, "the product of the talent of Vien. [118]But that great painter never saw the original and maybe you'd admire it less if you knew that this daub was copied from the statue of a woman."

[119]"But who is it?"

I hesitated.

"I want to know," she added, impetuously.

[120]"I believe," I replied, "that this Adonis is a . . . a relative of Mme de Lanty."

[121]I had the pain of seeing her rapt in the contemplation of this figure. She sat in silence; I sat down next to her and took her hand without her being aware of it! Forgotten for a painting! [122]At this moment, the light footsteps of a woman in a rustling dress broke the silence. [123]Young Marianina came in, and her innocent expression made her even more alluring than did her grace and her lovely dress; she was walking slowly and escorting with maternal care, with filial solicitude, the costumed specter who had made us flee from the music room [124]and whom she was leading, watching with what seemed to be concern as he slowly advanced on his feeble feet. [125]They went together with some difficulty to a door hidden behind a tapestry. [126]There, Marianina knocked softly. [127]At once, as if by magic, a tall, stern man, a kind of family genie, appeared. [128]Before entrusting the old man to the care of his mysterious guardian, [129]the child respectfully kissed the walking corpse, and her chaste caress was not devoid of that graceful cajolery of which some privileged women possess the secret.

[130]"Addio, addio," she said, with the prettiest inflection in her youthful voice.

[131]*She added to the final syllable a marvelously well-executed trill, but in a soft voice, as if to give poetic expression to the emotions in her heart.* [132]*Suddenly struck by some memory, the old man stood on the threshold of this secret hideaway. Then, through the silence, we heard the heavy sigh that came from his chest:* [133]*he took the most beautiful of the rings which adorned his skeletal fingers, and placed it in Marianina's bosom.* [134]*The young girl broke into laughter, took the ring, and slipped it onto her finger over her glove;* [135]*then she walked quickly toward the salon, from which there could be heard the opening measures of a quadrille.* [136]*She saw us:*

"Ah, you were here," she said, blushing.

After having seemed as if about to question us, [137]*she ran to her partner with the careless petulance of youth.*

[138]"What did that mean?" my young companion asked me. "Is he her husband? [139]I must be dreaming. Where am I?"

"You," I replied, "you, madame, superior as you are, you who understand so well the most hidden feelings, who know how to inspire in a man's heart the most delicate of feelings without blighting it, without breaking it at the outset, you who pity heartache and who combine the wit of a Parisienne with a passionate soul worthy of Italy or Spain—"

She perceived the bitter irony in my speech; then, without seeming to have heard, she interrupted me: "Oh, you fashion me to your own taste. What tyranny! You don't want me for myself!"

"Ah, I want nothing," I cried, taken aback by her severity. [140]"Is it true, at least, that you enjoy hearing stories of those vivid passions that ravishing Southern women inspire in our hearts?"

[141]"Yes, so?"

"So, I'll call tomorrow around nine and reveal this mystery to you."

[142]"No," she replied, "I want to know now."

"You haven't yet given me the right to obey you when you say: I want to."

[143]"At this moment," she replied with maddening coquetry, "I have the most burning desire to know the secret. Tomorrow, I might not even listen to you . . ."

[144]*She smiled and we parted; she just as proud, just as forbidding, and I just as ridiculous as ever. She had the audacity to waltz with a young aide-de-camp; and I was left in turn angry, pouting, admiring, loving, jealous.*

[145]"*Till tomorrow,*" *she said, around two in the morning, as she left the ball.*

[146]"*I won't go,*" *I thought to myself.* "*I'll give you up. You are more capricious, perhaps a thousand times more fanciful . . . than my imagination.*"

[147]*The next evening, we were both seated before a good fire* [148]*in a small, elegant salon, she on a low sofa, I on cushions almost at her feet, and my eyes below hers. The street was quiet. The lamp shed a soft light. It was one of those evenings pleasing to the soul, one of those never-to-be-forgotten moments, one of those hours spent in peace and desire whose charm, later on, is a matter for constant regret, even when we may be happier. Who can erase the vivid imprint of the first feelings of love?*

[149]"*Well,*" *she said,* "*I'm listening.*"

[150]"*I don't dare begin. The story has some dangerous passages for its teller. If I become too moved, you must stop me.*"

[151]"*Tell.*"

[152]"*I will obey.*"

[153]*Ernest-Jean Sarrasine was the only son of a lawyer in the Franche-Comté, I went on, after a pause. His father had amassed six or eight thousand livres of income honestly enough, a professional's fortune which at that time in the provinces, was considered to be colossal. The elder Sarrasine, having but one child and anxious to overlook nothing where his education was concerned, hoped to make a magistrate of him, and to live long enough to see, in his old age, the grandson of Matthieu Sarrasine, farmer of Saint-Dié, seated beneath the lilies and napping through some trial for the greater glory of the law; however, heaven did not hold this pleasure in store for the lawyer.*

[154]*The younger Sarrasine, entrusted to the Jesuits at an early age,* [155]*evidenced an unusual turbulence.* [156]*He had the childhood of a man of talent.* [157]*He would study only what pleased him, fre-*

quently rebelled, and sometimes spent hours on end plunged in confused thought, occupied at times in watching his comrades at play, at times dreaming of Homeric heroes. [158]*Then, if he made up his mind to amuse himself, he threw himself into games with an extraordinary ardor. When a fight broke out between him and a friend, the battle rarely ended without bloodshed. If he was the weaker of the two, he would bite.* [159]*Both active and passive by turns, without aptitude and not overly intelligent, his bizarre character* [160]*made his teachers as wary of him as were his classmates.* [161]*Instead of learning the elements of Greek, he drew the Reverend Father as he explained a passage in Thucydides to them, sketched the mathematics teacher, the tutors, the Father in charge of discipline, and he scribbled shapeless designs on the walls.* [162]*Instead of singing the Lord's praises in church, he distracted himself during services by whittling on a pew;* [163]*or when he had stolen a piece of wood, he carved some holy figure. If he had no wood, paper, or pencil, he reproduced his ideas with bread crumbs.* [164]*Whether copying the characters in the pictures that decorated the choir, or improvising, he always left behind him some gross sketches whose licentiousness shocked the youngest Fathers; evil tongues maintained that the older Jesuits were amused by them.* [165]*Finally, if we are to believe school gossip, he was expelled* [166]*for having, while awaiting his turn at the confessional on Good Friday, shaped a big stick of wood into the form of Christ. The impiety with which this statue was endowed was too blatant not to have merited punishment of the artist. Had he not had the audacity to place this somewhat cynical figure on top of the tabernacle!*

[167]*Sarrasine sought in Paris a refuge from the effects* [168]*of a father's curse.* [169]*Having one of those strong wills that brook no obstacle, he obeyed the commands of his genius and entered Bouchardon's studio.* [170]*He worked all day, and in the evening went out to beg for his living.* [171]*Astonished at the young artist's progress and intelligence, Bouchardon* [172]*soon became aware of his pupil's poverty; he helped him, grew fond of him, and treated him like his own son.* [173]*Then, when Sarrasine's genius was revealed* [174] *in one of those works in which future talent struggles with the effervescence of youth,* [175]*the warmhearted Bouchardon endeavored to*

235

restore him to the old lawyer's good graces. Before the authority of the famous sculptor, the parental anger subsided. All Besançon rejoiced at having given birth to a great man of the future. In the first throes of the ecstasy produced by his flattered vanity, the miserly lawyer gave his son the means to cut a good figure in society. [176]For a long time, the lengthy and laborious studies demanded by sculpture [177]tamed Sarrasine's impetuous nature and wild genius. Bouchardon, foreseeing the violence with which the passions would erupt in this young soul, [178]which was perhaps as predisposed to them as Michelangelo's had been, [179]channeled his energy into constant labor. He succeeded in keeping Sarrasine's extraordinary impetuosity within limits by forbidding him to work; by suggesting distractions when he saw him being carried away by the fury of some idea, or by entrusting him with important work when he seemed on the point of abandoning himself to dissipation. [180]However, gentleness was always the most powerful of weapons where this passionate soul was concerned, and the master had no greater control over his student than when he inspired his gratitude through paternal kindness.

[181]At twenty-two, Sarrasine was necessarily removed from the salutary influence Bouchardon had exercised over his morals and his habits. [182]He reaped the fruits of his genius by winning the sculpture prize [183]established by the Marquis de Marigny, the brother of Mme de Pompadour, who did so much for the arts. [184]Diderot hailed the statue by Bouchardon's pupil as a masterpiece. [185]The King's sculptor, not without great sorrow, saw off to Italy a young man [186]whom he had kept, as a matter of principle, in total ignorance of the facts of life.

[187]For six years, Sarrasine had boarded with Bouchardon. [188]As fanatic in his art as Canova was later to be, he arose at dawn, went to the studio, did not emerge until nightfall, [189]and lived only with his Muse. [190]If he went to the Comédie-Française, he was taken by his master. He felt so out of place at Mme Geoffrin's and in high society, into which Bouchardon tried to introduce him, that he preferred to be alone, and shunned the pleasures of that licentious era. [191]He had no other mistress but sculpture [192]and Clotilde, one of the luminaries of the Opéra. [193]And even this affair did not last.

[194]*Sarrasine was rather ugly, always badly dressed, and so free in his nature, so irregular in his private life,* [195]*that the celebrated nymph, fearing some catastrophe, soon relinquished the sculptor to his love of the Arts.* [196]*Sophie Arnould made one of her witticisms on this subject. She confessed her surprise, I believe, that her friend had managed to triumph over statuary.*

[197]*Sarrasine left for Italy in 1758.* [198]*During the journey, his vivid imagination caught fire beneath a brilliant sky and at the sight of the wonderful monuments which are to be found in the birthplace of the Arts. He admired the statues, the frescoes, the paintings, and thus inspired,* [199]*he came to Rome,* [200]*filled with desire to carve his name between Michelangelo's and M. Bouchardon's. Accordingly, at the beginning, he divided his time between studio tasks and examining the works of art in which Rome abounds.* [201]*He had already spent two weeks in the ecstatic state which overwhelms young minds at the sight of the queen of ruins,* [202]*when he went one evening to the Teatro Argentina,* [203]*before which a huge crowd was assembled.* [204]*He inquired as to the causes of this gathering* [205]*and everyone answered with two names: Zambinella! Jomelli!* [206]*He entered* [207]*and took a seat in the orchestra,* [208]*squeezed between two notably fat abbati;* [209]*however, he was lucky enough to be fairly close to the stage.* [210]*The curtain rose.* [211]*For the first time in his life, he heard that music* [212]*whose delights M. Jean-Jacques Rousseau had so eloquently praised to him at one of Baron d'Holbach's evenings.* [213]*The young sculptor's senses were, so to speak, lubricated by the accents of Jomelli's sublime harmony. The languorous novelties of these skillfully mingled Italian voices plunged him into a delicious ecstasy.* [214]*He remained speechless, motionless, not even feeling crowded by the two priests.* [215]*His soul passed into his ears and eyes. He seemed to hear through every pore.* [216]*Suddenly a burst of applause which shook the house greeted the prima donna's entrance.* [217]*She came coquettishly to the front of the stage and greeted the audience with infinite grace. The lights, the general enthusiasm, the theatrical illusion, the glamour of a style of dress which in those days was quite attractive, all conspired in favor* [218]*of this woman.* [219]*Sarrasine cried out with pleasure.*

[220]*At that instant he marveled at the ideal beauty he had hith-*

erto sought in life, seeking in one often unworthy model the roundness of a perfect leg; in another, the curve of a breast; in another, white shoulders; finally taking some girl's neck, some woman's hands, and some child's smooth knees, [221]without ever having encountered under the cold Parisian sky the rich, sweet creations of ancient Greece. [222]La Zambinella displayed to him, united, living, and delicate, those exquisite female forms he so ardently desired, of which a sculptor is at once the severest and the most passionate judge. [223]Her mouth was expressive, her eyes loving, her complexion dazzlingly white. [224]And along with these details, which would have enraptured a painter, [225]were all the wonders of those images of Venus revered and rendered by the chisels of the Greeks. [226]The artist never wearied of admiring the inimitable grace with which the arms were attached to the torso, the marvelous roundness of the neck, the harmonious lines drawn by the eyebrows, the nose, and the perfect oval of the face, the purity of its vivid contours and the effect of the thick, curved lashes which lined her heavy and voluptuous eyelids. [227]This was more than a woman, this was a masterpiece! [228]In this unhoped-for creation could be found a love to enrapture any man, and beauties worthy of satisfying a critic. [229]With his eyes, Sarrasine devoured Pygmalion's statue, come down from its pedestal. [230]When La Zambinella sang, [231]the effect was delirium. [232]The artist felt cold; [233]then he felt a heat which suddenly began to prickle in the innermost depth of his being, in what we call the heart, for lack of any other word! [234]He did not applaud, he said nothing, [235]he experienced an impulse of madness, [236]a kind of frenzy which overcomes us only when we are at the age when desire has something frightening and infernal about it. [237]Sarrasine wanted to leap onto the stage and take possession of this woman: his strength, increased a hundredfold by a moral depression impossible to explain, since these phenomena occur in an area hidden from human observation, seemed to manifest itself with painful violence. [238]Looking at him, one would have thought him a cold and senseless man. [239]Fame, knowledge, future, existence, laurels, everything collapsed.

[240]"To be loved by her, or die!" Such was the decree Sarrasine passed upon himself. [241]He was so utterly intoxicated that he no

longer saw the theater, the spectators, the actors, or heard the music. [242]*Moreover, the distance between himself and La Zambinella had ceased to exist, he possessed her, his eyes were riveted upon her, he took her for his own. An almost diabolical power enabled him to feel the breath of this voice, to smell the scented powder covering her hair, to see the planes of her face, to count the blue veins shadowing her satin skin.* [243]*Last, this agile voice, fresh and silvery in timbre, supple as a thread shaped by the slightest breath of air, rolling and unrolling, cascading and scattering, this voice attacked his soul so vividly* [244]*that several times he gave vent to involuntary cries torn from him by convulsive feelings of pleasure* [245]*which are all too rarely vouchsafed by human passions.* [246]*He was presently obliged to leave the theater.* [247]*His trembling legs almost refused to support him. He was limp, weak as a sensitive man who has given way to overwhelming anger. He had experienced such pleasure, or perhaps he had suffered so keenly, that his life had drained away like water from a broken vase. He felt empty inside, a prostration similar to the debilitation that overcomes those convalescing from serious illness.*

[248]*Overcome by an inexplicable sadness,* [249]*he sat down on the steps of a church. There, leaning back against a pillar, he fell into a confused meditation, as in a dream. He had been smitten by passion.* [250]*Upon returning to his lodgings,* [251]*he fell into one of those frenzies of activity which disclose to us the presence of new elements in our lives. A prey to this first fever of love derived equally from both pleasure and pain, he tried to appease his impatience and his delirium by drawing La Zambinella from memory. It was a kind of embodied meditation.* [252]*On one page, La Zambinella appeared in that apparently calm and cool pose favored by Raphael, Giorgione, and every great painter.* [253]*On another, she was delicately turning her head after having finished a trill, and appeared to be listening to herself.* [254]*Sarrasine sketched his mistress in every pose: he drew her unveiled, seated, standing, lying down, chaste or amorous, embodying through the delirium of his pencils every capricious notion that can enter our heads when we think intently about a mistress.* [255]*However, his fevered thoughts went beyond drawing.* [256]*He saw La Zambinella, spoke to her, beseeched her, he*

239

passed a thousand years of life and happiness with her by placing her in every imaginable position; [257]in short, by sampling the future with her. [258]On the following day, he sent his valet to rent a box next to the stage for the entire season. [259]Then, like all young people with lusty souls, [260]he exaggerated to himself the difficulties of his undertaking and first fed his passion with the pleasure of being able to admire his mistress without obstruction. [261]This golden age of love, during which we take pleasure in our own feeling and in which we are happy almost by ourselves, [262]was not destined to last long in Sarrasine's case. [263]Nevertheless, events took him by surprise [264]while he was still under the spell of this vernal hallucination, as naïve as it was voluptuous. [265]In a week he lived a lifetime, spending the mornings kneading the clay by which he would copy La Zambinella, [266]despite the veils, skirts, corsets, and ribbons which concealed her from him. [267]In the evenings, installed in his box early, alone, lying on a sofa like a Turk under the influence of opium, he created for himself a pleasure as rich and varied as he wished it to be. [268]First, he gradually familiarized himself with the overly vivid emotions his mistress's singing afforded him; [269]he then trained his eyes to see her, and finally he could contemplate her [270]without fearing an outburst of the wild frenzy which had seized him on the first day. As his passion became calmer, it grew deeper. [271]For the rest, the unsociable sculptor did not allow his friends to intrude upon his solitude, which was peopled with images, adorned with fantasies of hope, and filled with happiness. [272]His love was so strong, so naïve, that he experienced all the innocent scruples that assail us when we love for the first time. [273]As he began to realize that he would soon have to act, to plot, to inquire where La Zambinella lived, whether she had a mother, uncle, teacher, family, to ponder, in short, on ways to see her, speak to her, these great, ambitious thoughts made his heart swell so painfully that he put them off until later, [274]deriving as much satisfaction from his physical suffering as he did from his intellectual pleasures.

[275]"But," Mme de Rochefide interrupted me, "I still don't see anything about either Marianina or her little old man."

"You are seeing nothing but him!" I cried impatiently, like an author who is being forced to spoil a theatrical effect.

[276]For several days, I resumed after a pause, Sarrasine had reappeared so faithfully in his box and his eyes had expressed such love [277]that his passion for La Zambinella's voice would have been common knowledge throughout Paris, had this adventure happened there; [278]however, in Italy, madame, everyone goes to the theater for himself, with his own passions, and with a heartfelt interest which precludes spying through opera glasses. [279]Nevertheless, the sculptor's enthusiasm did not escape the attention of the singers for long. [280]One evening, the Frenchman saw that they were laughing at him in the wings. [281]It is hard to know what extreme actions he might not have taken [282]had La Zambinella not come onto the stage. She gave Sarrasine one of those eloquent glances [283]which often reveal much more than women intend them to. [284]This glance was a total revelation. Sarrasine was loved!

"If it's only a caprice," he thought, already accusing his mistress of excessive ardor, "she doesn't know what she is subjecting herself to. I am hoping her caprice will last my whole life."

[285]At that moment, the artist's attention was distracted by three soft knocks on the door of his box. [286]He opened it. [287]An old woman entered with an air of mystery.

[288]"Young man," she said, "if you want to be happy, be prudent. Put on a cape, wear a hat drawn down over your eyes; then, around ten in the evening, be in the Via del Corso in front of the Hotel di Spagna."

[289]"I'll be there," he replied, [290]placing two louis in the duenna's wrinkled hand.

[291]He left his box [292]after having given a signal to La Zambinella, who timidly lowered her heavy eyelids, like a woman pleased to be understood at last. [293]Then he ran home to dress himself as seductively as he could. [294]As he was leaving the theater, [295]a strange man took his arm.

"Be on your guard, Frenchman," he whispered in his ear. "This is a matter of life and death. Cardinal Cicognara is her protector and doesn't trifle."

²⁹⁶*At that moment, had some demon set the pit of hell between Sarrasine and La Zambinella, he would have crossed it with one leap. Like the horses of the gods described by Homer, the sculptor's love had traversed vast distances in the twinkling of an eye.*

²⁹⁷*"If death itself were waiting for me outside the house, I would go even faster," he replied.*

²⁹⁸*"Poverino!" the stranger cried as he disappeared.*

²⁹⁹*Speaking of danger to a lover is tantamount to selling him pleasures, is it not?* ³⁰⁰*Sarrasine's valet had never seen his master take so much care over his toilette.* ³⁰¹*His finest sword, a gift from Bouchardon, the sash Clotilde had given him, his embroidered coat, his silver-brocade waistcoat, his gold snuffbox, his jeweled watches, were all taken from their coffers,* ³⁰²*and he adorned himself like a girl about to appear before her first love.* ³⁰³*At the appointed hour, drunk with love and seething with hope,* ³⁰⁴*Sarrasine, concealed in his cape, sped to the rendezvous the old woman had given him. The duenna was waiting for him.*

"You took a long time," she said. ³⁰⁵*"Come."*

She led the Frenchman along several back streets ³⁰⁶*and stopped before a rather handsome mansion.* ³⁰⁷*She knocked.* ³⁰⁸*The door opened.* ³⁰⁹*She led Sarrasine along a labyrinth of stairways, galleries, and rooms which were lit only by the feeble light of the moon, and soon came to a door* ³¹⁰*through whose cracks gleamed bright lights and from behind which came the joyful sounds of several voices.* ³¹¹*When at a word from the old woman he was admitted to this mysterious room, Sarrasine was suddenly dazzled at finding himself in a salon as brilliantly lighted as it was sumptuously furnished, in the center of which stood a table laden with venerable bottles and flashing flagons sparkling with ruby facets.* ³¹²*He recognized the singers from the theater,* ³¹³*along with some charming women, all ready to begin an artists' orgy as soon as he was among them.* ³¹⁴*Sarrasine suppressed a feeling of disappointment* ³¹⁵*and put on a good face.* ³¹⁶*He had expected a dim room, his mistress seated by the fire, some jealous person nearby, death and love, an exchange of confidences in low voices, heart to heart, dangerous kisses and faces so close that La Zambinella's hair would have caressed his forehead throbbing with desire, feverish with happiness.*

[317]"Vive la folie!" *he cried.* "Signori e belle donne, *you will allow me to take my revenge later and to show you my gratitude for the way you have welcomed a poor sculptor."*

[318]*Having been greeted warmly enough by most of those present, whom he knew by sight,* [319]*he sought to approach the armchair on which La Zambinella* [320]*was casually reclining.* [321]*Ah! how his heart beat when he spied a delicate foot shod in one of those slippers which in those days, may I say, madame, gave women's feet such a coquettish and voluptuous look that I don't know how men were able to resist them. The well-fitting white stockings with green clocks, the short skirts, the slippers with pointed toes, and the high heels of Louis XV's reign may have contributed something to the demoralization of Europe and the clergy.*

"Something?" the Marquise replied. "Have you read nothing?"

[322]*La Zambinella, I continued, smiling, had impudently crossed her legs and was gently swinging the upper one with a certain attractive indolence which suited her capricious sort of beauty.* [323]*She had removed her costume and was wearing a bodice that accentuated her narrow waist and set off the satin panniers of her dress, which was embroidered with blue flowers.* [324]*Her bosom, the treasures of which were concealed, in an excess of coquetry, by a covering of lace, was dazzlingly white.* [325]*Her hair arranged something like that of Mme du Barry, her face, though it was partially hidden under a full bonnet, appeared only the more delicate, and powder suited her.* [326]*To see her thus was to adore her.* [327]*She gave the sculptor a graceful smile.* [328]*Unhappy at not being able to speak to her without witnesses present, Sarrasine* [329]*politely sat down next to her and talked about music, praising her extraordinary talent;* [330]*but his voice trembled with love, with fear and hope.*

[331]*"What are you afraid of?" asked Vitagliani, the company's most famous singer. "Go ahead; you need fear no rivals here." Having said this, the tenor smiled without another word. This smile was repeated on the lips of all the guests,* [332]*whose attention contained a hidden malice a lover would not have noticed.* [333]*Such openness was like a dagger thrust in Sarrasine's heart. Although endowed with a certain strength of character, and although nothing*

could change his love, [334]it had perhaps not yet occurred to him that La Zambinella was virtually a courtesan, [335]and that he could not have both the pure pleasures that make a young girl's love so delicious and the tempestuous transports by which the hazardous possession of an actress must be purchased. [336]He reflected and resigned himself. [337]Supper was served. [338]Sarrasine and La Zambinella sat down informally side by side. [339]For the first half of the meal, the artists preserved some decorum, [340]and the sculptor was able to chat with the singer. [341]He found her witty, acute, [342]but astonishingly ignorant, [343]and she revealed herself to be weak and superstitious. [344]The delicacy of her organs was reflected in her understanding. [345]When Vitagliani uncorked the first bottle of champagne, [346]Sarrasine read in his companion's eyes a start of terror at the tiny explosion caused by the escaping gas. [347]The love-stricken artist interpreted the involuntary shudder of this feminine constitution as the sign of an excessive sensitivity. The Frenchman was charmed by this weakness. [348]How much is protective in a man's love!

"My strength your shield!" Is this not written at the heart of all declarations of love? [349]Too excited to shower the beautiful Italian with compliments, Sarrasine, like all lovers, was by turns serious, laughing, or reflective. [350]Although he seemed to be listening to the other guests, he did not hear a word they were saying, so absorbed was he in the pleasure of finding himself beside her, touching her hand as he served her. He bathed in a secret joy. [351]Despite the eloquence of a few mutual glances, [352]he was astonished at the reserve La Zambinella maintained toward him. [353]Indeed, she had begun by pressing his foot and teasing him with the flirtatiousness of a woman in love and free to show it; [354]but she suddenly wrapped herself in the modesty of a young girl, [355]after hearing Sarrasine describe a trait which revealed the excessive violence of his character. [356]When the supper became an orgy, [357]the guests broke into song under the influence of the Peralta and the Pedro-Ximenes. There were ravishing duets, songs from Calabria, Spanish seguidillas, Neapolitan canzonettas. [358]Intoxication was in every eye, in the music, in hearts and voices alike. Suddenly an enchanting vivacity welled up, a gay abandon, an Italian warmth of feeling [359]incon-

ceivable to those acquainted only with Parisian gatherings, London routs, or Viennese circles. ³⁶⁰*Jokes and words of love flew like bullets in a battle through laughter, profanities, and invocations to the Holy Virgin or il Bambino.* ³⁶¹*Someone lay down on a sofa and fell asleep.* ³⁶²*A girl was listening to a declaration of love unaware that she was spilling sherry on the tablecloth.* ³⁶³*In the midst of this disorder,* ³⁶⁴*La Zambinella remained thoughtful, as though terror-struck. She refused to drink,* ³⁶⁵*perhaps she ate a bit too much; however, it is said that greediness in a woman is a charming quality.* ³⁶⁶*Admiring his mistress's modesty,* ³⁶⁷*Sarrasine thought seriously about the future.*

"She probably wants to be married," he thought. He then turned his thoughts to the delights of this marriage. His whole life seemed too short to exhaust the springs of happiness he found in the depths of his soul. ³⁶⁸*Vitagliani, who was sitting next to him, refilled his glass so often that, toward three in the morning,* ³⁶⁹*without being totally drunk, Sarrasine could no longer control his delirium.* ³⁷⁰*Impetuously, he picked up the woman,* ³⁷¹*escaping into a kind of boudoir next to the salon,* ³⁷²*toward the door of which he had glanced more than once.* ³⁷³*The Italian woman was armed with a dagger.*

"If you come any closer," she said, "I will be forced to plunge this weapon into your heart. ³⁷⁴*Let me go! You would despise me. I have conceived too much respect for your character to surrender in this fashion. I don't want to betray the feeling you have for me."*

³⁷⁵*"Oh no!" cried Sarrasine. "You cannot stifle a passion by stimulating it!* ³⁷⁶*Are you already so corrupt that, old in heart, you would act like a young courtesan who whets the emotions by which she plies her trade?"*

³⁷⁷*"But today is Friday," she replied,* ³⁷⁸*frightened at the Frenchman's violence.*

³⁷⁹*Sarrasine, who was not devout, broke into laughter.* ³⁸⁰*La Zambinella jumped up like a young deer* ³⁸¹*and ran toward the salon.* ³⁸²*When Sarrasine appeared in her pursuit,* ³⁸³*he was greeted by an infernal burst of laughter.*

³⁸⁴*He saw La Zambinella lying in a swoon upon a sofa. She was pale and drained by the extraordinary effort she had just made.*

³⁸⁵*Although Sarrasine knew little Italian,* ³⁸⁶*he heard his mistress saying in a low voice to Vitagliani: "But he will kill me!"*

³⁸⁷*The sculptor was utterly confounded by this strange scene. He regained his senses. At first he stood motionless; then he found his voice, sat down next to his mistress, and assured her of his respect. He was able to divert his passion by addressing the most high-minded phrases to this woman; and in depicting his love, he used all the resources* ³⁸⁸*of that magical eloquence, that inspired intermediary* ³⁸⁹*which women rarely refuse to believe.* ³⁹⁰*When the guests were surprised by the first gleams of morning light, a woman suggested they go to Frascati.* ³⁹¹*Everyone enthusiastically fell in with the idea of spending the day at the Villa Ludovisi.* ³⁹²*Vitagliani went down to hire some carriages.* ³⁹³*Sarrasine had the pleasure of leading La Zambinella to a phaeton.* ³⁹⁴*Once outside Rome, the gaiety which had been momentarily repressed by each person's battle with sleepiness suddenly revived. Men and women alike seemed used to this strange life, these ceaseless pleasures, this artist's impulsiveness which turns life into a perpetual party at which one laughed unreservedly.* ³⁹⁵*The sculptor's companion was the only one who seemed downcast.*

"Are you ill?" Sarrasine asked her. "Would you rather go home?"

"I'm not strong enough to stand all these excesses," she replied. "I must be very careful; ³⁹⁶*but with you I feel so well! Had it not been for you, I would never have stayed for supper;* ³⁹⁷*a sleepless night and I lose whatever bloom I have."*

"You are so delicate," Sarrasine said, looking at the charming creature's pretty face.

"Orgies ruin the voice."

³⁹⁸*"Now that we're alone," the artist cried, "and you no longer need fear the outbursts of my passion, tell me that you love me."*

³⁹⁹*"Why?" she replied. "What would be the use?* ⁴⁰⁰*I seemed pretty to you. But you are French and your feelings will pass.* ⁴⁰¹*Ah, you would not love me as I long to be loved."*

"How can you say that?"

"Not to satisfy any vulgar passion; purely. ⁴⁰²*I abhor men perhaps even more than I hate women.* ⁴⁰³*I need to seek refuge in friendship.* ⁴⁰⁴*For me, the world is a desert. I am an accursed crea-*

246

ture, condemned to understand happiness, to feel it, to desire it, and, like many others, forced to see it flee from me continually. [405]Remember, sir, that I will not have deceived you. [406]I forbid you to love me. [407]I can be your devoted friend, for I admire your strength and your character. I need a brother, a protector. Be all that for me, [408]but no more."

[409]"Not love you!" Sarrasine cried. "But my dearest angel, you are my life, my happiness!"

[410]"If I were to say one word, you would repulse me with horror."

[411]"Coquette! [412]Nothing can frighten me. [413]Tell me you will cost my future, that I will die in two months, that I will be damned merely for having kissed you."

[414]He kissed her, [415]despite La Zambinella's efforts to resist this passionate embrace.

[416]"Tell me you are a devil, that you want my money, my name, all my fame! Do you want me to give up being a sculptor? Tell me."

[417]"And if I were not a woman?" [418]La Zambinella asked in a soft silvery voice.

[419]"What a joke!" Sarrasine cried. "Do you think you can deceive an artist's eye? [420]Haven't I spent ten days devouring, scrutinizing, admiring your perfection? [421]Only a woman could have this round, soft arm, these elegant curves. [422]Oh, you want compliments."

[423]She smiled at him sadly, and raising her eyes heavenward, she murmured: "Fatal beauty!"

[424]At that moment her gaze had an indescribable expression of horror, so powerful and vivid that Sarrasine shuddered.

[425]"Frenchman," she went on, "forget this moment of madness forever. [426]I respect you, [427]but as for love, do not ask it of me; that feeling is smothered in my heart. I have no heart!" she cried, weeping. "The stage where you saw me, that applause, that music, that fame I am condemned to, such is my life, I have no other. [428]In a few hours you will not see me in the same way, the woman you love will be dead."

[429]The sculptor made no reply. [430]He was overcome with a dumb rage which oppressed his heart. He could only gaze with enflamed, burning eyes at this extraordinary woman. La Zambinella's weak

voice, her manner, her movements and gestures marked with sorrow, melancholy, and discouragement, awakened all the wealth of passion in his soul. Each word was a goad. [431]At that moment they reached Frascati. [432]As the artist offered his mistress his arm to assist her in alighting, [433]he felt her shiver.

"What is wrong? You would kill me," he cried, seeing her grow pale, "if I were even an innocent cause of your slightest unhappiness."

"A snake," she said, pointing to a grass snake which was sliding along a ditch. "I am afraid of those horrid creatures." Sarrasine crushed the snake's head with his heel.

[434]"How can you be so brave?" La Zambinella continued, looking with visible horror at the dead reptile.

[435]"Ah," the artist replied, smiling, "now do you dare deny you are a woman?"

[436]They rejoined their companions and strolled through the woods of the Villa Ludovisi, which in those days belonged to Cardinal Cicognara. [437]That morning fled too quickly for the enamored sculptor, [438]but it was filled with a host of incidents which revealed to him the coquetry, the weakness, and the delicacy of this soft and enervated being. [439]This was woman herself, with her sudden fears, her irrational whims, her instinctive worries, her impetuous boldness, her fussings, and her delicious sensibility. [440]It happened that as they were wandering in the open countryside, the little group of merry singers saw in the distance some heavily armed men whose manner of dress was far from reassuring. Someone said, "They must be highwaymen," and everyone quickened his pace toward the refuge of the Cardinal's grounds. At this critical moment, Sarrasine saw from La Zambinella's pallor that she no longer had the strength to walk; he took her up in his arms and carried her for a while, running. When he came to a nearby arbor, he put her down.

[441]"Explain to me," he said, "how this extreme weakness, which I would find hideous in any other woman, which would displease me and whose slightest indication would be almost enough to choke my love, pleases and charms me in you? [442]Ah, how I love

248

you," he went on. "All your faults, your terrors, your resentments, add an indefinable grace to your soul. [443]I think I would detest a strong woman, a Sappho, a courageous creature, full of energy and passion. [444]Oh, soft, frail creature, how could you be otherwise? [445]That angelic voice, that delicate voice would be an anomaly coming from any body but yours."

[446]"I cannot give you any hope," she said. [447]"Stop speaking to me in this way, [448]because they will make a fool of you. [449]I cannot stop you from coming to the theater; but if you love me or if you are wise, you will come there no more. [450]Listen, monsieur," she said in a low voice.

[451]"Oh, be still," the impassioned artist said. [452]"Obstacles make my love more ardent."

[453]La Zambinella's graceful and modest attitude did not change, but she fell silent as though a terrible thought had revealed some misfortune to her. [454]When it came time to return to Rome, she got into the four-seated coach, ordering the sculptor with imperious cruelty to return to Rome alone in the carriage. [455]During the journey, Sarrasine resolved to kidnap La Zambinella. He spent the entire day making plans, each more outrageous than the other. [456]At nightfall, as he was going out to inquire where his mistress's palazzo was located, [457]he met one of his friends on the threshold.

"My dear fellow," he said, "our ambassador has asked me to invite you to his house tonight. He is giving a magnificent concert, [458]and when I tell you that Zambinella will be there . . ."

[459]"Zambinella," cried Sarrasine, intoxicated by the name, "I'm mad about her!"

"You're like everyone else," his friend replied.

[460]"If you are my friends, you, Vien, Lauterbourg, and Allegrain, will you help me do something after the party?" Sarrasine asked.

"It's not some cardinal to be killed? . . . not . . . ?"

"No, no," Sarrasine said, "I'm not asking you to do anything an honest person couldn't do."

[461]In a short time, the sculptor had arranged everything for the success of his undertaking. [462]He was one of the last to arrive at the ambassador's, [463]but he had come in a traveling carriage drawn by

249

powerful horses and driven by one of the most enterprising vetturini of Rome. ⁴⁶⁴The ambassador's palazzo was crowded; ⁴⁶⁵not
without some difficulty, the sculptor, who was a stranger to everyone present, made his way to the salon where Zambinella was singing at that very moment.

⁴⁶⁶"Is it out of consideration for the cardinals, bishops, and abbés
present," Sarrasine asked, "that she is dressed like a man, that she
is wearing a snood, kinky hair, and a sword?"

⁴⁶⁷"She? What she?" asked the old nobleman to whom Sarrasine
had been speaking. "La Zambinella." "La Zambinella!" the Roman
prince replied. "Are you joking? ⁴⁶⁸Where are you from? ⁴⁶⁹Has
there ever been a woman on the Roman stage? And don't you know
about the creatures who sing female roles in the Papal States?
⁴⁷⁰I am the one, monsieur, who gave Zambinella his voice. I paid
for everything that scamp ever had, even his singing teacher. Well,
he has so little gratitude for the service I rendered him that he has
never consented to set foot in my house. ⁴⁷¹And yet, if he makes a
fortune, he will owe it all to me."

⁴⁷²Prince Chigi may well have gone on talking for some time;
Sarrasine was not listening to him. A horrid truth had crept into
his soul. It was as though he had been struck by lightning. He stood
motionless, his eyes fixed ⁴⁷³on the false singer. ⁴⁷⁴His fiery gaze
exerted a sort of magnetic influence on Zambinella, ⁴⁷⁵for the
musico finally turned to look at Sarrasine, ⁴⁷⁶and at that moment
his heavenly voice faltered. He trembled! ⁴⁷⁷An involuntary murmur escaping from the audience he had kept hanging on his lips
completed his discomfiture; ⁴⁷⁸he sat down and cut short his aria.
⁴⁷⁹Cardinal Cicognara, who had glanced out the corner of his eye
to see what had attracted his protégé's attention, then saw the
Frenchman: ⁴⁸⁰he leaned over to one of his ecclesiastical aides-de-
camp and appeared to be asking the sculptor's name. ⁴⁸¹Having obtained the answer he sought, ⁴⁸²he regarded the artist with great
attention ⁴⁸³and gave an order to an abbé, who quickly disappeared.

⁴⁸⁴During this time, Zambinella, having recovered himself,
⁴⁸⁵once more began the piece ⁴⁸⁶he had so capriciously interrupted;
⁴⁸⁷but he sang it badly, ⁴⁸⁸and despite all the requests made to him,

he refused to sing anything else. [489]This was the first time he displayed that capricious tyranny for which he would later be as celebrated as for his talent [490]and his vast fortune, due, as they said, no less to his voice than to his beauty.

[491]"It is a woman," Sarrasine said, believing himself alone. "There is some hidden intrigue here. Cardinal Cicognara is deceiving the Pope and the whole city of Rome!"

[492]The sculptor thereupon left the salon, [493]gathered his friends together, [494]and posted them out of sight in the courtyard of the palazzo. [495]When Zambinella was confident that Sarrasine had departed, he appeared to regain his composure. [496]Around midnight, having wandered through the rooms like a man seeking some enemy, [497]the musico departed. [498]As soon as he crossed the threshold of the palazzo, he was adroitly seized by men who gagged him with a handkerchief and drew him into the carriage Sarrasine had hired. [499]Frozen with horror, Zambinella remained in a corner, not daring to move. He saw before him the terrible face of the artist, who was silent as death.

[500]The journey was brief. [501]Carried in Sarrasine's arms, Zambinella soon found himself in a dark, empty studio. [502]Half dead, the singer remained in a chair, [503]without daring to examine the statue of a woman in which he recognized his own features. [504]He made no attempt to speak, but his teeth chattered. [505]Sarrasine paced up and down the room. Suddenly he stopped in front of Zambinella.

"Tell me the truth," he pleaded [506]in a low, altered voice. [507]"You are a woman? [508]Cardinal Cicognara . . ."

[509]Zambinella fell to his knees, and in reply lowered his head.

[510]"Ah, you are a woman," the artist cried in a delirium, "for even a . . ." He broke off. "No," he continued, "he would not be so cowardly."

[511]"Ah, do not kill me," cried Zambinella, bursting into tears. [512]"I only agreed to trick you to please my friends, who wanted to laugh."

[513]"Laugh!" the sculptor replied in an infernal tone. "Laugh! Laugh! You dared play with a man's feelings, you?"

[514]"Oh, have mercy!" Zambinella replied.

[515]"I ought to kill you," Sarrasine cried, drawing his sword with a violent gesture. [516]"However," he went on, in cold disdain, [517]"were I to scour your body with this blade, would I find there one feeling to stifle, one vengeance to satisfy? You are nothing. If you were a man or a woman, I would kill you, [518]but . . ."

Sarrasine made a gesture of disgust [519]which forced him to turn away, whereupon he saw the statue.

[520]"And it's an illusion," he cried. [521]Then, turning to Zambinella: "A woman's heart was a refuge for me, a home. Have you any sisters who resemble you? [522]Then die! [523]But no, you shall live. Isn't leaving you alive condemning you to something worse than death? [524]It is neither my blood nor my existence that I regret, but the future and my heart's fortune. Your feeble hand has destroyed my happiness. [525]What hope can I strip from you for all those you have blighted? You have dragged me down to your level. To love, to be loved! are henceforth meaningless words for me, as they are for you. [526]I shall forever think of this imaginary woman when I see a real woman." He indicated the statue with a gesture of despair. [527]"I shall always have the memory of a celestial harpy who thrusts its talons into all my manly feelings, and who will stamp all other women with a seal of imperfection! [528]Monster! [529]You who can give life to nothing. [530]For me, you have wiped women from the earth."

[531]Sarrasine sat down before the terrified singer. Two huge tears welled from his dry eyes, rolled down his manly cheeks, and fell to the ground: two tears of rage, two bitter and burning tears.

[532]"No more love! I am dead to all pleasure, to every human emotion."

[533]So saying, he seized a hammer and hurled it at the statue with such extraordinary force [534]that he missed it. He thought he had destroyed this monument to his folly, [535]and then took up his sword and brandished it to kill the singer. [536]Zambinella uttered piercing screams. [537]At that moment, three men entered [538]and at once the sculptor fell, stabbed by three stiletto thrusts.

[539]"On behalf of Cardinal Cicognara," one of them said.

[540]"It is a good deed worthy of a Christian," replied the French-

man as he died. ⁵⁴¹These sinister messengers ⁵⁴²informed Zambinella of the concern of his protector, who was waiting at the door in a closed carriage, to take him away as soon as he had been rescued.

⁵⁴³"But," Mme de Rochefide asked me, "what connection is there between this story and the little old man we saw at the Lantys'?"

⁵⁴⁴"Madame, Cardinal Cicognara took possession of Zambinella's statue and had it executed in marble; today it is in the Albani Museum. ⁵⁴⁵There, in 1791, the Lanty family found it ⁵⁴⁶and asked Vien to copy it. ⁵⁴⁷The portrait in which you saw Zambinella at twenty, a second after having seen him at one hundred, later served for Girodet's Endymion; you will have recognized its type in the Adonis."

⁵⁴⁸"But this Zambinella—he or she?"

"He, madame, is none other than Marianina's great-uncle. ⁵⁴⁹Now you can readily see what interest Mme de Lanty has in hiding the source of a fortune which comes from—"

⁵⁵⁰"Enough!" she said, gesturing to me imperiously. We sat for a moment plunged in the deepest silence.

⁵⁵¹"Well?" I said to her.

"Ah," she exclaimed, standing up and pacing up and down the room. She looked at me and spoke in an altered voice. ⁵⁵²"You have given me a disgust for life and for passions that will last a long time. ⁵⁵³Excepting for monsters, don't all human feelings come down to the same thing, to horrible disappointments? Mothers, our children kill us either by their bad behavior or by their lack of affection. Wives, we are deceived. Mistresses, we are forsaken, abandoned. Does friendship even exist? ⁵⁵⁴I would become a nun tomorrow did I not know that I can remain unmoved as a rock amid the storms of life. ⁵⁵⁵If the Christian's future is also an illusion, at least it is not destroyed until after death. ⁵⁵⁶Leave me."

"Ah," I said, "you know how to punish."

⁵⁵⁷"Am I wrong?"

"Yes," I replied, with a kind of courage. "In telling this story, which is fairly well known in Italy, I have been able to give you a fine example of the progress made by civilization today. They no longer create these unfortunate creatures."

[558]"Paris is a very hospitable place," she said. "It accepts everything, shameful fortunes and bloodstained fortunes. Crime and infamy can find asylum here; [559]only virtue has no altars here. Yes, pure souls have their home in heaven! [560]No one will have known me. I am proud of that!"

[561]And the Marquise remained pensive.

Paris, November 1830

II

Sequence of Actions (Act.)

Since actions (or proairetisms) form the main armature of the readerly text, we here recall the sequences as they were indicated in the text, without attempting to structure them further. Each term is followed by its lexia number. The sequences are presented according to the order of appearance of their first term.

TO BE DEEP IN   1: to be absorbed (2). 2: to come back again (14).

HIDING PLACE   1: to be hidden (6). 2: to come out of hiding (15).

TO MEDITATE   1: to be in the process of meditation (52). 2: to stop meditating (53).

TO LAUGH   1: to burst out laughing (53). 2: to stop (62).

TO JOIN   1: to sit down (63). 2: to sit next to (65).

TO NARRATE   1: to know the story (70). 2: to know the story (120). 3: to offer to tell (140). 4: to suggest a rendezvous for telling a story (141). 5: to discuss the time of the rendezvous (142). 6: to agree to the rendezvous (145). 7: to reject the rendezvous (146). 8: to have accepted the rendezvous (147). 9: to command to tell (149). 10: to hesitate to tell (150). 11: to repeat the command to tell (151). 12: command accepted (152). 13: castrating effect of the narration (552).

QUESTION I   1: to ask oneself a question (94). 2: to verify (95).

TO TOUCH   1: touching (95). 2: reaction (97). 3: generalized reaction (99). 4: to flee (100). 5: to hide (101).

TABLEAU 1: to look around (107). 2: to perceive (108).

TO ENTER 1: to announce oneself by a sound (122). 2: the entrance itself (123).

DOOR I 1: to reach a door (125). 2: to knock (126). 3: to appear at a door (to open it) (127).

FAREWELL 1: to entrust (before leaving) (128). 2: to embrace (129). 3: to say farewell (130).

GIFT 1: incite (or be incited) to the gift (132). 2: to give the gift (133). 3: to accept the gift (134).

TO LEAVE 1: to want to leave (135). 2: to delay (136). 3: to leave again (137).

BOARDING SCHOOL 1: to go away to boarding school (154). 2: to be expelled (165).

CAREER 1: to go to Paris (167). 2: to study with a great master (169). 3: to leave the master (181). 4: to win a prize (182). 5: to be praised by a great critic (184). 6: to leave for Italy (185).

LIAISON 1: to have a liaison (192). 2: indication of the end of the liaison (193). 3: end of the liaison (195).

JOURNEY 1: to depart (197). 2: to travel (198). 3: to arrive (199). 4: to stay (200).

THEATER 1: to enter (the building) (202). 2: to enter the hall (206). 3: to be seated (207). 4: curtain up (210). 5: to hear the overture (211). 6: entrance of the star (216). 7: greeting of the star (217). 8: the star's aria (230). 9: to leave (246). 10: to return home (250).

QUESTION II 1: a fact to be explained (203). 2: to inquire (204). 3: to receive an answer (205).

DISCOMFORT 1: to be squeezed, made uncomfortable (208). 2: to feel nothing (214).

PLEASURE 1: proximity to the desired object (209). 2: madness (235). 3: tension (237). 4: apparent immobility (238). 5: isolation (241). 6: embrace (242). 7: to be penetrated (243). 8: ejaculation (244). 9: emptiness (247). 10: sadness (248). 11: to recuperate (249). 12: conditions for repetition (258).

SEDUCTION 1: ecstasy (213). 2: extraversion (215). 3: intense pleasure (219). 4: delirium (231). 5: delirium 1: cold (232). 6: delirium 2: heat (233). 7: delirium 3: silence (234).

TO DECIDE 1: mental condition of the choice (239). 2: to propose an alternative (240).

WILL-TO-LOVE (impulsive enterprise) 1: proposal of the enterprise (240). 2: to draw, interim activity (251). 3: to rent a theater box (contemplative activity) (258). 4: to pause (260). 5: interruption of the undertaking (263). 6: indication of terms composing the interlude (264). 7: morning, to sculpt (265). 8: evening, the sofa (267). 9: to accustom the ear (268). 10: to train the eye (269). 11: result (270). 12: protection of the induced hallucination (271). 13: alibi and prorogation (273). 14: résumé (276).

WILL-TO-DIE 1: proposal of the project (240). 2: to flout a warning (297). 3: accept any risk (412). 4: predictive, in the form of a provocation of fate (413). 5: to comment on one's death in advance (524). 6: to die to women (530). 7: to die to feeling (532). 8: to die to art (533). 9: to assume one's death (540).

DOOR II 1: to knock (285). 2: to open (286). 3: to enter (287).

RENDEZVOUS 1: to arrange a rendezvous (288). 2: to give assent to the messenger (289). 3: to thank, to tip (290). 4: to give assent to the person offering the rendezvous (292). 5: rendezvous kept (304).

TO LEAVE 1: a first locality (291). 2: a second locality (294).

DRESSING 1: to want to dress (293). 2: to dress (300).

WARNING 1: to give a warning (295). 2: to ignore it (297).

MURDER 1: designation of the future murderer (295). 2: indicating the victim (479). 3: request for information (480). 4: information received (481). 5: evaluation and interior decision (482). 6: secret order (483). 7: entrance of the murderers (537). 8: murder of the hero (538). 9: signature of the murder (539). 10: final explanation (542).

HOPE 1: to hope (303). 2: to be disappointed (314). 3: to compensate (315). 4: to hope (316). 5: to compensate (317). 6: to be disappointed (328). 7: to compensate (329). 8: to hope (330). 9: to compensate (to resign oneself) (336).

ROUTE 1: to set out (305). 2: to walk along (305). 3: to penetrate (309). 4: to arrive (311).

DOOR III 1: to stop at (306). 2: to knock (307). 3: to open (308).

ORGY 1: precursory signs (310). 2: rhetorical statement (313). 3: supper (337). 4: initial calm (339). 5: wines (345). 6: nomination of the orgy (356). 7: to sing (357). 8: to abandon oneself (denominative statement) (358). 9: to abandon oneself

(1) unbridled talk (360). 10: to let oneself go (2) to sleep (361). 11: to abandon oneself (3) to spill wine (362). 12: to abandon oneself (denominative reprise) (363). 13: end (dawn) (390).

CONVERSATION I   1: to approach (319). 2: to sit down (329). 3: to talk (329).

CONVERSATION II   1: to sit side by side (338). 2: to chat (340).

DANGER   1: act of violence, sign of a dangerous character (355). 2: victim's fear (364). 3: victim's repeated fright (378). 4: victim's premonitory fear (386). 5: persistent fear (395). 6: premonition of misfortune (453). 7: reaction of fright (476). 8: feeling of threat (487). 9: to become calm (495). 10: continued uneasiness (496).

RAPE   1: conditioning of the ravisher (369). 2: to carry off the victim (370). 3: to change locale (371). 4: to have premeditated the abduction (372). 5: victim's armed defense (373). 6: victim's flight (380). 7: change of locale (381). 8: pursuit (382). 9: failure of the rape, return to order (387).

EXCURSION   1: proposal (390). 2: agreement (391). 3: hiring of carriages (392). 4: collective gaiety (394). 5: to arrive at the destination (431). 6: to stroll in the woods (436). 7: return (454).

AMOROUS OUTING   1: to get into the same carriage (393). 2: tête-à-tête conversation (395). 3: to want to kiss (414). 4: to resist (415). 5: to come to an end (431). 6: to assist in alighting from the carriage (432). 7: separate return (454).

DECLARATION OF LOVE   1: request for an avowal (398). 2: to elude the requested avowal (399). 3: first basis for declining (fickleness) (400). 4: second basis for declining (exigency) (401). 5: third basis, exclusion (404). 6: forbid to love (406). 7: friendship, not love (407). 8: protestation of love (409). 9: gift of life (413). 10: gift of art (416). 11: fourth basis for declining (physical impediment) (417). 12: disclaimer of the disclaimer (419). 13: command to forget (425). 14: to remain silent (429). 15: command to give up (446). 16: command to be silent (447). 17: final dismissal (449).

KIDNAPPING   1: decision and plans (455). 2: preliminary information (456). 3: recruiting accomplices (460). 4: arrangements made (461). 5: rapid means of escape (463). 6: gathering of the accomplices (493). 7: ambush (494). 8: the victim's inno-

III

Summary of Contents

c. Analyze a single text (VI); this analysis has a theoretical value (VI); it serves to dispel the illusion that the text contains insignificant things and that structure is merely a "pattern" (VI, XXII).

d. Move gradually through the tutor text, starring digressions which signal the inter-textual plural (VI).

e. Forgo establishing a deep and ultimate structure for the text (VI) and in reconstituting the paradigm of each code aim at multiple structures (XI, XII); prefer structuring to structure (VIII, XII); seek out the play of the codes, not the plan of the work (XXXIX).

4. *Method II: Operations*

a. Dividing the textual continuum into brief, contiguous fragments (lexias) is arbitrary, but useful (VII).

b. What we seek to identify: the meanings, signifieds in each lexia, or their connotations. Various approaches to connotation: definitional, topical, analytical, topological, dynamic, historical, functional, structural, ideological (IV).

c. Analysis provides material for various criticisms (VIII, LXXXI). This does not imply liberality, conceding some truth to each form of criticism, but observance of the plurality of meanings as being, not as deduction or tolerance (II).

d. The text chosen: Balzac's *Sarrasine* (X and Appendix I).

II. THE CODES

1. *The code in general* (xii).

a. The perspective vanishing point of the codes (VI, XII, LXVII). Continue the buttressing of the codes: critical problems: infinite thematids (XL); the Balzacian text (XC); the author as text (XC), not as god (LXXIV).

b. The "already-written" (XII, XXXVI).

c. The code as an anonymous voice (XII, LXIV). Irony as a voice (XXI).

2. *Code of Actions, Voice of Empirics* (lxxxvi)

a. Setting up a sequence of actions is to name it (XI, XXXVI).

b. The Empiric code is based on various branches of knowledge (LXVII). No other proairetic logic but the already-written, already-seen, already-read, already-done (XI), trivial or novelistic (XI), organic or cultural (XXVI, LXXXVI).

c. Expansion of the sequence: the tree (LVI), the interweaving (LXVIII).

d. Functions: repleteness (XLVI), depreciation (XLV). The code of actions principally determines the readability of the text (LXXXVI).

3. *Hermeneutic Code, Voice of Truth* (LXXXIX)

a. Hermeneutic morphemes (XI, XXXII, LXXXIX). Proposition of truth articulated like a sentence (XXXVII); accidentals, disorder, confusion, formlessness of terms (XXXVII, XLVIII).

b. Structural paths of falsehood (1): equivocation, double understanding (LXII); metonymic falsehood (LXIX).

c. Structural paths of falsehood (2): false proofs, tricks: narcissistic proof (LXI), psychological proof (LXIII), aesthetic proof (LXXII).

d. Structural paths of falsehood (3): casuistry of the discourse (LX).

e. To delay truth is to constitute it (XXVI, XXXII).

4. *Cultural or Referential Code, Voice of Science* (LXXXVII)

a. The proverb and its stylistic transformation (XLIII).

b. Codes of Knowledge, school texts, farrago (LXXXVII).

c. Cultural Codes as ideological specters (XLII).

d. Oppressive function of reference through repetition (vomiting of stereotypes, LIX, LXXXVII), or neglect (LXXVIII).

5. *Semes or connotative signifieds, Voice of the Person* (LXXXI)

a. Naming of semes, thematics (XL).

b. Textual distribution of semes (XIII). The portrait (XXV).

c. Collection of semes: person, character (XXVIII, LXXXI).

d. Semes, inductors of truth (XXVI).

6. *The Symbolic Field*

a. The body, site of meaning, sex, and money: whence the critical privileges apparently granted the symbolic field (XCII).

b. Reversibility: the subject perfused in the text (LXX); the symbolic field reached by three entrances, without order of precedence (XCII).

c. Rhetorical entrance (meaning): Antithesis (XIV) and its transgressions: supplement (XIV), paradigmatic conflagration (XXVII, XLVII, LXXIX).

d. Poetic entrance (creation, sex)
  1] The lubricated body (XLIX), the reassembled body (L, LI).
  2] Duplicative chain of bodies (XXIX). Beauty (XVI, LI, LXI). Posterity (XVIII).
  3] Term and problems of the duplicative code: the masterpiece (LII); the beyond and short (XXX); the chain (XXXI, LXXXV); deficiency and underneath (theory of realistic art) (XXIII, L, LIV, LXXXIII, LXXXVIII).

e. Economic entrance (trade, Gold). Passage from index to sign (XIX). Narrative as subject of a contract (XCI); upsetting the economy (XCII).

f. Generalized problem: castration as a camp (XVII), as metonymy (XXIX), as pandemic (LXXXVIII, XCII). The castrating figure: the "gossip" (LXXXIX). Metonymic collapse (XCII).

7. *The Text*
The text as a braid, woven of voices, codes (LXVIII): stereophony (VIII, XV) and polytonality (XV).

III. THE PLURAL

1. *The plural text as a whole*
The triumphant plural (II, V). The modest plural (VI) and its diagram: the score (XV).

2. *Reductive determinations*
  a. Solidarities: holding (LXVI), overdetermination (LXXVI), coherent dispersion (XIII).
  b. Plenitude: to complete, to close, to predicate, to conclude (XXII, XXVI, XXXII, XLVI, LIV, LXXIII); to fill meaning, art (LXXXIV); to redound (XXXIV); to think

(XCIII). Character as illusion of plenitude: the Proper Name (XXVIII, XLI, LXXXI); character as effect of reality (XLIV); character determined by motive (LVIII). Completude, nausea, outmoded (XLII, LXXXVII).

c. Closings: classic writing prematurely cuts off the codes (LIX); the insufficient role of irony (XXI). Hermeneutic and proairetic codes, agents reducing the plural (XV).

3. *Multivalent and reversible determinations*

a. Reversibilities and multivalences: symbolic area (XI, XV, XCII).

b. The figure. Character as discourse (LXXVI), as accomplice of discourse (LXII). Figure, reversible order (LXXVIII).

c. The *dissolve* of voices (XII, XX).

d. Uncertain meanings (XXXIII, LXXVI). Transcriptability (Euphemism) (LIII).

e. Ambiguities of representation. What is presented is not operable (XXXV). "Flattened representation": narrative treating itself (XXXVIII, LXX, XCI).

f. Countercommunication. Play of destinations (LVII), the division of listening (LXII, LXIX), literature as "noise," cacography (LVII, LXII).

4. *Performance*

Some successes of classic narrator: wide syntagmatic difference between affirmative semes (XIII), uncertainty of meanings, confusion of operative and symbolic (XXXIII, LXX), explaining the explainer (LXXIV), the ludic metaphor (XXIV).

5. *The readerly text and writing*

a. The ideological role of the sentence: lubricating the semantic articulations, linking connotations in the "phrased," removing denotation from play, it yields meaning, with the security of an "innocent" nature: language, syntax (IV, VII, IX, XIII, XXV, LV, LXXXII).

b. Appropriation of meaning in the readerly text: classification, nomination (V, XXXVI, XL, LVI); obsessional defense against the logical "defect" (LXVI); confrontation of codes: the "scene" (LXV), the declaration of love (LXXV), objectivity and subjectivity (forces without affinity with the text) (V).

c. False unleashing of the infinity of codes: irony, parody (XXI, XLII, LXXXVII). Beyond irony, the irreparable force of meaning: Flaubert (XXI, LIX, LXXXVII).

d. Writing: with regard to the reader (I, LXIV), its "proof" (LIX), its power: dissolve all metalanguage, any submission of one language to another (XLII, LIX, LXXXVII).

"To a greater or lesser degree every man is suspended upon narratives, on novels, which reveal to him the multiplicity of life. Only these narratives, often read in a trance, situate him before his fate. So we ought to seek passionately to find what narratives *might be.*

"How to orient the effort through which the novel *renews, or, better, perpetuates itself.*

"The concern for various techniques which cope with the satiety of familiar forms does occupy the mind. But I am putting it badly —if we want to know what a novel can be—*that a basis should first be perceived and well marked. The narrative that reveals the possibilities of life does not necessarily appeal, but it reveals a moment of* rage, *without which its author would be blind to its* excessive possibilities. *I believe it: only suffocating, impossible trial provides the author with the means of attaining the distant vision the reader is seeking, tired of the tight limitations conventions impose.*

"How can we linger over books to which obviously the author was not constrained?

"I wanted to formulate this principle. I will not argue it.

"I shall confine myself to giving some titles that respond to my statement (some titles . . . I could give others, but disorder is the measure of my intent): Wuthering Heights, The Trial, Remembrance of Things Past, The Red and the Black, Eugénie de Franval, l'Arrêt de Mort, Sarrazine [sic], The Idiot . . ."[1]

GEORGES BATAILLE
Foreword to Le Bleu du ciel
J.-J. Pauvert, 1957, p. 7

[1] *Eugénie de Franval,* by the Marquis de Sade (in *Crimes de l'Amour*); *l'Arrêt de Mort,* by Maurice Blanchot; *Sarrazine* [*sic*], a story by Balzac that is relatively little known but is one of the high points of his work. G.B.

IV

Key